SKEPTICAL ENGAGEMENTS

SKEPTICAL ENGAGEMENTS

Frederick Crews

New York   Oxford
OXFORD UNIVERSITY PRESS
1986

OXFORD UNIVERSITY PRESS

Oxford   New York   Toronto
Delhi   Bombay   Calcutta   Madras   Karachi
Petaling Jaya   Singapore   Hong Kong   Tokyo
Nairobi   Dar es Salaam   Cape Town
Melbourne   Auckland

and associated companies in
Beirut   Berlin   Ibadan   Nicosia

Published by Oxford University Press, Inc.,
200 Madison Avenue, New York, New York 10016

Oxford is a registered trademark of Oxford University Press

Library of Congress Cataloging-in-Publication Data
Crews, Frederick C.
Skeptical engagements.
Bibliography: p.   Includes index.
1. Psychoanalysis—Addresses, essays, lectures.
2. Freud, Sigmund, 1856–1939—Addresses, essays, lectures.   I. Title.
BF173.F85C73 1986   150.19′5   86–1391
ISBN 0–19–503950–5

9 8 7 6 5 4 3 2 1

Printed in the United States of America
on acid-free paper

for Adolf Grünbaum
in friendship and gratitude

Acknowledgments

Skeptical Engagements has been so long in the making that I cannot remember all the acts of kindness that smoothed my path. Two figures were so important, though, that they deserve special mention. One is Adolf Grünbaum, who rekindled my interest in psychoanalytic questions, criticized some of my draft essays with his famous persistence, and gave me a model of the thinker who always puts rational considerations first. And then there is Elizabeth Crews, to whom I owe everything. My working definition of good fortune is to discover that your best friend is also the keenest and most demanding editor you have ever known.

Many other people have given me varying doses of support and encouragement, helpful criticism, and constructive disagreement. Few if any would subscribe to every contention in this book, but all have kept me going. My thanks go especially to Paul Alpers, Wayne Booth, Helene Boyd, William Chace, Peter Collier, Morris Eagle, Edward Erwin, Jacob Fuchs, Gerald Graff, Stephen Greenblatt, Alan Gribben, Nathan Hale, Jr., E. D. Hirsch, Jr., J. Allan Hobson, Sidney Hook, Albert Hutter, Martin Jay, Phillip Johnson, Hugh Kenner, Steven Knapp, Larry Laudan, Robert Lescher, David Leverenz, John Limon, Elaine Maimon, Leo Marx, Susan Meigs, Gerald Mendelsohn, Leonard Michaels, John R. Miles, the late Ernest Nagel, Cornelia Nixon, Hershel Parker, Ellen and Robert Pinsky, Norman Rabkin, Ralph W. Rader, Adena Rosmarin, William McKinley Runyan, Mark Shechner, Robert Silvers, William P. Sisler, Henry Nash Smith, Murray Sperber, George Starr, Frank J. Sulloway, Eric Sundquist, Peter J. Swales, John L. Traugott, Ian Watt, and Alex Zwerdling.

Contents

Introduction

This volume, my first collection of essays and occasional pieces since *Out of My System* (1975), represents approximately a decade's-worth of reflection about books and ideas that have stirred my interest. Some of the books just happened along, thanks to editors who wanted them reviewed; but when I became engaged with them, I nearly always found myself reverting to the themes of my self-initiated essays. Those themes are the specific failings of Freudian psychoanalysis; the nature, appeal, and consequences of closed, self-validating doctrines; the resultant indispensability of an empirical (evidence-oriented) point of view; and the dubious effects of literary-critical methods that spurn that point of view. The several themes really come down to just one: the fear of facing the world, including its works of literature, without an intellectual narcotic ready at hand.

My equipment for understanding the power of that fear was acquired the hard way, through trying to work myself free of a seductive dogma that had promised quick, deep knowledge. For a decade or so I was convinced that psychoanalysis, with its distrust of appearances and its stoic willingness to face the unspeakable, was a useful adjunct to my skeptical principles. Only in halting stages did I come to reverse that opinion and acknowledge that Freudianism is a faith like any other. But throughout the process I was publishing my ever-changing judgments of the Freudian tradition, and when I came to put my essays together in *Out of My System*, I used the sequence of chapters as a kind of fever chart. By the end of the book, as one reviewer tartly observed, the Freudian ground I could still stand on was no larger than a postage stamp.

This experience of conversion followed by self-deprogramming explains why psychoanalysis occupies a central place in *Skeptical*

Engagements, a book which does not change its mind about anything. Freudianism has become for me the paradigmatic example of a doctrine that compels irrational loyalty. But of course it is not the most consequential of such modern systems; that honor belongs to Marxism, to which I turn my attention in Chapters Eight and Nine. Marxism and psychoanalysis, I gradually came to see, make the same type of combined moral and "scientific" appeal, and, thanks to the fact that neither movement was founded on a truly empirical basis, their troubled intellectual histories are significantly alike. That is, in both cases the need for flight from potential disconfirmation has dictated a characteristically pseudoscientific conceptual elaboration, hairsplitting, and excommunicative bickering. And ironically, each doctrine has attracted recent academic admirers through the very fudging of its original claims.

Though *Skeptical Engagements* exhaustively sets forth the grounds for my defection from psychoanalysis, many readers—not all of them adamant Freudians—will be reluctant to take my statements at face value. *Their* skepticism will tell them to distrust someone who began by overrating a theory that everyone knows to contain its stronger and weaker points, and who then proceeded to heap abuse on that very theory in its entirety. Is this not a classic reaction formation, a product of what one of my Freudian detractors has called "the zeal of the convert of negation" (Thompson, 16)? As the Marxist psychoanalyst Joel Kovel put it in a recent public debate with me, Crews on Freud is probably just another case of "The God That Failed."

Kovel's analogy was striking, and it sent me back to *The God That Failed: Six Studies in Communism* (1950) to see how appropriate the parallel might be. I had read that book in the mid-Fifties and been strongly impressed by it, but since the mid-Sixties I had heard it mentioned only with sarcastic contempt. Rereading it in 1985, I found it more persuasive than ever—especially the contributions by Arthur Koestler, Richard Wright, Ignazio Silone, and Stephen Spender. Not one of them had written in the overcompensating spirit implied by Kovel's allusion; on the contrary, they recognized that they had been driven toward Communism by the collapse of pre-1914 values and the sorry state of capitalism, and they still seemed dazed by the Party's inability to make room for the "undisciplined" contributions of eager intellectuals.

Yet those saddened writers also marveled at their own former readiness to swallow all fundamental doubts and go on believing, in Koestler's words, that "the Party could only be changed from inside" (Koestler et al., 73). That sounded all too familiar to me; I had frequently been urged by uneasy Freudians to remember whose side I was on and not "go over to the positivists." And having been subjected to a good deal of diagnostic condescension since my apostasy, which Freudians have treated more as a symptom than as an intellectual stand, I could appreciate why the contributors to *The God That Failed* were sure they understood more about the Communist mentality than any Kremlinologist ever would. Closed systems show their true face to those who want out.

It was only after breaking with psychoanalysis that I grasped that the *ad hominem* approach to dissent, which I was suddenly encountering at every turn, is not really a behavioral lapse to which certain Freudian partisans happen to be susceptible. Rather, it is an imperative emanating from the heart of the psychoanalytic vision. Just as Marxism divides humankind into those people illumined by proletarian consciousness and those entrapped in capitalist false consciousness, so Freudianism can acknowledge only deep knowers—roughly, the analyzed—and the repressed. Hence at the moment of falling away I ceased to exist as an eligible critic of Freudian shortcomings; my file was simply rerouted, as it were, to the "Repressed" bin.

I plead guilty, then, to exhibiting the God That Failed syndrome. Like Koestler and Silone, I can no longer regard my abandoned faith primarily as a cluster of propositions, some of which must of necessity be more sensible than the others. I see it rather as a movement that channels thought in ways that are meant to perpetuate, not a scientific truth or a revolutionary passion, but the movement itself, which has long since forgotten what it was orginally supposed to be about. Nevertheless, not expecting others to take my word for this understanding of psychoanalysis, in Chapters One through Five I take pains to show why Freudian propositions, even the mildest-looking ones, have not been significantly corroborated.

Since students of literature will be reading this book, however, I know that I face another credibility problem. Some colleagues oppose my current position by holding up against me my own psychoanalytic study of Nathaniel Hawthorne, *The Sins of the Fathers* (1966). Insofar as they find that book convincing, they fail to understand how I can now turn my back on it. The shortest answer is that I see no need to repudiate the whole book. Much of its emphasis—for example, on the egregiously moralistic tradition of Hawthorne criticism and on the manifest psychological tone of Hawthorne's fiction—owes nothing uniquely to Freudian theory. And in pointing out that Hawthorne's concern with furtive sexuality, incest, and moral masochism was akin to Freud's, I was not applying psychoanalytic method but simply mentioning what any reader of both authors can still ascertain.

The Sins of the Fathers went astray, however, by gratuitously relegating much of that concern on Hawthorne's part to his repressed unconscious and by wielding Freudian symbol interpretation with unwarranted confidence. I think I could recast the argument more modestly today, giving more weight to Hawthorne's background, milieu, and audience and to his conscious irony; the psychological themes would still come out much the same. And by drawing on recent studies such as Gloria C. Erlich's *Family Themes and Hawthorne's Fiction* (1984) and Philip Young's more speculative *Hawthorne's Secret* (1984), I could provide other possible reasons for Hawthorne's sexual preoccupation than the oedipal one I highlighted in 1966.

Still, there remains Hawthorne's impressive-looking "anticipation of Freud," which at least one recent critic (Adams) takes to be a sign that Freud's ideas must be right. But Hawthorne and Freud were both immersed in the psychological atmosphere of Romanticism; the fact that they shared a thematic emphasis proves only that a *Zeitgeist* can pass across continents and decades. In fact, one of Freud's most beguiling stratagems was to point to the surprising and delightful corroboration of his "clinical findings" by great works of literature and philosophy that he had supposedly read only afterwards. As Henri Ellenberger (1970) and others have shown, the reason psychoanalysis appears to validate earlier authors is that it was partly derived from them. In any event, if we want to justify the application of Freudian ideas to literature, we have to show not that they were anticipated but that they are well-founded and free of fatal confusions.

Yet well-foundedness is itself a confusing concept for many humanists and even some social scientists. A minority of them hold that there is no such thing as an empirically warranted idea, and many others feel that Freud's contribution to our culture is just too precious and familiar, too entwined with our sense of the modern, to deserve being subjected to potentially humbling interrogation.

Freud, they are sure, was "one of us," the kind of thinker who penetrates directly to intuitive truth and sees the nuances and tragic ironies that are lost on data mongerers.

In one sense this is a fitting apprehension of Freud, who mimicked the diction and the deterministic lawgiving of natural science, as he conceived it, but slyly thumbed his nose at scientific prudence. His magnum opus, for example, was self-consciously anti-inductive in its affinities, embracing the wisdom of poets and the folklore of popular dream interpretation, invoking hellish powers in its famous epigraph, and even tauntingly calling to mind astrology (*Sterndeutung*) in its very title, *Die Traumdeutung* (Ellenberger, 452). That, we might say, was the "cocaine" side of an extraordinarily embattled and imperious mind, at once clouded and indomitable. It was not by adding to our scientific knowledge but rather by concocting an ingenious witches' brew of speculative neurophysiology, mythic conceptualizing about subterranean psychic agents, literary charm, debaters' tricks, mendacious therapeutic claims, and spicy and grotesque sexual tales that Freud eventually captured the fancy of a civilization—or rather, of those of its members who were trying to modernize their morals and see through all "sublimations," including the resented achievements of mainstream science.

Even so, Freud never doubted one rule of cardinal importance: since psychoanalysis purports to offer laws of mental functioning, it must be judged by the same empirical criteria as any other would-be scientific theory. Freud did everything he could to postpone and befuddle such judgment, but he accepted its appropriateness in principle. This acquiescence was not what Jürgen Habermas (1971) has perversely called a "scientistic self-misunderstanding" on Freud's part, but rather a simple recognition that a science of mental causes and effects would have to be discarded if its claims never received corroboration.

The case against psychoanalysis made by *Skeptical Engagements*, then, is an unabashedly empirical one—no less so than that of my friend Adolf Grünbaum, to whom the book is gratefully dedicated. Readers familiar with Grünbaum's pathbreaking *The Foundations of Psychoanalysis* (1984), however, will note that I am trying to take a step beyond its argument. Grünbaum, looking at Freudian tenets one by one, emphasizes the absence *thus far* of cogent support for those ideas that have turned out—no thanks to their proponents—to be experimentally or epidemiologically test-

able. In theory, though by no means in actual expectation, Grünbaum contemplates the remote possibility that eventually some
psychoanalytic concepts or hypotheses will be shown to have been
"serendipitously" cogent—a prospect that certain Freudians (e.g.,
Edelson, Lieberson) have clung to like drowning men.

I think, with Frank Cioffi (1970, 1985), that it is less useful
to imagine such a miraculous rescue than it is to emphasize how,
in practice, any given Freudian inference could be just as plausibly
replaced by another one. If this is so, then psychoanalysis is not
appreciably different in epistemic rigor from the reading of tea
leaves, and the eventual discovery of some corroborated Freudian
assertions can no more alter a negative verdict on the method than
would the fortune teller's lucky guess. I therefore focus on the ambiguous and opportunistic character of the whole Freudian system,
in which any given proposition, however testable in theory, is pre-
served from risk by escape clauses, vague interpretations, or even
outright contradictions. What chiefly matters is not that we count
the hits and misses in that cluster-bomb assault on truth, but that
we show the illegitimacy of reasoning in the self-indulgent Freudian style.

It is this interest in willful, arbitrary assertion that links
Parts I and II of *Skeptical Engagements*. Over the past fifteen years
or so, my own field of literary study has been invaded by a strong
and widening current of anti-empiricism. In the very period when
I was being beset by factually based misgivings about psychoanalysis, many of my colleagues were deciding to cast their lot with
impressive-sounding doctrines, structuralist and poststructuralist,
that had arisen within Continental philosophy, anthropology, linguistics, politics, criticism, and psychoanalysis itself. Those doctrines tacitly or openly subordinated the pursuit of corroborated
knowledge to the swift overthrow of bourgeois illusions, which
they replaced with no less debatable but more sweeping and dogmatic assertions. Chapters Six through Nine characterize this
theoretical explosion and explain why, in my opinion, we should
be extremely wary of its claims.

To "do theory" these days, as that expression is understood
by department chairs who hope to load their ranks with a full
panoply of "theorists," is not to maintain a thesis against likely
objections, but rather to strike attitudes that will identify one as
a loyal follower of some figure—a Roland Barthes, a Jacques Derrida, a Michel Foucault, a Jacques Lacan, a Fredric Jameson—who

has himself made unexamined claims about the nature of capitalism or patriarchy or Western civilization or the collective unconscious or the undecidability of knowledge. Such gurus are treasured, I suspect, less for their specific creeds than for the invigorating Nietzschean scorn they direct at intellectual prudence. The rise of "theory" has resulted in an irrationalist climate in the strictest sense—that is, an atmosphere in which it is considered old-fashioned and gullible to think that differences of judgment can ever be arbitrated on commonly held grounds.

When this position of rational undecidability is stated in a comprehensible way, it possesses a semblance of plausibility. Indeterminists, as I call them, contend that the "evidence" that might favor one critical interpretation over another will always be itself an artifact of an interpretation. All literary argument, then—indeed, all argument whatsoever—is considered circular. By citing such apparent cognitive radicals as Thomas Kuhn (1970) and Paul Feyerabend (1970), the indeterminists even manage to suggest that science itself, our model of orderly progress, lurches from paradigm to paradigm spurred by extrinsic, prejudicial factors.

Extending the indeterminist argument to scientific discovery, however, has been a self-damning as well as a typical arrogation. As I maintain in Chapter Nine, where Kuhn's actual "sociology of rationality" is defended against its misinterpreters, the undoubted achievements of twentieth-century science are sufficient testimony against the envious proposal that scientists possess no evidential basis for choosing between rival ideas. The truism that all facts are theory-laden is irrelevant; what counts is whether a given piece of evidence, when judged by an expert community possessing common values and rules, is sufficiently independent of the particular theories in conflict. Recognizing that fact, we could return to literary study and show that there, too, just as in science, appeals are often successfully made to evidential points—biographical, historical, bibliographical, linguistic—that stand outside the arena of competing interpretations. It is only by choosing the most ambiguous literary examples—a typical anti-empirical tactic—that indeterminists can purport to show the contrary.

Moreover, as E. D. Hirsch, Jr. (1967, 1976) and others have explained, the vanguard position of cognitive nihilism can only be managed through a logical trick, one that Gerald Graff has named the "Poststructuralist Two-Step." In step one, the theorist asserts a total undecidability between propositions, and anyone who doubts his claim is accused of being stuck in the outmoded Cartesian dualism of subject and object, whereby the facts of the world are innocently thought to lie "out there." But since the theorist is himself a subject making a claim that he wants to be deemed objectively true, he must take a discreet hop toward the cognitive center. In step two, then, he implies that for himself alone the truth is accessible after all, thanks merely to his watchfulness against the biases he finds in others.

But the Poststructuralist Two-Step is not as novel as it looks. In one form or another, it characterizes the whole "School of Suspicion"—the line of radically anti-consensual philosophy that runs from Marx, Freud, and Nietzsche through Heidegger to Derrida and Foucault. All of those thinkers described a general human state of epistemic occlusion—of inevitable subjection to the warping effects of class membership or species-wide cowardice or the repressed unconscious or the hermeneutic circle or the prison-house of language; yet each, in the act of making his claims, implied that a superior mind, his own, was unaffected by those forces. Marxism and Freudianism became the modern movements *par excellence* that induced fervid belief by holding out this double promise: enlightenment for you and me, darkness for the others.

My reply to the School of Suspicion is that its Romantic, individualistic model of the search for knowledge has been erroneous from the start. The turn toward nihilism is unavoidable if we begin by picturing the single mind alone with the enigmatic universe on one side and a meager stock of metaphors on the other. My own starting point is an acknowledgment that we do, by now, know a great many things with enough assurance to profit from their consequences. We know them, not because the isolated mind is a reliable instrument or because some magus has bequeathed us his vision, but because our disciplinary communities have evolved ways of choosing shrewdly between an array of (mostly poor, often foolish) cognitive opportunities.

If I dwell on anti-empirical movements rather than on positive gains, it is because such movements can poison the cooperative atmosphere that makes knowledge a feasible project. Regrettably, my own field has led the way in lending them sanctuary and prestige. Squinting in the unaccustomed limelight of publicity, well-intentioned colleagues have not known whether to be ashamed or proud of the grandiose claims now made for literary interpretation as the queen of techniques for overturning common sense.

And so, by and large, they have lamely tried to adapt themselves to "new insights" whose sources they do not examine. When I notice that some of those "insights" depend on long-discredited Freudian dogma, I feel obliged to warn against misapprehensions that are all too familiar to me.

"Crews, Stannard, and their sympathizers," one recent commentator has remarked, "must have noticed on their way to bury psychoanalysis that traffic going the other way is nearly bumper to bumper" (Weiland, 709). If everyone agrees that traffic patterns should set our intellectual direction, the case is closed. But this book presupposes that things are not yet that far gone. I address my arguments to readers who still cherish common sense and who suspect that schemes of drastic liberation are not always what they claim to be. Would it not be truly liberating to rehabilitate the empirical spirit and demand that literary theorists, psychoanalysts, and others show us why we should be expected to believe them? If *Skeptical Engagements*, though only a collection of previous encounters, nevertheless has a practical end in view, it is to make that prospect more attractive.

Works Cited

Adams, Michael Vannoy. 1983. "Pathography, Hawthorne, and the History of Psychological Ideas." *ESQ*, 29: 113–126.

Cioffi, Frank. 1970. "Freud and the Idea of a Pseudo-Science." In *Explanation in the Behavioural Sciences*, ed. Robert Borger and Frank Cioffi. Cambridge: Cambridge University Press. Pp. 471–499.

———. 1985. "Psychoanalysis, Pseudo-Science and Testability." In *Popper and the Human Sciences*, ed. G. Currie and A. Musgrave. Dordrecht: Nijhoff. Pp. 13–211.

Crews, Frederick. 1966. *The Sins of the Fathers: Hawthorne's Psychological Themes*. New York: Oxford University Press.

———. 1975. *Out of My System: Psychoanalysis, Ideology, and Critical Method*. New York: Oxford University Press.

Edelson, Marshall. 1984. *Hypothesis and Evidence in Psychoanalysis*. Chicago: University of Chicago Press.

Ellenberger, Henri F. 1970. *The Discovery of the Unconscious: The History and Evolution of Dynamic Psychiatry*. New York: Basic Books.

Erlich, Gloria C. 1984. *Family Themes and Hawthorne's Fiction: The Tenacious Web*. New Brunswick: Rutgers University Press.

Feyerabend, Paul. 1970. *Against Method*. Minneapolis: University of Minnesota Press.

Grünbaum, Adolf. 1984. *The Foundations of Psychoanalysis: A Philosophical Critique.* Berkeley: University of California Press.

Habermas, Jürgen. 1971. *Knowledge and Human Interests*, trans. Jeremy J. Shapiro. Boston: Beacon.

Hirsch, E. D., Jr. 1967. *Validity in Interpretation.* New Haven: Yale University Press.

———. *The Aims of Interpretation.* Chicago: University of Chicago Press.

Koestler, Arthur, and Ignazio Silone, André Gide, Richard Wright, Louis Fischer, and Stephen Spender. 1950. *The God That Failed: Six Studies in Communism*, intro. Richard Crossman. London: Hamish Hamilton.

Kuhn, Thomas S. 1970. *The Structure of Scientific Revolutions*, 2d ed. (1st ed. 1962.) Chicago: University of Chicago Press.

Lieberson, Jonathan. 1985. "Putting Freud to the Test." *New York Review of Books*, 31 January, pp. 24–28.

Thompson, Thomas H. 1984. "Freud Redux: Psychoanalysis Turned Inside Out." *North American Review*, December, pp. 14–28.

Weiland, Steven. 1983. "Relations Stop Nowhere: Cases and Texts, Critics and Psychoanalysis." *College English*, 45: 705–723.

Young, Philip. 1984. *Hawthorne's Secret: An Un-Told Tale.* Boston: Godine.

I

The Freudian Temptation

1

The Liberal Unconscious

This essay-review of Erik H. Erikson's Life History and the Historical Moment *(1975) marks a stage in my own life history. Relatively hesitant though it is in tone, this is the first of my writings that can be considered resignedly anti-psychoanalytic. Though I ended by asking Freudians for "an unsparing reassessment" of the tradition I had recently abandoned, I sensed that no such self-examination was foreseeable and that, in any event, my misgivings had already hardened into convictions.*

It is fitting that my break with psychoanalysis was announced, however discreetly, through a discussion of Erikson's career. In the line of psychoanalytic evolution that I had favored—the one that runs from Freud's clinical theory through the refinements and complications of American ego psychology—Erikson stands out as the suavest and most adaptable of spokesmen. If anyone could have met my wish for a nondogmatic, humanistic version of psychoanalysis that would nonetheless reaffirm Freud's most daring discoveries, it would have been Erikson. By 1975, however, I could see that Erikson's eclecticism depended for its air of wisdom on stylistic artifices whose spell could not survive much cold attention. To acknowledge the empirical vacuum in Erikson's seductive oeuvre *was also to recognize that I had no other Freudian direction in which to turn.*

The appearance of another collection of Erik Erikson's incidental pieces, loosely connected in theme, is not in itself an event of great significance—not, certainly, one to be compared with the arrival of the brilliant and novel studies on which his reputation mainly rests: *Childhood and Society, Young Man Luther, Gandhi's Truth.* It has

3

been six years now since Erikson's last major book, and though everything he writes merits attention, his career has recently been in a phase of clarification, consolidation, and response to criticism. Erikson the author has lately become much occupied with Erikson the figure: with the benevolent adjuster of social polarities (as in his cautious and labored encounter with Huey Newton at Yale); with the prophet and catalyst of a "new identity" for Americans and others,[1] and with the psychohistorical pioneer whose well-intentioned dicta, twisted by partisan opponents, must be patiently restated, not without an occasional note of injured majesty.

Now we have Erikson's most explicitly personal book, in which he directly discusses his early life and career, spars posthumously with Freud, recounts the origin and methodology of his research into Gandhi, and politely rebukes the feminists who took him to task for theorizing about the "inner space" of womankind. In these conference papers, addresses, and reviews, Erikson always has at least one eye on his reputation. It is, in short, his own achievement, rather than any new area of inquiry, to which our attention is now persistently directed. A prior concern with Erikson is requisite if *Life History and the Historical Moment* is to take on importance.

No one who cares about the vicissitudes of Freudian thought, however, will lack that concern. For Erikson above all other ego psychologists has turned psychoanalysis, a doctrine plagued by mechanism, reification, and arbitrary universalism, into a reasonably flexible tool for addressing historical particulars. It is Erikson, again, who has expanded and most clearly systematized Freud's ideas about early development, making all those zones, modes, modalities, and stages look less like crackpot categories than like ordinary observables of childhood. And it is Erikson who has done most to combat the gloom imparted to psychoanalysis by Freud's temperamental bias. The currency of such Eriksonian terms as "basic trust," "identity crisis," and "moratorium" may remind us how successful he has been in urging a nondeterministic view of crises and their solutions. His success has been won through vivid and delicately handled examples—not just in the three famous books, but also in essays that subtly blend analytic penetration and restraint. He is at once the most resourceful, the most humane, and not coincidentally the most popular of all Freud's heirs.

Erikson's prestige is the more remarkable because psychoanalysis as an intellectual movement has plainly fallen on hard times.

There is wide agreement that the logic of Freudian reasoning is suspiciously loose; that its data are too private and inferential to be scientifically trustworthy; that many of its particular assertions, especially regarding women, have owed more to ideology and superstition than to clinical fact; and that its lingering appeal to Freud's personal word leaves it only partly responsive to new knowledge. Though the individual Freudian may—and too often does—shrug off these criticisms, their cumulative effect has been to jeopardize his whole style of thinking. Psychoanalysis finds itself conceding one failing after another in the hope that some shrunken core of method or insight will be considered salvageable. Except for ponderously whimsical Parisian recastings of Freud's "text," only Erikson's fledgling discipline of psychohistory seems capable of stirring excitement today. And it is clear to most observers that psychohistory is far from invulnerable to the criticism that has been besetting psychoanalysis on every side.

If Erikson has thrived in this worsening climate, part of the reason may be that he has managed to join in the dissent from orthodoxy without forsaking the most promising aspects of psychoanalysis—its attentiveness to signs of conflict, its hospitality to multiple significance, its ideas of ambivalence, identification, regression, and projection. Nothing in his gracious prose suggests that he feels threatened by an acknowledgment of the more quirky and culture-bound side of Freudianism. He himself has come to accept the idea that a theory of trauma and dysfunction cannot be considered a general psychology, and his display of scruples inspires confidence in his own more modest and qualified use of that theory.

Nor does Erikson wish to deny that psychoanalysis is among other things an instrument of social and political advocacy. Several chapters of *Life History*, along with previous essays, are marked by an awareness of Freud's biases and of the partisan function of psychoanalysis "in the cultural and ideological controversies of our time." Indeed, Erikson welcomes this function, claiming that psychoanalysis cannot be a healing art without "directly intervening in the processes by which values are formed and transmitted in society." Unlike the classic Freudian, who pretended to be practicing value-neutral medicine while he was promoting a *Weltanschauung*, Erikson appears to know just where his clinical principles cease and his moral commitment begins.

That moral commitment must itself be counted among the

reasons for Erikson's public acclaim. Unlike Freud, who could not always suppress his scorn for mortal folly, Erikson is patently a friend of humankind. He remains unmesmerized by those psychic recesses that prompted Freud to brood about a primal crime, hereditary guilt, and an incurable panhuman lust for war. Erikson instead hopes to instill enlightened and pacific ideals in a species which may yet repay his faith in its unfulfilled promise of nobility. His emphasis falls on the altruistic strivings of youth, the satisfaction of motherhood, the dignity and wisdom of age, the indispensability of the nuclear family, and the need for harmony among the nations, which will surely outgrow their immature divisiveness. Readers who think of Erikson as having derived these perceptions from deep psychological research are bound to feel relieved that the nightmare of Freudian fatalism has been dispelled at last.[2]

Not everyone, however, is prepared to regard Erikson's achievement in this generous light. Those who dissent from particular ingredients of his ethical vision, or whose wariness is aroused by the coinciding of that vision with educated middle-class opinion, have already begun to wonder whether he hasn't contrived a shrewd but specious compromise between Freudianism and liberal ideology. The suspicion is rude, even shocking; yet once it has been entertained, Erikson's writings are curiously helpless to drive it away. It is clear that he has grafted his own virtue-oriented scheme of development onto Freud's drive-oriented one, but his objective basis for doing so is far from readily apparent.

In order to refute his detractors, Erikson must be able to show, not merely assert, that he has drawn his ideas from replicable scientific findings; otherwise the debate immediately reduces to an exchange of unsupported claims. But here the empirical weakness of the Freudian tradition lets him down. As psychoanalysis is gradually demoted from a science to a body of challengeable propositions, fewer and fewer readers will be satisfied by Erikson's personal assurance that he has seen and circumvented the methodological pitfalls. Erikson himself, after all, has debunked the physicalistic pretensions of psychoanalysis, spurned its main interpretative expectation (which is that primitive and infantile concerns will always be found to underlie complex and adult ones), and depicted it as one movement among many that have derived a new "truth" out of emergent cultural forces. How then can he offer his own neo-Freudian conclusions as the fruits of psychoanalytic investigation? Has he, in his psychohistorical researches, discovered that certain Freudian ideas are permanently and cross-culturally valid?

No forthright answer to this question can be extracted from Erikson's works. Unlike his late friend David Rapaport, who brought to psychoanalytic theorizing a dry Kantian rigor, he has been by disposition a peacemaker among competing ideas. He is, by his own account in *Life History*, someone with a propensity for "moving on," taking inspiration where he finds it while indefinitely postponing the choice of "belonging anywhere quite irreversibly." What drew him toward psychoanalysis was not its conceptual niceties but, he says, Freud's speculative "freedom and enjoyment of inquiry," with which he has always felt "a particular and maybe peculiar identification." Yet Erikson is not quite ready to admit that his ideas originated in that unconstrained license to generalize. Rather, he falls back ambiguously on the very authority he would seem to have demystified—the authority of psychoanalysis as a reliable scientific method.

It is, oddly enough, because he is preeminently a moralist that Erikson needs to keep that empirical authority alive. The strong cultural influence that psychoanalysis exerted for decades, and that Erikson hopes to retain, was facilitated by Freud's sincere but mistaken conviction that he was an ethically neutral scientist. The selfishness and undependability he ascribed to the unconscious impressed people because they thought of him not as an anti-utopian social philosopher but as a conscientious explorer sending back reports from an alarmingly savage territory. If readers had been able to penetrate his scientistic vocabulary of drives, cathexes, and mechanisms, they would have seen immediately that psychoanalysis is a socially engaged doctrine—and their interest in it would have been more guarded. Erikson's root concepts, in contrast to Freud's, are explicitly moral, and he openly aspires to guide his readers toward certain sociopolitical values; but for this very reason he cannot bear to part with the myth of the psychoanalyst as scientist. In order to be heard with the respect to which renowned Freudians have long been accustomed, he must swallow his evident misgivings and do what he can to keep that myth alive.

Erikson's method of handling historical problems implies an awareness that the a priori nucleus of Freudian ideas is highly suspect. Yet he repeatedly calls psychoanalysis a "science," one which "will take generations to find proper forms of verification," but which meanwhile has managed to cast light on "man's central motivations." The analyst's consulting room, he says, is also "a psychologist's laboratory," and "clinical verification . . . is always of the essence in any conceptual shift in psychoanalysis." If we ask what this verification consists of—how, for example, it can be disentangled from the ideological influence that Erikson concedes and actually applauds as a means of keeping psychoanalysis adaptable to "humanist enlightenment"—we are met only with a smoke-screen of temporizing rhetoric.

This rhetoric consists largely of hedged assertions that psychoanalysis includes, or should include, "methods of observing its own functioning in the cultural-historical process." "Precisely because it knows how to study the importance of oversimplified world views for the management of anxiety in each person and community, and especially so as it becomes aware of its own historical fate in such changing world images," psychoanalysis "may have the built-in correctives" for "pseudo-ethical" distortions of its concepts. Which is to say that the psychoanalyst may attain a kind of objectivity by noticing, and somehow making allowance for, the very ideologizing of clinical doctrine that Erikson encourages him to indulge.

The murkiness of this position should be readily apparent. If the consulting-room "laboratory"—a laboratory whose forms of proof may be worked out several generations from now—has yielded certain concepts that Erikson correctly finds redundant and indefensible, how can we imagine that "built-in correctives" will spare psychoanalysis from ideological warping?

It is true that Freudians have always prided themselves on what Erikson approvingly calls their "disciplined subjectivity," namely, their alertness to the effects of transference and countertransference; and in *Life History* he calls grandly for an extension of self-analysis to the psychohistorian's "*re-transference* on former selves" and even to "*cross transferences* from one reviewer of the same subject to another." But all this punctilio appears quite empty when we realize that the analyst may overlook a given instance of unconscious projection on his part; left alone with his good intentions and his belief in his own acuteness, he possesses nothing resembling the intersubjective checking whereby genuine sciences bring the individual theorizer to logical and empirical account. That Erikson himself is unusually self-aware, no one would deny. But by ascribing a special self-corrective acumen to a movement whose cultural relativity he has helped to expose, he risks too much of his credit in a dubious cause.

Whenever Erikson brings himself to the verge of admitting that psychoanalysis has no adequate means of weeding out folklore, we can be sure to find a tepid non sequitur allowing the point to slip vaguely away. Thus one chapter of *Life History* ends with this inconclusive paragraph:

> Psychoanalysis represents a very special admixture of "laboratory" conditions, methodological climate, and personal and ideological involvement. Other fields may claim to be governed by radically different admixtures and certainly by much less subjective kinds of evidence. But I wonder whether they could insist, at any time, on a total absence of any one of the ingredients described here.

The obvious rejoinder is that "other fields" make no claim that their adherents are immune to passion and fashion; what they claim is allegiance to certain criteria of falsification which psychoanalysis, by virtue of the inaccessibility of its data and the open-endedness of its logic, must necessarily forgo. But here and elsewhere, Erikson does not stay for an answer. He leaves us to infer, erroneously, that "personal and ideological involvement," since it can be detected in scientists of every sort, poses no fundamental obstacle to the verification of Freudian ideas.

If Erikson were merely being generous toward a discipline he admired from a distance, his equivocations about psychoanalysis would have only a peripheral interest. In fact, however, he is more committed to the Freudian mode of drawing inferences than one might gather from his tentative-sounding prose. The key debility in that mode is its fatal readiness to corroborate any number of incompatible hunches about a given phenomenon, which can, according to the analyst's whim, be taken to mean either what it seems to mean, or exactly the opposite, or some other idea which it has supposedly "displaced."

Erikson's habit is to take just enough advantage of the pliability in Freudian reasoning to gain a privileged angle on his subject—and then to highlight his forbearance in not following through with an orthodox reductionist interpretation. Hoping, for example, to show that the Ahmedabad mill strike was "the Event" in the emergence of Gandhi's vocation, he found support in Gandhi's telltale "wish to 'play it down' "—that is, in the fact that the strike receives no special emphasis in Gandhi's autobiography or elsewhere in his writings.[3] With the concepts of resistance and denial ready at hand, the psychohistorian can place his central dramatic emphasis wherever he pleases. It is small recompense when he sensitively discusses and cautions against the arrogance of method which he nevertheless continues to exercise.

Despite the contrast he repeatedly implies between Freud's narrow views and his own open-mindedness, Erikson from the beginning has embraced some of the more dogmatic points of Freudian doctrine. The epigenetic scheme articulated in *Childhood and Society* presumes, along with Freud and Abraham, that there are real "stages of the libido" corresponding to the imagery of adult patients and that the ground plan of human character is demarcated by certain constants: the potentially traumatic conflicts over feeding, elimination, phallic assertion, and, in females, an inceptiveness which is apt to make a girl "more dependent and more demanding" (Erikson 1963, 90). "Freud's findings regarding the sexual etiology of a mental disturbance," declared Erikson a quarter-century ago, "are as true for our patients as they were for his . . ."; and he chooses this very passage to reaffirm in his latest work, as if to restore a solidarity with Freud that he might seem to have long since demolished.

There is, in an ironical sense, justice in the statement that the sexual etiology of neurosis remains as true as ever, for Freud never demonstrated that etiology in the first place. He merely chose to reconstruct determinative infantile crises on the basis of "screen memories" and leading themes in his patients' emphatically coaxed and edited associations. Virtually the entire Freudian theory of childhood was devised by remote and chancy inference, without direct observation of children themselves. In *Childhood and Society* Erikson accepted that theory in most of its essentials, using his own work with children not to test the theory but to provide anecdotal illustration of it. To be sure, he then went on to argue that intrapsychic factors alone give only a partial account of any patient's situation. What he did not do, however, was to inquire whether ordinary childhood development ought to be characterized by rubrics borrowed from the study of extraordinary adult breakdown. As opposed, say, to the more observation-based formulations of Piaget, Erikson's ideas about the stages of childhood have a distinctly scholastic air.

But there is nothing derivative about the uniquely Eriksonian successors to those stages. On the contrary, they seem to have been invented *ex nihilo*. I refer to the highly moralized struggles between "intimacy and distantiation," "generativity and stagnation," "integrity and despair," and so forth. Without disclosing the evidence that made him settle on each pair of terms instead of some other pair, Erikson has presumed to set forth a complete life plan for his species, irrespective of cultural differences. Like Freud in promulgating the death instinct, he has directly translated his world view into "science."

That world view, as we have already seen, is in some respects opposite to Freud's, and one must admire the ingenuity with which Erikson appears to anchor it in Freud's work. Where Freud is reductive and "originological," Erikson is expansive and teleological, depicting both the individual and the human race as growing toward the realization of predestined ideals. Those ideals, embodying everything that leads *"outward* from self-centeredness to the mutuality of love and communality, *forward* from the enslaving past to the utopian anticipation of new potentialities, and *upward* from the unconscious to the enigma of consciousness," are a concise summation of the liberal-Protestant ethos that Erikson found so attractive when he arrived in the New World. He has paid America the honor of deciding that its favorite virtues are, in some unexplained sense, immanent in human nature.

A skeptical reader may feel entitled to be told how Erikson knows that the "guiding vision" now required by humankind is already enacting itself in history. But rather than defend his teleology in detail, Erikson appears content with the reflection that psychoanalysis and prophecy traditionally go hand in hand. Indeed, he tries to convince himself that Freud's speculations were secretly in alignment with his own. Freud, he divines, anticipated "a new morality . . . which in our time may well (again, because it must) evolve from psychoanalytic and ecological considerations." And when his persuasive energy falters, Erikson is not above enlisting the support of Freudian ideas that he has elsewhere explicitly rejected. For instance:

> If I, furthermore, postulate a built-in developmental aim of adult maturity in the individual life cycle and an intrinsic socio-evolutionary goal of one specieshood for mankind, I may, again, remind you that Freud pointed to the recurrent self-assertion of Eros as a power binding larger and larger units of mankind together, and this just when he was tragically aware of the periodical and ever more efficient destructiveness of Thanatos.

What Freud is here said to have been tragically aware of is an "instinct" that Erikson, earlier in the same volume, characterizes as "a grandiose contradiction in terms." But when one posits intrinsic socio-evolutionary goals for mankind, one can't be finicky in one's choice of corroborating references.

It should be borne in mind that Erikson's hollowest pronouncements are all of recent date—bearing witness, perhaps, only to a certain overexposure to *Daedalus* conferences on large and timely issues. The usefulness of his concepts remains unaffected by any doubts we may harbor about his world-unifying Gandhian ambitions. At the same time, however, the prevalence of unsupported moralizing in Erikson's late writings is bound to raise new questions about his early ones. How independent of popular opinion has Erikson ever been? Has his ideological outlook followed from his psychology, or rather did it help to dictate that psychology?

Take, for example, Erikson's central (though still inadequately defined) concept of identity. He has previously told us that he first began speaking of "identity crises" when observing ego-impaired veterans in the early 1940s (Erikson 1968, 16–17). But from his latest book we learn that the ideological imperatives of those years also left their stamp on his idea. "In the Roosevelt era," he recalls, "we immigrants could tell ourselves that America was once more helping to save the Atlantic world from tyranny." The best hope for resistance to the tide of fanaticism and authoritarianism seemed to lie in the "expansively open . . . 'national character' " of his newly adopted country. "What now demanded to be conceptualized . . . called for a whole new orientation which fused a new world image (and, in fact, a New World image) with traditional theoretical assumptions." Erikson does not say that he produced "identity" expressly to meet this political requirement, and that is most unlikely. Yet the term was launched on a prevailing updraft of nationalistic idealism, and Erikson was plainly eager to ride that current himself.

Rereading *Childhood and Society* today, we cannot miss its nakedly political, almost allegorical emphasis—its sunny view of the resourceful American personality, threatened only by "Momism and bossism"; its cautionary examples of German and Russian characterological rigidity; its blunt advice that we watch for renewed attempts by Germans to solve their identity problems at the world's expense and its enthusiasm for foiling Communism by exporting American ideals to foreign masses, who must be convinced "that—from a very long-range point of view—their protestantism is ours and ours, theirs" (Erikson 1963, 402).

In thus combining American chauvinism and hypotheses about national character, Erikson was indulging in a well-established and, by the Forties, highly mobilized academic pursuit. The study of "culture and personality," founded at Yale in the Thirties by Edward Sapir and Erikson's mentor John Dollard, had concentrated at first on primitive societies and global questions about variability in human nature. By the Forties, however—when, according to Robert Coles, Erikson was writing papers on "submarine psychology" and the most productive ways of interrogating German prisoners (Coles, 43–44)—this hybrid of anthropology, sociology, and psychology had yielded a victory garden of instrumental projects, from prediction of German feelings about saturation bombing to what Margaret Mead called "the most notable contribution" of national-character research during the war, namely, exploration of "the relationship between preserving the Emperor and obtaining a simultaneous and complete surrender of all the Japanese armed forces" (Mead, 75). Soon after the war, predictably, the Russian "national character" became irresistibly fascinating, with sponsorship of culture-and-personality studies shifting from the prewar Bureau of Indian Affairs to policy institutes, RAND, the Office of Naval Research, and the Air Force.[4]

At Yale, Berkeley, and Harvard, as well as in his government service, Erikson was in contact with the mainstream of culture-and-personality research, and *Childhood and Society*, with its progress from the Sioux and Yurok through Hitler to Gorky, can be read in part as a précis of the field's development. Erikson, too, briefly studied Indians, not just under the auspices of the Bureau of Indian Affairs but from the BIA's tacit cultural vantage. In his original report on the Yurok he noted enthusiastically (despite the fact that he "was not able to make relevant observations on Yurok childhood as it is today") that "the Yurok child, under proper treatment, has a much shorter way to go in adaptation to white standards than does the child of other tribes" (Erikson 1943, 283+n.). And the pathology which, thanks to close study of one film about Gorky's childhood, he was able to detect in those baby-swaddling Russian peasants ("Is the Russian soul a swaddled soul?") and their steely Bolshevik masters—"our cold, our dangerous adversaries"—accorded well with many another diagnosis of incurable Soviet irrationality (Erikson 1963, 388, 399).

After the mid-Sixties, for reasons that need no rehearsing, Erikson appears to have changed his mind about the bumptious, eternally adolescent American character and its evangelical destiny. Instead of worrying only that happy-go-lucky Americans might be too impressionable, he now suspects that our myth of the "do-it-yourself personality" rationalizes "the reactionary possession of privileged interests and organized powers" (Erikson 1974, 104). At times he even implies that the whole country is a menace whose collective sickness embraces, in Marcusean style, "the *repression* of inner conflict in those who overadjust to power, the *suppression* of adversary opinions, and the ready *oppression* of foreign people" (Erikson 1974, 111). In short, Erikson appears to have accommodated himself to the New Left with the same alacrity with which he formerly became "Americanized."

What is bothersome here is not the mere change in Erikson's outlook. Few social thinkers went through the Sixties with their ideology intact, and no special glory attaches to those who did. My point is rather that we must note the extent to which Erikson's psychological ideas have tagged behind his swerving politics. For Erikson suddenly appears uneasy, not just with the specific American myth of the self-made man, but with the very concept of national identity. Attachment to one's nation is now regarded as acquiescence in the paranoid projectiveness whereby each artificial grouping vents its craziness on the others. It is in this period of retreat from his Cold War patriotism that Erikson has discovered mankind's inborn program of evolving toward "one specieshood." When national pride is battered, universalism is revealed to be nature's immutable law.

Readers whose political consciousness is not advancing at the same rate as Erikson's cannot help but observe how sharply his recent characterological findings differ from his earlier ones. As one former disciple, David Gutmann, remarks:

> . . . in the early 60's Erikson saw the modal American as a decent and fundamentally reasonable individual. . . . Today he sees him as a dangerous and primitive psychological type, externalizing his rage and frustrations through sadistic forays against outsiders who represent metaphors of his own impotence. Which of these two versions is the correct one? Can American life and particularly the American character possibly have changed so drastically in so short a time? (Gutmann, 62)

For Gutmann the first Erikson was right and the second one is wrong about our national disposition. More searchingly, we must ask whether his notions in either epoch have been sufficiently independent of the prevailing political mood.

When that mood turns divisive and acrimonious, not even the supremely adaptable Erikson can spare himself from controversy. His gathering troubles are well represented by a chapter of *Life History* that is given over to an ingenious, appealing, but finally empty defense of his now notorious essay, "Womanhood and the Inner Space." Considered simply in relation to psychoanalytic orthodoxy, that essay was a progressive document, denying the universality of "female masochism," minimizing penis envy and "female castration," and allowing for constructive roles in addition to the reaffirmed one of mothering. Yet it was also a heavily tendentious declaration, insisting, on the basis of no substantial evidence, that women's achievements are bound to reflect "the implications of what is biologically and anatomically given" (Erikson 1968, 292). And this blow was cushioned with prose that would have aroused suspicion in a milkmaid:

> The singular loveliness and brilliance which young women display in an array of activities obviously removed from the future function of childbearing is one of those esthetic phenomena which almost seem to transcend all goals and purposes and therefore come to symbolize the self-containment of pure being—wherefore young women, in the arts of the ages, have served as the visible representation of ideals and ideas and as the creative man's muse, anima, and enigma. (Erikson 1968, 283)

In defending his besieged essay, Erikson shows that his feminist critics overlooked numerous qualifications with which he had characteristically blunted his thesis. Yet the critics would hardly have warmed to his reasoning if they had followed it more minutely. For though Erikson was desperately sincere in urging women to expand their public influence, his purpose in doing so was not to recognize female equality but to shore up his own crumbling utopianism. Unnerved in recent years by the proclivity of male leaders, especially American ones, for aggressive foolhardiness, Erikson has appealed to inward-looking womankind to rescue his dream of universal cooperation. What was once entrusted to a nation is now handed along to a sex—provided only that the sex go on behaving like its innately nurturant, enclosing self. This large compliment, needless to say, is lost on women who are weary of serving fantasy roles and who are trying precisely not to be evaluated according to their genital morphology.

Psychoanalytic theory would have meant little to him, Erikson confesses in *Life History*, without "Freud's phenomenological and literary approach, which seemed to reflect the very creativity of the unconscious." In that "literary" approach lie both the immediate charm and the long-term vulnerability of Erikson's work. He is, at his best, remarkably skillful in capturing the essence of a personality, finding a key detail and drawing out its significance, identifying the large pattern that was too pervasive for the method-bound to recognize. But he remains impressionistic and improvisational when straightforward logic would be welcome. From the beginning he has been less a sober clinical researcher than a virtuoso, mingling sensitive observations with a blend of Freudian dogma, conventional sentiment, and engrossing self-dramatization.

The resultant mixture looks rather volatile, and doubly so now that Erikson has raised the proportion of moralizing and apologetics to empirical psychology. It becomes harder to remain awestruck as he exhorts us to "the redirection of much of human instinctuality," affects to find in the militancy of youth and women a necessary penultimate phase before "one specieshood" comes to pass, and meanwhile scurries to silence his detractors by accusing them of "re-repression of the obvious."

Unfortunately for all of us who have been intellectually drawn toward psychoanalysis, very little remains obvious in the legacy of Freud. It is also unfortunate that Erikson, who has done so much to reveal that fact, requires us to forget it if we are to endorse his prophetic aspirations. The task that lies before people of Freudian inclination today is not the intuiting of new psychosocial trends, much less the coaxing of world libido into sublimated channels, but the unsparing reassessment of psychoanalysis itself. Where that reassessment will end, perhaps no one can say; but that it cannot be contained within the limits preferred by Erikson is obvious indeed.

Notes

1. See Erikson 1973, 1974.
2. For an idea of how far such gratitude may be taken, see Coles. One

must read several pages into Coles's chapter entitled "The Mahatma" to be quite sure who is intended.

3. Erikson's mercurial tendency is especially visible in his handling of this issue. Throughout *Gandhi's Truth* the capitalized Event is accorded a momentous historical and biographical weight. Now, in *Life History*, Erikson surprisingly rebukes his critics for assuming "that because [the mill strike] became important for me, I also consider it *the* Event in Gandhi's life." Four pages later, however, he is once again referring to how he "made sense of the meaning of the Event in Gandhi's life." The bewildered reader must decide for himself how, if at all, these statements can be reconciled.

4. For an outline of such developments, see Singer.

Works Cited

Coles, Robert. 1970. *Erik H. Erikson: The Growth of His Work*. Boston: Little, Brown.

Erikson, Erik H. 1943. *Observations on the Yurok: Childhood and World Image*. University of California Publications in Archaeology and Ethnology, 35, no. 10, pp. 257–301.

———. 1963. *Childhood and Society*, 2d ed. (1st ed. 1950.) New York: Norton.

———. 1968. *Identity: Youth and Crisis*. New York: Norton.

———. 1970. *Gandhi's Truth: On the Origins of Militant Nonviolence*. New York: Norton.

———. 1973. *In Search of Common Ground: Conversations with Erik H. Erikson and Huey P. Newton*. New York: Norton.

———. 1974. *Dimensions of a New Identity: The 1973 Jefferson Lectures in the Humanities*. New York: Norton.

———. 1975. *Life History and the Historical Moment*. New York: Norton.

Gutmann, David. 1974. "Erik Erikson's America." *Commentary*, September, pp. 60–64.

Mead, Margaret. 1951. "The Study of National Character." In *The Policy Sciences: Recent Developments in Scope and Method*, ed. Daniel Lerner and Harold D. Lasswell. Stanford: Stanford University Press. Pp. 70–85.

Singer, Milton. 1961. "A Survey of Culture and Personality Theory and Research." In *Studying Personality Cross-Culturally*, ed. Bert Kaplan. New York: Harper & Row. Pp. 9–90.

2

Analysis Terminable

I wrote this essay in 1980 to explain the grounds of my disaffection from psychoanalysis. Though "Analysis Terminable" brought a heated response from practicing analysts and other Freudians, I have not been persuaded to alter any of its contentions or to state them more demurely. In a postscript to this chapter I include my reply (Commentary, October 1980) to the most challenging of my essay's detractors.

What is chiefly new here, among my various discussions of psychoanalysis, is the emphasis on therapeutic as well as theoretic deficiencies. I had known from the outset of my Freudian studies that the aggregate curative record was dismal, but I had previously skirted the subject; the explanatory merit of psychoanalytic theory—my central concern—had seemed to stand apart from any healing pretensions. But Adolf Grünbaum, whose influence is first acknowledged in this essay, helped me to see that, in Freud's own reasoning at least, unique therapeutic efficacy was an indispensable warrant for the otherwise vulnerable postulates of his psychology. Since no such unique efficacy has been found, the indifferent therapeutic record turns out to be an important mark against the theory itself.

I

To people who take their cues from the intellectual fashions of academe, any speculation about the decline and fall of psychoanalysis must seem premature or downright perverse. Freud's name, along with those of Nietzsche and Heidegger, has never evoked more automatic reverence than it does today, and the Continental thinkers, from Jürgen Habermas and Paul Ricoeur to Jacques Derrida and Jacques Lacan and the late Roland Barthes, who for the moment strike literary commentators as most advanced, are all Freudians in their various ways. Partisans of psychoanalysis can take comfort, furthermore, from an unabated outpouring of "applied analysis" in the form of psycholiterary, psychobiographical, and psychohistorical studies which, if not always a credit to the tradition, attest to the continuing seductiveness of Freud's ideas.

But given the diminished standing of psychoanalysis as a psychiatric modality and a theory of mind, it is questionable how much longer the Freudian vogue can last. Bodies of purportedly scientific thought, however dazzling they may be to people who take ideological inspiration from them, ultimately depend for survival on empirical support for their claims. So, indeed, do all disciplines that intend to describe and account for experience in nontranscendent terms, whether or not they aspire to be recognized as sciences. After nearly a century, psychoanalysis has received only trifling and debatable corroboration—and much devastating criticism. If that criticism has yet to make an impact on literary intellectuals, we can anticipate that even they will eventually get the point.

In the United States at least, there are many signs that psychoanalysis has been falling out of favor. The number of applicants for therapy and training has declined, and perspicacious Freudians have been complaining that the brightest, most scientifically creative young doctors are no longer drawn toward their specialty. One of the central concepts of Freudianism, neurosis, has been pronounced devoid of meaning by the canonical *Diagnostic and Statistical Manual* of the American Psychiatric Association.[1] The authority of Freud, uniquely important to the morale of his followers, has been eroded by a flood of books detailing his logical and empirical mistakes, his frailties of temperament, and his deafness to reasonable objections. The proliferation of psychoanalytic schools and splinter groups has undermined confidence that the movement as a whole rests on commonly secured scientific grounds. Feminists have convincingly challenged the Freudian picture of their sex as condemned by anatomy to masochism and penis envy. And decisive advances in our knowledge of the waking and sleeping brain, providing revolutionary insights into dream activity, psychotic states, the localization of functions, and the chemistry of pain and pleasure, have not only supplied more reliable means of characterizing the mind, but have established an embarrassing contrast with the vacuous Freudian research tradition, which has failed to yield a single authenticated discovery.

Although these developments, taken collectively, would appear to be ominous, most psychoanalysts continue to act as if no sum of setbacks and concessions could fundamentally damage their institution. In displaying such confidence they follow Freud himself, who on diverse occasions proposed that the whole of his metapsychology could be safely discarded, that neurophysiology would one day obviate his psychological postulates, that factors beyond the purview of psychoanalysis attach people to their neuroses, and that an analyst can have little expectation of undoing a complex. Those statements contradicted promises Freud made between and after his seizures of modesty. To the faithful, however, they appear not as confessions of frustration or as reflections on the vigorous claims that they negate, but as signs of an enviable openmindedness. By the same token, some analysts feel that with each new debunking of a Freudian hypothesis, their discipline makes a smaller target for future snipers.

Psychoanalysis can indeed make do without any given item of doctrine. The reason, however, lies not in the strength of its other, demonstrated, claims, but in the ambiguous state of its thoery and in the public's willingness to grant that an entrenched psychiatric institution must possess a core of valid findings. That willingness is in the process of crumbling. As it does so, we can only become more acutely aware that Freud's putative science of mind lacks a firm empirical basis, is riddled with gratuitous assumptions, and relies for its prestige on therapeutic expectations that seem to be met at least as well by rival and less tortuous forms of treatment.

II

I myself, among other one-time Freudians, supposed for years that the well-foundedness of psychoanalysis as a theory could be judged apart from any disallowed claims for psychoanalysis as a therapy. I professed agnosticism toward the therapy while maintaining that the theory had proved its independent merits as a psychology. Freudian theory, however, has always been tied epistemologically to the "clinical findings" of individual psychotherapy, and its many counterintuitive postulates took hold as a means of accounting for the triumphant therapeutic results claimed by psychoanalysts. If those results were to prove exaggerated, and if it were shown that the Freudian clinical situation is epistemologically compromised by the therapist's presuppositions, then the whole necessity for positing the deep structures and mechanisms of the Freudian unconscious would dissolve.

The therapeutic claims of psychoanalysis, it must be understood, are *differential*. That is, Freudians maintain that their regimen, by far the most expensive and time-consuming of some two hundred competing therapies, demonstrates its value by effecting permanent improvements, as opposed to the mere symptomatic relief, or even outright "symptom substitution," that results from quicker treatments. The idea is that psychoanalysis alone roots out the source of the patient's suffering by giving him conscious access to his long-repressed traumatic experiences in the first years of life.[2] Although not every psychoanalyst feels confident enough to make that boast, every orthodox practitioner depends on it for his livelihood. For if one therapy worked about as well as another, only people with severely impaired reasoning, or with motives other than a wish to be speedily cured, would choose the one that is most disruptive of their budgets and work schedules.

Because of intrinsic difficulties in comparing long-term outcomes of diverse therapies, one cannot say for certain whether any modality is superior to another. It is significant, however, that existing studies, even when they have made no allowance for the vastly longer duration of Freudian treatment, have failed to note any meaningful advantage of that treatment over its myriad competitors.[3] Researchers have established a likelihood that psychoanalysis *and all other psychotherapies* are statistically better than no intervention at all, but this scarcely constitutes an endorsement of Freudianism. On the contrary, if all psychotherapies were to be judged about equally effective, psychoanalysis would rank as the least efficient of therapies, bar none. As for "symptom substitution," it appears to be at least as common in former patients of psychoanalysis as in others. Indeed, it pervades Freud's own case histories, which are to a remarkable extent a record of confessed or implied failure.[4]

More importantly, the tentatively supported equivalence of therapeutic outcomes places in jeopardy the claim of psychoanalysis *to succeed because its psychological theory is singularly correct.* An overwhelmingly plausible alternative view is that all therapies succeed, insofar as they do, for reasons other than the unique causal factors specified in their accompanying theories. It is easy to imagine such reasons—for instance, that patients who seek therapy have already decided to take themselves in hand, or that any explanation offered in tandem with a promise of symptom relief can be happily embraced, or simply that a hired friend is better than none.[5] In short, theories that enter into therapies probably act as welcome placebos. If so, the theories not only remain unsubstantiated by therapeutic success; they are positively erroneous in isolating curative factors that are wide of the mark.

The fact that psychoanalysis frequently "works" is therefore less corroborative than some contented former patients think it is. Faith healing "works," too, as Freud ruefully acknowledged in deferring to the superior results achieved at Lourdes. Just as a successful laying on of hands demonstrates nothing about Christ's mercy, so the propositional content of psychoanalysis remains undemonstrated by a successful case history—or by any number of them. If psychoanalysis is to justify its distinctly exotic theory, it must show that the unique features of that theory are well authenticated by facts that do not lend themselves to any simpler explanation.

Unfortunately, however, the situation that produces nearly all psychoanalytic evidence—the clinical interview—is epistemologically contaminated to an extreme degree. It would be hard to find a data-gathering arrangement less conducive to the empirical ideal of neutralizing the investigator's bias. Psychoanalysts, like other therapeutic practitioners, perceive their patients through the categories of the thoery that outsiders regard as questionable—and the theory in this instance is notorious for its encouragement of premature conclusions. A Freudian can as readily find "evidence" of libidinal cathexes and repressed imagos as a Jungian can locate the anima, the shadow, and the persona. Neither group, we can be sure, will ever stumble across "evidence" for the existence of the other's postulated entities.

Freudian analysts would have us believe that their patients get better because they have raised repressed memories to consciousness and achieved a maturing insight into their formerly buried conflicts. But as Freud himself sometimes feared, there are indications that some of the materials eventually "recovered" from a patient's "repressed unconscious" may be artifacts of insistent suggestion on the analyst's part. Doubts have been raised whether the memory impressions of early infancy survive *at all* (Kagan 1971, 1978)—to say nothing of whether they possess pathogenicity for outbreaks of neurosis several decades later. Moreover, in the words of two pro-Freudian but understandably troubled reviewers of research, "Investigators have found that individuals will enthusiastically accept bogus interpretations as accurate descriptions of their own personalities" (Fisher and Greenberg 1977, 364). Other researchers have found experimental evidence suggesting that introspective confirmation of the causes of one's own thoughts and feelings is beyond the capacity of exceptional as well as ordinary people (see Nisbett and Wilson). Without such confirmation from the patient, an analyst's inferences that certain early traumatic experiences were pathogenic must remain conjectural. Putting these considerations together with the failure of psychoanalysis to indicate any substantial advantage over other treatments, we can say that no grounds whatever exist for believing that recovery of the repressed is specifically therapeutic—or indeed that "the repressed" is an applicable term.

In linking therapeutic success to indifferent or spurious factors, psychoanalysis is no more disingenuous than any number of therapies that invite their clients to merge with the collective unconscious, regress to infancy, relive their births, or identify their previous incarnations. It does stand out, however, as the therapy that places fundamental stress on *analysis of the resistance*. The resistance in question issues in a reluctance to accept the therapist's most assured guesses about the patient's psychodynamics and their relation to "remembered" or reconstructed infantile experiences. Thus, the patient's balking at interpretive hints that may be misguided or even silly is taken as a sign of resurgent conflict with parents and siblings. The dissolving of this allegedly atavistic uncooperativeness—a recalcitrance which may in fact attest to the patient's unsurrendered common sense—is considered to be the analyst's infinitely painstaking task. Uniquely among recipients of psychotherapy, then, the Freudian client has his treatment prolonged and pays handsomely for the privilege of having some of his objections set aside, even though they may be entirely warranted.

If psychoanalysis, as its most fervent supporters have said, really is "the" cure for personality disorders, we must wonder why it has confined its benefits to the relatively healthy as well as the relatively affluent. The best indicators for success as a psychoanalytic patient, according to the Freudian investigators already cited, are "youth, education, intelligence, motivation, time, money, and a relative lack of profound personality disturbance" (Fisher and Greenberg 1977, 303). Yet even among this elite, psychoanalysis has not been able to show differentially impressive results. And it has on its books an exceptional share of the walking wounded. Everyone around the Freudian community knows patients who have become addicted to their analyses, clinging to a fruitless, financially draining dependency for ten, fifteen, or even twenty years without being either "cured," discharged as incurable, or referred to another form of treatment. Although Freud himself, in his late, pessimistic paper "Analysis Terminable and Interminable," recommended setting an arbitrary concluding date for stubborn cases, a significant number of analysts have dealt with their own protracted failure by calling the patient's efforts incomplete and by represcribing the very medicine that had failed to take effect.

III

When we turn from the state of the therapy to that of the theory, we find that the taint of subjectivism is pervasive. The problem begins with Freud, who took little care for self-consistency and whose writings, in the assessment of one distinguished psychoanalyst, were "formulated in a bewilderingly unsystematic way" (Rubinstein, 31). Because he believed, furthermore, that the clinical dialogue provided all the testing of hypotheses that scientific rigor could require, Freud continually overrated the empirical basis of his ideas—even to the point of maintaining that he had confounded genetic theory by discovering in his patients inherited memory traces from the dawn of civilization. Although few of his followers have accepted that judgment, nearly all of them have shared in the naïve methodological assumption that lay behind it—namely, the belief that hypotheses about the deepest structure of the human mind can be confirmed by what patients reveal to their analysts through "free association" and reports of dreams.

In logic, there is no need for contemporary psychoanalysts to repeat Freud's errors of fact or to emulate his overconfidence in drawing conclusions. In practice, however, analysts have not proved capable of subjecting Freud's ideas to the unsparing criticism that would typify a genuinely empirical discipline. Though most ana-

lysts differ from Freud on various particulars, they show no eagerness to confront the general, long-familiar epistemological objections to his work. The reason, we may suppose, is that their own
work rests not only on Freud's scientific authority as a ground-
breaker but also on the questionable rules of inference drawing
that he devised. The unwritten imperative of psychoanalytic reform is to salvage as much of Freud as possible, in appearance if
not in substance. As we will see in a characteristic example, metapsychology has consequently choked itself with provisos and ad-
denda that are meant to reverse Freud's deterministic emphasis
without seeming to do so. Much of psychoanalytic thought is by
now a palimpsest of hazy, mutually jostling notions, not one of
which has been shown by an adequately designed empirical study
to be the most likely explanation of a given phenomenon.

To be sure, some researchers who began with Freudian sympathies and who neglected to test for plausible alternatives to, say,
repression and castration anxiety believe they have proved the explanatory value of such concepts.[6] Unreconstructed critics, however, have had little trouble exposing the fallaciousness of such
proofs.[7] And still others have reviewed the whole standing of psychoanalysis as knowledge and found it to be nugatory. In an important series of recent articles, the eminent philosopher of science
Adolf Grünbaum has inquired whether psychoanalysis meets currently accepted canons of inductivism.[8] His judgments will be
gathered in a book to be entitled *The Foundations of Psychoanalysis*.
While Grünbaum does not rule out the logical possibility that some
Freudian hypotheses may one day be supported, he finds that for
now psychoanalysis rests on no solid evidence and that its purported clinical confirmations are open to the most fundamental
doubts. Nor can we overlook the stunning pronouncement made in
1975 by the Nobel prizewinner in medicine P. B. Medawar: "[D]oc-
trinaire psychoanalytic theory is the most stupendous intellectual
confidence trick of the twentieth century: and a terminal product as
well—something akin to a dinosaur or a zeppelin in the history of
ideas, a vast structure of radically unsound design and with no posterity" (Medawar, 17).

Against this bleak prospect, defenders of psychoanalysis assert that forbearance is in order. Their movement, they say, is still
young; it is as yet a "protoscience," groping with forgivable clum-
siness toward an adequate means of framing its discoveries. We are
asked to look forward to a time when conscientious Freudians will

have made peace with the scientific mainstream by simplifying the theory and submitting the remaining core of propositions to the most demanding empirical tests. Then, presumably, we will have avoided discarding valuable, hard-won insights along with early misconceptions. Every champion of the movement can point to a favorite branch of revisionism that has supposedly made a good beginning toward this goal.

After nine decades of sectarianism and self-isolation from the broader scientific community, however, psychoanalysis would hardly seem to be "proto" anything. The record to date suggests that when analytic theorists undertake to replace one of Freud's implausible ideas, they do so without benefit of methodological safeguards against further error. Unlike demonstrably empirical discoveries, furthermore, psychoanalytic reforms rarely bring the warring Freudian factions together; nearly every change has meant a further sundering, a new occasion for dogmatic belief within a subset of the faithful. This fission has been caused, not by the exuberant youthfulness that Freudians ascribe to their discipline, but by the fact that it is not, strictly speaking, a discipline at all. That is to say, psychoanalysis as usually elaborated eschews the means of discriminating warrantedly between rival hypotheses about mental functioning and paths to symptom removal. As for the "hard-won insights" that we should hesitate to dismiss, most of those that may actually possess merit were current before Freud's time and will presumably remain accessible in the future.[9]

Two factors condemn innovative Freudian metapsychologies to the subjectivism that yields one unresolvable quarrel after another. The first is that psychoanalytic reformers have only their own taste to guide them in deciding which metapsychological concepts to perpetuate and which to challenge. Notions like "id" and "Oedipus complex" and "pleasure principle" take their meaning from a network of postulates that generate no straightforward behavioral consequences. Thus the presence or absence of such consequences in a given instance cannot serve as a test of theoretical adequacy. On the contrary, the elasticity of Freudian interpretive rules, whereby any phenomenon can bear either its manifest meaning or an opposite meaning or some third, "displaced," meaning, enables every interpreter to convince himself that his concepts are backed by evidence. This absence of constraints encourages the riding of hobbyhorses instead of a principled adjudication of differences.

And second, most psychoanalytic theoreticians have relied on "findings" that will be forever unavailable to outside parties. The Freudian community retains its self-respect by assuming that the author of a paper, because he has been analyzed and officially trained, has acquired an objectivity and scrupulousness rarely found among the laity. But with the best will in the world, a Freudian innovator meets no methodological barrier against the temptation to misinterpret, embroider, or censor his essentially secret case histories. Scientific responsibility is thus lodged precariously not in the watchdog process whereby investigators check the replicability of one another's announced results, but in individuals telling self-serving anecdotes about anonymous patients. In a community operating by such rules, metapsychological innovation comes cheaply—and is prized no less cheaply by guardians of established views.

Let us suppose, however, that reformers could persuade their colleagues to do without high-level metapsychology and restrict themselves to those concepts that provide a quasi-phenomenological account of therapist–client relations—concepts such as resistance, transference, repression, and regression. Could psychoanalysis get by on that minimal basis? Some revisionists think so, but they overlook the fact that even these terms are shot through with implications about infantile sexuality, the alleged stages of libidinal development, the early-traumatic etiology of neurosis, and the analyst's privileged insight into that etiology. Psychoanalysis as a drawn-out regimen presupposes those ideas; without them, there would be no conceivable justification for the laborious and costly task of anamnesis.

If psychoanalysts wish to continue practicing under the old rules, therefore, they cannot afford to go very far toward admitting how little they really know about the mind. To most present-day analysts, Freud's system is at once reassuring in its apparent conferral of authority and embarrassing in many of its details. The analysts' best hope of preserving their elevated standing in a rapidly changing society is to patch over the more obvious defects in classic psychoanalytic thought while continuing to maintain that they understand what causes and cures mental instability, what the basic instincts are, how sexual identity is formed, and so forth. We will see, however, that such ad hoc repair not only fails to go far enough; in some cases it makes matters worse by taxing the theory with overcomplication and by drawing attention to the flaws it is intended to cover.

IV

To examine the liabilities of psychoanalytic reform at close range, let us consider one of the most respected of contemporary theorists, Heinz Kohut. Though Kohut is less well known to the public than a Fromm or an Erikson, among the cognoscenti he comes nearer to fitting the image of a properly *Freudian* innovator. His two major works, *The Analysis of the Self* (1971) and *The Restoration of the Self* (1977), have a large and grateful following, and recently he has acknowledged his eminence by issuing a two-volume collection of papers, graced by a 106-page introduction by Dr. Paul H. Ornstein extolling what is now said to be "the leading paradigm of psychoanalysis" (Kohut 1978, 91).[10] Needless to say, there is room for dispute on that point; psychoanalytic theory is so easy to play variations on that anyone with a handful of followers could think he had revolutionized the field. But if Freud's couch were passed along like the throne of St. Peter, it might well find itself today in Dr. Kohut's office in Chicago.

It is not just Kohut's stature but also his deference to empirical values that makes him an appropriate figure for assessing the future of psychoanalysis. In his papers he repeatedly admonishes his colleagues against hasty conclusions and unnecessarily rigid views. He is careful to reject biological explanations of psychologically described events, and he tries wherever possible to rely on tangible phenomena rather than on abstract reconstructions. One of his main concerns within the American Psychoanalytic Association, furthermore, has been the promotion of research. And unlike some analysts, he does not hesitate to point out areas in which psychoanalysis has shown itself deficient. By manner, at least, no one would inspire more confidence in the capacity of Freudians to set their house in order.

Sadly, however, Kohut's empirical scruples turn out to be mostly cosmetic—a matter of scientistic rhetoric rather than true rigor. Psychoanalysis in its current state is already, for him, "this great new edifice of human thought" (695), "this new sun among the sciences of man" (684), "the science that reaches farthest into the breadth and depth of the human soul" (683–84), and the rightful candidate to become "man's scientific leader" (682). Nothing in his writings suggests awareness of the key defect in his "science," namely, the fact that we have typically been asked to take an analyst's word both for the raw data he reports and for the correctness of his interpretations.

On the contrary, Kohut refers with assurance to "the laboratory of psychoanalytic treatment" (523), as if analysts in their fifty-minute hours were properly testing the debatable hypotheses of Freudianism instead of applying familiar and notably compliant rules of interpretation. And when he calls for more research, he has in view not controlled studies that might determine which concepts deserve to survive, but mere consolidation and publication of what analysts have already learned "from the clinical situation" (602). To be sure, Kohut worries about bias in research—but he does so along the quaint diagnostic lines established by Freud. One researcher, he tells us, may have reacted so strongly against his early sadistic impulses that he is too compassionate to be objective (607), and another may suffer from "a libidinal hypercathexis in the visual-cognitive area" (608) and so lack balanced judgment. In Kohut's perspective, the problem of skewed results apparently vanishes as soon as the investigator has achieved "mastery and integration of infantile precursors of his research interest" (608).

I have mentioned as one of the handicaps of psychoanalysis its intellectually compromising subservience to Freud. Kohut, true to his role as an enlightened adviser to the movement, discusses this very problem at some length. Analysts in training, he says, encounter Freud as "the great father-figure and teacher of our science" (796), and thus they acquire "an attitude of firmly established identification with an idealized figure (or, in reaction formation, of rebelliousness against this identification)" (796). As Kohut sees it, this confusion of emotional dependency with the scientific posture is a warping force, inducing the individual psychoanalyst either to rubber-stamp Freud's ideas or to subvert them by hitting on some gratuitous novelty to emphasize.

One might expect Kohut, therefore, to be especially wary of idolizing Freud. Such is not the case. Psychoanalysts, he announces, are lucky "because in this finite life we are able to participate in the work of one of the few geniuses of mankind, a participation which in our field appears to me to be more intimate and profound than in most other sciences" (393). As we will see, Kohut senses that his own ideas are in crucial respects opposed to Freud's; like other revisionists, he faces the psychological and rhetorical problem of diverging from the "genius" while continuing to share in his glory. The solution is to take on faith great chunks of doctrine that are not immediately at issue and to appease Freud's offended ghost with hyperbolical praise.

Thus, for example, Kohut asks why Freud thought that female sexuality is an outcome of thwarted phallic strivings rather than a natural biological development. Could it be that the master had a "circumscribed blindspot" (228) on this issue? Kohut raises the possibility only to wave it away without discussion. It must have been an admirable "reliance on clinical evidence" (228) that kept Freud from exercising common sense: "Penetrating beyond the feminine attitudes and feelings of his patients, he regularly found the struggle over phallic strivings, and, *while he accepted biological bisexuality*, he rejected the postulate of a preceding psychological phase of femininity without psychological evidence for it" (228). Kohut does not allow that Freud's "penetrations" may have been tendentious, or that "evidence" supplied by indoctrinated adult patients may not necessarily be evidence of an infantile stage of development, or that Freud's acceptance of "biological bisexuality" was just as arbitrary as his decision to make penis envy the *raison d'être* of femininity. Ordinary empirical prudence must be stifled in deference to "the great father-figure and teacher of our science."[11]

More is involved in such kindness than filial homage, however. If Kohut were to grant the full extent of Freud's interpretive whimsy, he would be disavowing his own right to base conclusions about early childhood on remarks made by supine grownups. Kohut must remain convinced that psychoanalytic theory is objectively dictated by facts that impress themselves upon the clinician who is schooled to listen empathically and ponder introspectively. Indeed, Kohut is so enamored of this idea that he thinks empathy "should become the guiding ideal of all the sciences . . . the scientist's commitment to it should take the place of the pride in his methodological and technological expertness which he has felt up to now" (703). Without flinching, he tells us that "Freud's attitude concerning the development of female sexuality is only one of many examples of his faithful adherence to the introspective and empathic method of observation" (228–29). Yet neither Freud nor Kohut would be able to explain how introspection and empathy generate adequate controls for error and *idées fixes*, much less how they enable the Freudian thinker to make inferences about psychic energy, stages of infancy, various kinds of libido, oedipal and pre-oedipal fixations, and the rest of the leaden conceptual baggage that psychoanalysis carries wherever it goes. Nor could they explain why analysts, if their tools of investigation are indeed superior to those of experimental natural science, remain divided within squabbling sects, each with its boast of having corrected the others' faulty understanding of the mind.

Kohut himself is the founder of one such sect, purportedly the guardian of fundamental advances in therapy as well as theory. His contribution has been to rescue narcissism from its lowly place in Freudian thought and to endow it with its own special drive, its hitherto neglected vicissitudes (the "narcissistic disturbances"), its ideal line of normal development, and a happy ending, namely, the production of a wholeness that Kohut designates as "the self." Kohut, Ornstein, and others now regard "the psychology of the self" as a second and superior half of the great theoretical edifice begun by Freud. Until he himself came along, Kohut reflects, psychoanalysis saw only "Guilty Man," in conflict with his libidinal drives. Now we can also deal precisely with "Tragic Man," whose goal is not gratification but self-realization. At last psychoanalysis can "attempt to make contributions—*scientific* contributions—to the understanding of some of the most important activities of man, such as his religions or his art, that do not dissolve these activities into their elemental constituents and, by doing so, become blind to their essential significance . . ." (923–24).[12]

Like other Freudian explorers, Kohut tells us little about the procedures he followed in arriving at his discoveries. From what he does say, however, we can discern the outlines of a characteristic pattern. In his case as in some others, the analyst's starting point is apparently a perception of indifferent therapeutic success—a perception he keeps to himself until after the breakthrough, whereupon he becomes more or less candid about past failures, though not about present ones. Thus Kohut reveals that for some fifteen years before 1974, he had felt "increasingly stumped" (888) by as many as half of his cases. (One looks in vain for any acknowledgment of that fact in papers written during the period.) Goaded to try new ideas, the analyst decides to attach extra importance to some element of behavior or theory—in this case narcissism—that earlier investigators have overlooked or considered incidental. Then, still believing that whatever he learns from analytic sessions must be direct evidence of infantile development, he links the newly central factor to the "archaic experiences" that his patients have supposedly recovered from their repressed depths.

To the analyst's delight, everything falls into place; the patient who is destined to become the latest Dora eventually accedes to his interpretive hints and feels, presumably, that the stalled analysis must be getting somewhere at last. The treatment then proceeds according to the customary Sisyphean technique, but with an altered vocabulary and a different set of assumptions about the nature of the patient's woes, the root causes of trouble, and the signs of progress and backsliding. Certain forms of childishness on the patient's part, for example, are now considered productive, for they indicate revival of the conflicts that have just been granted theoretical preeminence.

Needless to say, the new point of view is no less spuriously confirmed by "clinical results" than the one it has supplanted. In evaluating his apparent success, the analyst is unlikely to wait until he can learn whether the "cure," if any, was only temporary. Nor will he inquire whether his own enthusiasm may have served as a placebo, or whether an extant rival theory might have yielded the same results, or whether Dora may have simply gotten older and more resigned to other people's obsessions, or whether he should take into account those patients who have resisted his new line of coaxing and have thus failed to ratify his destiny as a medical pioneer. And in writing up his scientific advance for the edification of his colleagues, he of course provides no data to support the claim of sharply increased therapeutic success. To do so would be to break with Freud's precedent and to imply that there may be something lax about the trusting atmosphere that enables each reporting analyst, whether or not he is a competent therapist, to have a turn at innovation.

Kohut is typical in another important respect as well: he does everything he can to minimize the extent of his departure from orthodoxy. As a holistic concept, Kohut's idea of selfhood is contradictory in spirit to the mechanistic, trifurcated model of mind developed by Freud. Potentially, then, Kohut is as much a schismatic as Jung, who stood Freudian theory on its head. He tells us, however, that he built his new system keeping in mind that "the new psychology of the self must remain in an unbroken continuum with traditional psychoanalytic theory to preserve the sense of the historical continuity of the group self in the psychoanalytic community" (937). For a sentimental or political reason, in other words, Kohut was determined to *insert his ideas into* the preexisting framework of metapsychology, whether or not they belonged there.

That is precisely what he did, with results that defy succinct description. Dr. Ornstein's labyrinthine introduction traces the stages of Kohut's delicate progress toward conceiving of *two* selves—in effect, one for Freud and one for Kohut. The "narrower" self, as Ornstein notes, is "embedded (albeit somewhat loosely) in a mental-apparatus psychology and ego psychology," while the broader or Kohutian one "is conceptually independent from and has moved beyond drive theory and ego psychology" (98). As a concordat with the Freudian establishment, this arrangement has much to recommend it. As a supposed psychological finding, it requires the faith of a Bernadette.

Kohut's practice, to speak bluntly, is always to throw a bone to Freud while saving the choicest, most humanistic-looking morsels of theory for himself. Thus he fully accepts Freud's account of the psychoneuroses, in which a repressed drive is seeking satisfaction, but charts as his own territory the more congenial narcissistic disorders, in which "an injured, narcissistic *ego* is seeking *reassurance*" (22). The mind, it seems, is a creaky contraption when working for Freud but a soulful being when working for Kohut. Again, instead of challenging Freud's murky idea of libido, Kohut tactfully avers that there are two kinds of libido, one leading to the traditional Freudian terminus of "object love," the other leading to self-love and onward to selfhood, a realm where the penurious economy of Freudian energy expenditure is nowhere to be seen. And if just two selves seem insufficient to placate the orthodox, Kohut is willing to supply more—provided everyone agrees that he holds the patent on the best one. "We recognize," he says,

> the simultaneous existence of contradictory selves: of different selves of various degrees of stability and of various degrees of importance. There are conscious, preconscious, and unconscious selves; there are selves in the ego, the id, and the superego; and we may discover in some of our patients contradictory selves, side by side, in the same psychic agency. Among these selves, however, there is one which is most centrally located in the psyche; one which is experienced as the basic one, and which is most resistant to change. I like to call this self the "nuclear self." (96)

As this passage suggests, there are no limits to the complication that psychoanalytic reformers will add to already dubious postulates in order to avoid an open break with tradition. So long as analysts want simultaneously to free themselves from Freud's biologism and to bask in its remaining prestige, they will continue

ornamenting the stark branches of id psychology with "selves"—
and with neutralized energies, and desexualized drives, and integra-
tive functions, and conflict-free spheres of the ego—without noticing that they are creating, not a credible metapsychology, but a
Rube Goldberg apparatus that bears no examinable relation to experience.

V

Freud explained intellectual resistance to psychoanalysis in terms
of injured human pride. His discovery that our minds are enthralled
by repressed wishes, as he announced without undue humility on
his own part, was the third great blow to anthropocentrism following those administered by Copernicus and Darwin. Yet it is curious
how readily many of us absorbed the putative insult and defended
it as what it distinctly is not, a scientifically confirmed truth. The
real question to be resolved is not why people resisted a doctrine
that found in every physician a deflected sadist, in every artist a
former dabbler in his own feces, in every infant a murderous and
incestuous schemer, in every decent act the sublimation of a barbaric impulse. The question is rather why so many people fell
cheerfully into line with these and equally lurid ideas, expounded
with no more proof than the say-so of a compelling stylist.

Any answers are bound to be partial and conjectural. Yet I
think we can recognize certain nonrational appeals within psychoanalysis, even if we cannot assign them relative degrees of importance. It would seem, for example, that for many intellectuals psychoanalysis has been, not a blow to human pride in general, but a
means of elevating pride among a corps of privileged knowers who,
by subscribing to the Freudian movement, rescue themselves from
doubt and insignificance. It is as a cathartic and redemptive science
that psychoanalysis has claimed our loyalty. "Normal science" is
dry and impersonal, narrow in focus, and increasingly incompre-
hensible to the envious humanist. Psychoanalysis, by contrast, offers each of its believers a total vision that spans the entire history
of our species, links biology and psychology, and unveils the inner-
most scandalous wishes animating heroes and ordinary folk, great
works of art, and whole systems of law, philosophy, mythology,
and religion. What is so humbling about that? Could Faust have
asked Mephistopheles to show him much more?[13]

In part, then, we can suppose that psychoanalysis survives because it feeds extravagant intellectual hopes. It is energized not by the skeptical spirit but, as Freud knew in calling himself a conquistador, by a wish to overleap barriers and arrive at a comprehensive, countertraditional system of insight. Perhaps that is why armchair radicals, at a time when psychoanalysis as a therapy and science is in full retreat, can still base whole books on the most extreme elements of Freudian theory, such as polymorphous perversity and the death instinct. The reason they are not dissuaded by empirical criticism may be that their aim is precisely to have done with the restraining effects of empiricism. If I read them correctly, they wish to wield terms of discourse implying a realm of essence beneath and opposed to the visible world—a realm which, if we could only set it free, would work the overthrow of every tyranny of custom, tradition, and entrenched privilege. So, too, the "hermeneutic" school, which conceives of psychoanalysis only as a means of performing abstruse manipulations of texts, appears to have distilled from Freudianism its will to explanatory power while openly proclaiming the irrelevance of corroboration.

That sense of special power may be felt even by circumspect Freudians who eschew deep theory and try to confine themselves to such relatively accessible concepts as denial, projection, and identification. I was myself such a Freudian for a decade or so—excited yet also made wary by the prospect of holding a master key to interpretation. I remember taking comfort from the analysts' rhetoric of meticulous devotion to fact, even while I deplored some of the shortcomings I have mentioned here. To be a cautious Freudian was to have the best of both worlds: allegiance to transpersonal standards of knowledge and a head start toward certainty. Possessing that head start, or the illusion of it, a partisan of psychoanalysis will understandably hesitate to entertain more than selective doubts about his doctrine.

Finally, many veterans of therapy have their own reasons for clinging to the faith. They have had what they call confirming experiences—crystallizations of emotion, flashes of self-recognition, and enhanced insight into people or problems that had been troubling them. We need not doubt the genuineness of these catharses; the prolonged strain intrinsic to a Freudian patient's situation, combined with the analyst's disapproval of conventional, self-protective responses, probably sharpens the analysand's perceptions, however temporarily. What needs doubting is whether such experiences, which can be approximated in any number of other therapies or even in outright brainwashing, really ought to count as "confirming." Memorable though they may be, they prove nothing at all about the correctness of Freudian theory or the long-run usefulness of the therapy. Try telling that, however, to someone who thanks his analysis for his sanity and who now sees the work of id and ego everywhere, much as his counterpart a few centuries ago detected the equally confirming influence of angels and devils.

For several reasons, then, a rush of defections from the Freudian ranks seems unlikely. Yet psychoanalysis, I would expect, will fade away just as mesmerism and phrenology did, and for the same reason: its exploded pretensions will deprive it of recruits. If most people cannot readily forgo an entire world view that has sustained them, they find it easy enough to avoid the strange-looking intellectual fashions of another era. Psychoanalysis, once so familiar that, in Erich Heller's words, "it comes close to being the systematic consciousness that a certain epoch has of the nature and character of its soul" (Heller, 35), is in the process of becoming strange. There is no reason to believe, much less to hope, that the process will be reversed.

Whether or not my prediction is accurate, there is an immediate moral to be drawn: a concern for empirical standards should make us reconsider the habit of borrowing bits and pieces of psychoanalytic thought for ad hoc explanatory purposes. Perhaps some Freudian ideas, pried loose from their context of presumptions about mental hydraulics and libidinal development, may eventually prove to have some merit. If so, it will be because they have won a test against concepts that take less for granted and fit better with inductive sense. In the meanwhile, we would do well to struggle along without recourse to instant "depth." When we do, we will find that we have sacrificed, not complexity of understanding, but something nearly opposite: a pretended intimacy with realities that cannot be captured in the crude and monotonous language of Freudian explanation.

Notes

1. Critics have pointed out that the third edition of *DSM* (1980), like its predecessors, reflects political as well as medical and scientific opinion. Quite true: when smoking replaces homosexuality as a mental aberration, more of the credit must go to caucuses than to new findings. For that very

reason, however, we can safely regard the *DSM's* demotion of "neurosis" as a sign of waning psychoanalytic influence.

2. In Anna Freud's words, "In competition with the psychotherapies [analysts] are justified to maintain that what they have to offer is unique, i.e., thoroughgoing personality changes as compared with more superficial symptomatic cures" (Freud, 17).

3. See Luborsky et al., Goldberger et al., and Bergin and Lambert.

4. Freud, according to two sympathetic observers, "never presented any data, in statistical or case form, that demonstrated that his treatment was of benefit to a significant number of patients he himself saw," and he "chose to demonstrate the utility of psychoanalysis through descriptions of largely unsuccessful cases" (Fisher and Greenberg 1977, 285, 281).

5. Why does the contest between psychotherapies appear to end in a dead heat? "The most potent explanatory factor is that different forms of psychotherapy have major common elements—a helping relationship with a therapist is present in all of them, along with other related, nonspecific effects such as suggestion and abreaction" (Luborsky et al., 1006).

6. Observers who believe that at least a modest handful of Freudian hypotheses have been experimentally supported include Fisher and Greenberg (1977), Kline, and Silverman. Although the claims advanced by these Freudians are open to challenge, their acceptance *in toto* would lend only marginal credence to general psychoanalytic theory.

7. The *locus classicus* of Freudian investigations that rule out common-sense alternatives is a study purporting to show that, because a number of female college students dreamed of penises, the concept of penis *envy* has received significant support. The same study confirmed that women tend to dream about weddings and babies, i.e., "displaced penis envy." For an authoritative discussion of this and other poorly conceived investigations, see Eysenck and Wilson.

8. See especially Grünbaum. I am indebted to Professor Grünbaum not only for several ideas in the present essay, but also for searching criticisms of my various drafts.

9. See, e.g., Whyte.

10. Subsequent parenthetical page numbers without other attribution will cite the continuously paginated volumes of Kohut 1978; all quoted italics appear in the original text.

11. Kohut does worry that Freud's theory strains credulity by asking us to believe that every little girl in the history of the world has responded with "envy, shame, rage, and denial" (785) to her genital incompleteness. Natural selection, however, comes to the rescue. Perhaps, Kohut suggests, "in the prehistorical past of the human race those females of the species who reacted with greater sensitivity to the experience that they had no penis had a higher survival rate" (785).

12. In practice, however, Kohut treats works of art just as previous analysts have, mining them for points of likeness to his favorite ideas. He asserts, for example, that paranoia arises genetically from the incapacity of a child's "self-objects" (parents) "to mirror the child's total self," and he adds: "Kafka described this situation poignantly in *Metamorphosis*: Gregory Samsa experiences himself as nonhuman while his parents in the next room

speak about him in the third person singular" (743n.). Had they spoken about "Gregory" in some other person or number, they might have been beyond even Dr. Kohut's help.

13. The replies of several pro-Freudian acquaintances to a draft of this essay have illustrated the correlation between psychoanalytic allegiance and animus against "normal science." My respondents uniformly declared that since their interest in Freudianism was not a scientific one, my animadversions about the dubious scientific status of psychoanalysis were wasted on them. They did not care to recognize that I am here criticizing psychoanalysis, not for the technicality of failing to qualify as a science, but for being so conceptually muddled and empirically dubious that it does not warrant our belief. "Science," which many Freudians conveniently confuse with materialism or positivism or behaviorism, is their straw man—an antithesis to the humanistic spirit that binds them, however irrationally, to psychoanalysis, for both Freud and humanism strike them as championing the beleaguered imagination.

POSTSCRIPT

Since "Analysis Terminable" makes use of Seymour Fisher and Roger P. Greenberg's *The Scientific Credibility of Freud's Theories and Therapy*, I was especially interested in Fisher and Greenberg's published retort to the article. As they pointed out, their 1977 book had tried to indicate how much evidence has been garnered for various psychoanalytic ideas, considered piecemeal. Some of Freud's formulas, they wrote in 1980—for example, those regarding "Oedipal dynamics, the oral and anal character structures, and the family pattern basic to male homosexuality"—had emerged from their book with a verdict of "fairly good scientific support." Treating this judgment of their own as indisputable, Fisher and Greenberg then held it up against "Analysis Terminable":

> Crews's demands that we dismiss all of Freud's ideas as nonsense simply duplicate the rigid and unreasonable attitude he attributes to the psychoanalytic establishment. Orthodox psychoanalysts require that Freud's ideas be swallowed whole and Mr. Crews wants them to be completely regurgitated. The passion in Mr. Crews's presentation, with its use of words like "silly," "naïve," "vacuous," and "crude," is exactly what a scientific appraisal should avoid. The unending dispute between pro- and anti-Freudians will never cease as long as extremists continue to shout at us in loud, unreasonable tones (Fisher and Greenberg 1980, 17).

In reply, and as a conclusion to my response to the other published correspondents, I wrote the following:

Let me focus now on Seymour Fisher and Roger P. Greenberg, for these writers have an understanding of empirical issues far superior to the one prevailing in the psychoanalytic community at large. They have produced what I regard as the most illuminating—and also the most sobering—book ever written from a pro-Freudian point of view. Despite their avowed prior sympathy for "a dynamic [i.e., psychoanalytic] understanding of the causes of a patient's difficulties and a therapy based on that understanding" (*Credibility*, 274), Messrs. Fisher and Greenberg recognize that nothing in the Freudian tradition can be taken on faith. Nor do they share Dr. Soll's trust in classical Freudian dream interpretation, or Dr. Barglow's and Dr. Offenkrantz's evident belief that the mere taping of psychoanalytic sessions endows them with scientific rigor. And they freely grant what Dr. Rebner refuses to see, that Freud often bullied his patients into "overcoming their resistance" to interpretations that later turned out to be wrong.

These co-authors show that Freud's case histories weigh *against* his therapeutic claims; that "clinical evidence" is totally unavailing for the validation of any psychoanalytic construct; that Freudian therapy, even when no allowance is made for its longer duration, more selective criteria for accepting patients, and higher dropout rate, has failed to show better results than *any* of its two hundred-plus competitors; that experiments have cast doubt on some psychoanalytic ideas; and that some others are, on their face, too cloudy or improbable to merit consideration in a principled study. If my other critics would read *The Scientific Credibility of Freud's Theories and Therapy* with care, they would find much reluctantly stated backing for my own argument.

But why then do Messrs. Fisher and Greenberg characterize me as an extremist? The objection cannot be my mere use of adjectives such as "crude" and "vacuous," for such language may be entirely appropriate to a given "scientific appraisal." Nor can it be my "demands that we dismiss all of Freud's ideas as nonsense," for I made no such demands. What I did say is that although psychoanalysis in general does not merit our credence, some Freudian ideas "may eventually prove to have some merit," provided they can win a test against "concepts that take less for granted and fit better with inductive sense." If that is an extremist position, then the entirety of modern science is extremist.

The source of trouble, I gather, is my negative prognosis for the psychoanalytic movement. As critical sympathizers with that movement, Messrs. Fisher and Greenberg still *hope* (337) that some evidence favoring its therapy may yet turn up, and they prefer to think that miscellaneous "supported" psychoanalytic notions establish the respectability of Freudian thought. In reply, I submit, first, that the co-authors' own assessment of comparative studies makes their hope for the therapy look utopian; second, that the suspect manner in which psychoanalytic theory sprang up and evolved reduces the credibility of its untested portions; third, that even a crackpot theory will look "confirmed" in certain respects if it is sufficiently vague, ambitious, and laced with cynicism about human folly; and fourth and most important, that the specific validations claimed by Messrs. Fisher and Greenberg rely on an insufficiently critical use of the hypothetico-deductive method of theory testing.

This last point may appear inconsistent after my praise for the *negative* findings of these co-authors. But there is no contradiction. Messrs. Fisher and Greenberg, in exercising higher empirical standards than earlier pro-Freudian evaluators of research such as Paul Kline, have discredited a great number of seemingly corroborative studies. Yet their criteria for *accepting* positive findings are radically faulty, for Messrs. Fisher and Greenberg abandon their skepticism *as soon as a given Freudian hypothesis is well matched by a predicted consequence*. The flaw here—one that virtually nobody within the psychoanalytic movement appears able to grasp—is that some other extant hypothesis may do an even better job of accounting for the same consequence. In the words of Eysenck and Wilson . . . :

> Most workers in the field seem to believe that having made a deduction from Freudian theory, and carried out a study which more or less gives results in partial agreement with prediction, this is the end of the story. They fail to consider the duty incumbent upon any scientist to consider alternative hypotheses which might equally well, or better, explain the results found. (Eysenck and Wilson, 386–87)

It is regrettable that even the most scrupulous of Freudian sympathizers have marred their work by neglecting this key requirement. If Messrs. Fisher and Greenberg had kept in mind the necessity of weighing alternative explanatory hypotheses, they would probably have been compelled to endorse Eysenck and Wilson's carefully reasoned conclusion that "There is not one study which one could point to with confidence and say: 'Here is definitive support of this or that Freudian notion . . .'" (Eysenck and Wilson, 392).

Finally, since my motives for writing a "cruel" and even "murderous" essay have been questioned, let me point out that psychoanalysts—who, judging from these letters, have been recovering nicely—are not the only parties involved. As a teacher, I am concerned to spare students and others the intellectual befuddlement that I myself endured in my Freudian period. As a member of a society steeped in Freudian platitudes, I would like people to know that the guilt dispensed by psychoanalytic theorists to striving women and to the parents of homosexuals, "neurotics," and psychotics can be plausibly declined. And then of course there are the Freudian patients and prospective patients, many of whom have remained unaware of therapeutic alternatives to plunging their savings into the protracted and dubiously relevant task of stirring up ancient grievances. If "Analysis Terminable," my first published statement about psychoanalysis since 1975 and the only one that deals with therapy, is of use to some of these people, I will be able to endure the charge of having administered cruel and unusual punishment to Freud's complacent heirs.

Works Cited

American Psychiatric Association. 1980. *Diagnostic and Statistical Manual of Mental Disorders*, 3d ed. Washington, D.C.: American Psychiatric Association.

Bergin, Allen E., and Michael Lambert. 1978. "The Evaluation of Therapeutic Outcomes." In *Handbook of Psychotherapy and Behavior Change: An Empirical Analysis*, ed. Sol L. Garfield and Allen E. Bergin. New York: Wiley.

Eysenck, Hans, and Glenn D. Wilson. 1973. *The Experimental Study of Freudian Theories*. London: Methuen.

Fisher, Seymour, and Roger P. Greenberg. 1977. *The Scientific Credibility of Freud's Theories and Therapy*. New York: Basic Books.

———. 1980. Letter, *Commentary*, October, pp. 17–18.

Freud, Anna. 1969. *Difficulties in the Path of Psychoanalysis*. New York: International Universities Press.

Goldberger, Leo, Roger Reuben, and George Silberschatz. 1976. "Symptom Removal in Psychotherapy: A Review of the Literature." *Psychoanalysis and Contemporary Science*, 5: 513–536.

Grünbaum, Adolf. 1979. "Epistemological Liabilities of the Clinical Appraisal of Psychoanalytic Theory." *Psychoanalysis and Contemporary Thought*, 2: 451–526.

Heller, Erich. 1976. "Observations on Psychoanalysis and Modern Literature." In *Psychiatry and the Humanities*, Vol. 1, ed. Joseph H. Smith. New Haven: Yale University Press. Pp. 35–50.

Kagan, Jerome. 1971. *Change and Continuity in Infancy*. New York: Wiley.

———. 1978. "The Baby's Elastic Mind." *Human Nature*, January, pp. 66–73.

Kline, Paul. 1972. *Fact and Fantasy in Freudian Theory*. London: Methuen.

Kohut, Heinz. 1971. *The Analysis of the Self: A Systematic Approach to the Psychoanalytic Treatment of Narcissistic Personality Disorders*. New York: International Universities.

———. 1977. *The Restoration of the Self*. New York: International Universities Press.

———. 1978. *The Search for the Self: Selected Writings of Heinz Kohut: 1950–1978*, 2 vols., ed. Paul H. Ornstein. New York: International Universities Press.

Luborsky, Lester, Barton Singer, and Lise Luborsky. 1975. "Comparative Studies of Psychotherapies: Is It True That 'Everyone Has Won and All Must Have Prizes'?" *Archives of General Psychiatry*, 32: 995–1008.

Medawar, P. B. 1975. "Victims of Psychiatry." *New York Review of Books*, 23 January, p. 17.

Nisbett, Richard E., and Timothy Wilson. 1977. "Telling More than We Can Know: Verbal Reports on Mental Processes." *Psychological Review*, 84: 231–59.

Rubinstein, Benjamin B. 1975. "On the Clinical Psychoanalytic Theory and Its Role in the Inference and Confirmation of Particular Clinical Hypotheses." *Psychoanalysis and Contemporary Science*, 4: 3–57.

Silverman, Lloyd H. 1976. " 'The Reports of My Death Are Greatly Exaggerated.' " *American Psychologist*, 31: 621–637.

Whyte, Lancelot Law. 1960. *The Unconscious Before Freud*. New York: Basic Books.

3

The Freudian Way
of Knowledge

*This essay, published in the summer of 1984, owed its first impetus
to the celebrated* New Yorker *articles by Janet Malcolm that are
mentioned in its opening paragraphs. In the wake of those articles,
I was asked to join a public forum consisting of one or two psychoanalysts, a feminist, an expert in child abuse, and Jeffrey Masson—
the chief object of Malcolm's subtle ridicule—in a debate about
Freud's abandoned "seduction theory." Though no analysts could
be persuaded to appear, the event took place in February 1984
before a huge Berkeley audience, drawn chiefly by the prospect of
seeing the flamboyant troublemaker whose escapades in the Freud
Archives and in countless women's beds had afforded such amusement to Malcolm's readers.*

*The event proved lively enough, but many spectators must
have gone away disappointed. What occurred was not a circus but
a serious discussion, focused mainly on the implications of Freud's
decision, in adopting the idea of the Oedipus complex, to trace incest wishes to infancy and to grant them a momentous causal efficacy. My own participation consisted in stating my general objections to psychoanalysis, in explaining why I found the argument of
Masson's* The Assault on Truth *unconvincing, and in nevertheless
expressing some sympathy for Masson as a fellow target of Janet
Malcolm's poison pen. A year earlier Malcolm had referred to
"Analysis Terminable" as "the notorious hatchet job on psychoanalysis [by] the neo-Freudophobe Frederick Crews," grouping me,
in a revealing trio of adjectives, with other "tendentious, irrational,
unanalyzed" disbelievers in Freud's discoveries (Malcolm 1983a,
96).*

The "seduction theory" furor ended by whetting my curiosity

*about Freud biography. With few exceptions, that field has been
dominated by writers who follow Ernest Jones in taking Freud's
scientific greatness and healing power as given, and who therefore
swallow virtually everything that Freud himself asserted about his
empirical scruples and his heroic originality. Yet when one looks at
the record without such presuppositions, a very different picture
begins to take shape.*

*Freudians who have read this essay tell me that they cannot
go along with a reduction of psychoanalysis to a cocaine-induced
aberration on Freud's part. Neither can I; no such claim is made
here, and indeed it is specifically rejected (page 65). I must mention, nonetheless, that the uncensored Freud–Fliess letters, now in
print at last (Harvard University Press, 1985), fully corroborate
the importance of cocaine to Freud in the crucial decade of the
1890s.*

> Freud is a man given to absolute and exclusive formu-
> lations: this is a psychical need which, in my opinion,
> leads to excessive generalization.—JOSEPH BREUER, 1907
> (Cranefield, 320)

I

For many connoisseurs of high-level gossip, irony, and scandal,
some of the brightest moments of 1983 were provided by Janet
Malcolm's spellbinding articles in *The New Yorker* entitled "Trouble in the Archives." The articles, as my readers will probably
recall, dealt with the uproar surrounding the firing of Jeffrey Moussaieff Masson as Projects Director of the Freud Archives, an important collection in the Library of Congress which has been
largely restricted from scholars' view for periods extending as far
ahead as the year 2102. As Malcolm related, however, Masson, a
brash, newly accredited lay analyst, had made himself something
of a Trojan horse within that citadel. Dr. Kurt Eissler, the vener-
able guardian of the Archives and Freud idolator *extraordinaire*,
had been smitten by the glib and cunning Masson, and on Eissler's
advice the late Anna Freud had permitted Masson to inspect documents in her own possession that seemed to contradict received views
about the early Freud. Malcolm fashioned an intriguing narrative

out of Eissler's paternal doting upon Masson and their subsequent falling out over Masson's unsanctioned broadcasting of his new heterodoxy. And in her second article she trumped her portrait of the slick adventurer Masson with an even more unlikely figure, Masson's nemesis, Peter Swales—a high school dropout, a veteran of the rock music and drug cultures, and a self-made Freud scholar of colossal pretensions whose allegedly crude attempts to discredit Freud, as satirically depicted by Malcolm, looked like a *reductio ad absurdum* of Masson's own.

Most readers, including nearly every reviewer of Masson's subsequent book on Freud, took Malcolm's articles to be merely a neutral report, though an exceptionally piquant one. They failed to notice the pro-Freudian advocacy in those articles—typified, for example, in the following feat of logic: "The critics of psychoanalysis argue that people who have been analyzed are 'brainwashed' into 'believing in' psychoanalysis. But the same could be said of people who have come to a sympathetic understanding of Beethoven's genius through learning to play his piano sonatas" (Malcolm 1983b, I:80). Nor did they observe that Malcolm herself characterized her work as "a cautionary tale" (I:80) and that she drew the moral explicitly. There will always be Adlers and Jungs and Massons, Malcolm advised, whose quirks of temperament leave them vulnerable to a disease she named as "virulent anti-Freudianism" (I:121–22).

The further implication of Malcolm's articles—now developed into a book, *In the Freud Archives* (1984)—was that if you want to tear down Freud you will get no further than those hapless Snopeses of scholarship, Masson and Swales. That at any rate was Malcolm's fervent wish. All of her writings on psychoanalysis, whether narrative or expository, are works of what is known in Washington as damage control (Malcolm 1981, 1983a, 1983b). They anticipate objections or negative developments, grant that the Freudian movement is indeed troubled, and then slam the door on the critics, asserting, with Freud himself, that apostates and the unanalyzed cannot be expected to say anything reasonable about her favorite therapy and theory.

That, in my experience, is a characteristic maneuver of the militant analyzed when they are grappling with doubts. Virtually any negative insight can be entertained, but at a certain moment the pull of the leash is felt and the provisional skeptic finds him- or herself trotting along at Freud's heels as faithfully as ever. Mal-

colm's book, *Psychoanalysis: The Impossible Profession* (1981)—
so acute in its damning revelations of intellectual and institutional
decrepitude and so devotional in its final tone—is a classic of the
genre. We will see that such short-circuiting of the critical faculty
is not an incidental feature of the Freudian tradition.

Masson's own book, *The Assault on Truth: Freud's Suppression of the Seduction Theory* (1984), while it reads like an attack
on Freud, turns out to be no less cricumscribed by the Freudian
Weltanschauung than are Malcolm's works. Masson castigates
Freud for having abandoned his so-called seduction theory, namely,
that all hysterias are caused by repressed memories of molestation
in childhood. At times Masson seems to urge that Freud changed
his mind consciously to curry favor with the colleagues he had
previously alienated; elsewhere the motive appears to have been
an unconscious wish to exculpate his friend Wilhelm Fliess in the
Emma Eckstein affair (of which more below). But never once does
it occur to Masson that there may be more than two candidates for
an explanation of "neurosis." Nor was this possibility raised in any
of the (mostly hostile) reviews that came to my attention. Masson
and his antagonists agreed that Freud must have been either right
about neurosis before 1897 or right about neurosis thereafter.

Yet that assumption is not only unnecessary in view of competing theories but dubious on its face. Both of Freud's etiologies
posited a gap of many years between infantile causes and adult
effects. Freud wished us to believe that mental traumata suffered
by a relatively undeveloped organism have no immediately detectable influence on that organism yet are somehow retained
within it for toxic release at a stage of fuller development. He himself abandoned his 1895 "Project for a Scientific Psychology"
(Freud 1954) chiefly because he was unable to conceive of a neurological mechanism to account for that deferred action (Sulloway,
123–31). Nor has any physiological vehicle of repression turned
up in the nine subsequent decades. Surely that fact points to a
grave vulnerability in Freudian theory. Yet Freud's sway among the
opinion makers of our culture, many of whom are veterans of
analysis, remains so strong that the whole flap over "seduction"
has come and gone with scarcely a murmur of misgiving about the
repression etiology of neurosis.

Moreover, all parties to the debate over "seduction" have
shared a radically faulty sense of the way Freud reached his scientific judgments. Taking his apologetics at face value, they have

assumed that he drew theoretical conclusions directly from clinical observation, deciding after x number of cases that his patients had fallen ill through molestation but after $x + n$ cases that the preponderance of evidence now lay on the other side. The dispute, then, has been over which set of Freud's observations was the accurate one. But this narrow inductivist perspective overlooks the remoteness of Freud's inferences from any data available to him in the consulting room. While he may or may not have been able to tell whether his patients had been abused in early childhood, the leap to calling such events (or fantasies) neurosogenic had to be largely one of faith. Or rather, it was a matter of which books and papers he happened to have been taking as his guide to an informed view of the topic.

In *Freud, Biologist of the Mind*, Frank Sulloway has shown that when Freud abandoned the seduction etiology he was swayed by the sexological theories of Albert Moll, whose influence he tried to disguise (Sulloway, 310–15), and of Havelock Ellis, whose influence he belatedly acknowledged. In his *Three Essays on Sexuality* (1905) Freud credited narratives such as Ellis's with having "led me to make the modification in my aetiological hypotheses" (S.E., 7:190–91n.)—that is, with having persuaded him to throw over the seduction theory. As we will see, that is just the barest glimpse into Freud's actual indebtedness to popular thinkers of his day. For now, my point is that Freud's supporters and detractors alike have been beguiled by the "empirical" window-dressing of his ideas and have underestimated their actual deductive, speculative, and derivative origins. In other words, they have failed to grasp that "the structure of Freud's published arguments is often the exact reverse of the actual genesis of his ideas" (Sulloway, 421).[1]

We remain, then, largely unacquainted with the founder of psychoanalysis, whose steps of reasoning, as opposed to his brilliant but untrustworthy rhetoric, have been glimpsed only by a handful of scholars. Yet without having to wait for the promised publication of the unabridged Freud–Fliess letters, we can discern that Freud studies have entered a volatile period and that there can be no turning back from historically informed understanding. For we have now been granted a tantalizing glimpse of the real Freud of the later 1890s, in the very years when psychoanalysis was being conceived. That picture is so different from the canonical view that a general adjustment of perspective is inevitable. The present essay is a sketch of this new Freud and an assessment of the eventual effect of such understanding on accepted wisdom about the roots of psychoanalysis and its credibility as a general psychology.

II

I begin with the episode that momentarily clouded Janet Malcolm's horizon and that forms the core of Jeffrey Masson's otherwise unimpressive book: the Emma Eckstein case. That episode, which the original editors of Freud's letters to Fliess tried to suppress but which Max Schur brought to scholarly attention in 1966 (Freud 1954; Schur 1966), reveals a Freud totally at odds with the accepted image of the kindly healer and sage. We will see that the Eckstein case leads to fundamental questions about Freud's therapeutic style, his scientific ethics, his feelings about women, his handling of evidence, and his loyalty to notions that even the most fervent contemporary Freudian would have to consider outlandish.

In 1895 Freud summoned from Berlin his beloved friend and hero Wilhelm Fliess, a Berlin nose and throat specialist and biological visionary whom he had known since 1887, to operate on the nose of Freud's patient Emma Eckstein, probably thanks to Freud's identification of her as a victim of Fliess's favorite syndrome, the "nasal reflex neurosis." This affliction, according to Fliess, manifested itself variously in headaches, in neuralgic pains in the shoulders, arms, and stomach, in cardiac and respiratory irregularity and poor digestion, and in reproductive dysfunctions such as difficult menstruation (Freud 1954, 5; Sulloway, 139–40). As one might suppose from this array of symptoms, Fliess was rarely at a loss to discover that one of his patients had a nasal reflex neurosis.

The underlying causes, too, could be various; but like many physicians of the day, including Freud himself, Fliess was convinced that the abominable practice of masturbation was often to blame for otherwise unexplained complaints. It was good, then, to overrule the patient's protestations of innocence and to talk her out of masturbating; that was presumably Freud's role in the Emma case (Masson, 59, 77–78). But a full nasal reflex neurosis also called for direct intervention against the nose—for the nose as understood by Fliess was in fact a secondary sex organ and was thus presumably a site of referral of unhygienic uses of libido. Fliess's arsenal against the nasal reflex neurosis included three treatments of increasing gravity: applications of cocaine to the nasal membranes, cauterization of the "genital spots" within the nose, and finally the Eckstein operation, removal of the turbinate bone from the nose.

Today, of course, the nasal reflex neurosis cannot be found in any diagnostic manual. In a new book which is unfortunately marred by overstatements, E. M. Thornton (1984) has intriguingly proposed that the key to the syndrome was cocaine, which, when repeatedly applied to the nasal membranes and thence absorbed directly into the bloodstream, can eventually bring about most of the indicated symptoms. We do know for certain that both Freud and Fliess liberally prescribed cocaine for any number of initial complaints (Jones, 78–97, 309; Schur 1972, 69, 81, 83, 84, 95, 99). If Thornton is right, Freud and Fliess involved at least some of their patients in a chain of calamities whereby early applications of cocaine led to aggravated and expanded symptoms which then called for more cocaine, cauterization of the tissue damaged by the cocaine, and eventual surgery. In a word, the "cure" may have ended by causing most of the reported symptoms.

Emma Eckstein's bone removal appears to have been Fliess's first venture in major surgery. He returned to Berlin soon after the operation, leaving Freud to cope with postoperative complications that passed over into the grotesque. Fliess, as it was eventually revealed, had left half a meter of gauze inside the remains of Emma's nose, and Emma nearly died from the resultant infection. As she continued to hemorrhage in subsequent months, possibly as a result of further cocaine therapy, Freud gradually subdued his mortification over Fliess's malpractice and began *blaming Emma's unconscious* for this seemingly perverse refusal to stop bleeding. "I shall be able to prove to you," he triumphantly wrote Fliess, "that you were right; her hemorrhages were hysterical, brought on by *longing*, probably at the 'sexual period' (out of sheer resistance that *Frauenzimmer* has not yet given me the dates) . . ." (Schur 1966, 80). Or again: "she renewed the hemorrhage as an unfailing means of reawakening my affection" (81).

Even pro-psychoanalytic readers of such passages have been alarmed by Freud's having taken Fliess's side against Eckstein, and Masson justifiably calls Freud's diagnostic efforts here an early sign of his tendency to treat the patient as a liar. Feminists in particular have alleged that Freud's interpretation of Emma Eckstein's hemorrhaging as hysterical typifies his misogynistic bias. Terms like

Frauenzimmer (roughly, "broad") hardly contradict that charge. Yet these criticisms, grave as they are, do not squarely address the overwhelming question implicit in the whole matter. Did not Freud here display a fundamental and characteristic willfulness as an investigator—a willfulness that would undermine the standing of his "genuine discoveries" made in the immediately following years?

When Freud tells Fliess that he will be able to "prove" that Emma's bleeding is hysterical and is governed by "the sexual period," he is referring not to menstruation but to Fliess's now discredited numerological theory, which alleged a complex periodicity in all biological processes based on the numbers 28 and 23, representing respectively the female and male biological cycles.[2] Here we see Freud not only applying the theory to Emma but doing so before having extracted "the dates" from her—dates she is withholding from "resistance," a concept that was later to do yeoman service in putting recalcitrant critics as well as patients in their place.

What the Eckstein case reveals above all is a monomaniacal quality in Freud, a tendency to generalize too hastily while slighting any factors, especially organic ones, that might lead to a diagnosis other than his own. To be sure, such an attitude superficially resembles the boldness of a genuine scientific pioneer, for all such thinkers leap beyond the data lying before them. Thus it is not necessarily damning that Freud, as he told Fliess, considered himself "actually not at all a man of science, not an observer, not an experimenter, not a thinker. I am by temperament nothing but a *conquistador*, an adventurer . . . —with all the inquisitiveness, daring, and tenacity characteristic of such a man" (Schur 1972, 201). But as Freud truly remarked to his fiancée in 1884, "the temperament of an investigator needs *two* fundamental qualities: he must be sanguine in the attempt, *but critical in the work*" (Jones, 80; emphasis added). What if Freud turns out to have been a *conquistador* who tilted at windmills? Did his drive toward self-justification habitually warp his judgment and weaken his scruples, as it assuredly did in the Eckstein affair?

III

Once we have mustered the willingness to question Freud's scientific prudence, there is no shortage of telling material to pass in review. Consider, for example, his recognized yet often neglected cocaine phase, which is thought to have lasted from 1884 to 1887. (We will see that it actually lasted through the time when he was concocting psychoanalysis.) Freud in the mid-Eighties was not merely a recreational user of the newly synthesized drug in its highest-grade pharmaceutical form and a profligate dispenser of samples to friends, relatives, and patients, but also the most bigoted of cocaine evangelists (Jones, 78–97). His papers on the subject advocated virtually limitless cocaine applications for every complaint from indigestion, neurasthenia, weak libido, and hysteria to diabetes and syphilis (Freud 1974, 65–73). And though his panegyrics ceased after worldwide cocaine abuse had become so infamous that Freud himself was being denounced as the bringer of a scourge to humankind (Jones, 94), the little-known truth is that he made no substantial recantation of his disastrous advice. If he was rash and self-deluded in 1884, by 1887, when his last cocaine paper appeared, he was cowardly, evasive, and criminally negligent.

These are strong words. But let us reflect on Freud's consistent urging that cocaine be used to wean morphine addicts from their habit. That advice was based partly on American reports which he uncritically accepted and partly on his own administering of cocaine to his friend and colleague Ernst Fleischl von Marxow, whose reaction to the drug he was able to witness at close range for the rest of Fleischl's life. The Fleischl case constitutes a macabre sign of Freud's reluctance to accept criticism and to moderate his claims in the interest of curbing medical malpractice.

Both Freud and Fleischl himself thought for a while that cocaine had cured him of morphine dependency (Freud 1974, 144). Freud thereupon drew up a jaunty paper including an apparent reference to that cure, which had featured, he said, "rapid withdrawal from morphine under cocaine treatment" in a mere twenty days. "No cocaine habituation set in," wrote Freud. "On the contrary, an increasing antipathy to the use of cocaine was unmistakably evident" (Freud 1974, 117). But by June 1885, Fleischl, on top of his unabated morphine addiction, was injecting cocaine in daily doses roughly a hundred times stronger than Freud himself was occasionally taking to alter his mood (Jones, 91), and he was experiencing insomnia, fainting fits and convulsions, and hallucinations of white snakes crawling across his skin. Freud repeatedly sat up all night with him observing in anguish these effects, as he privately acknowledged, of his own intervention. Yet in the face

of this horrific refutation of his claims, Freud did nothing to forestall publication of his "Fleischl" paper two months later. "It seems
to have met with considerable success," observes Freud's adoring
biographer Ernest Jones. "Freud was gratified at *The Lancet* ab-
stracting it" (Jones 92).

Ernst Fleischl von Marxow clung to life through six more
years of indescribable suffering. Yet in his last cocaine paper of
1887, replying to his now clamorous critics, Freud still refused to
correct his erroneous earlier report—except to indicate vaguely that
some patients "get hold of the drug themselves" and abuse it
(Freud 1974, 172). Scoffing at substantial and tragic testimony to
the contrary, he added mistakenly that only morphine addicts can
become addicted to cocaine. Thus Freud still encouraged his physician readers to believe they could prescribe cocaine as a virtual
panacea. And though he now deemed it "advisable" (Freud 1974,
175) to forgo subcutaneous injections, he did not even hint that he
himself had previously been the leading advocate of precisely that
measure, which he had pronounced "quite harmless" (Freud 1974,
109). Rather than admit an error, Freud for the rest of his life tried
to suppress his authorship of the offending paper—a strategy that
the ever loyal Jones, who liked to write of Freud's "flawless integrity," tactfully ascribed to "unconscious repression" (Jones, 327,
96). Already by the 1880s, we must conclude, Freud showed a pattern of making extravagant curative claims, brushing aside opposing evidence, covering his tracks, and blithely violating the physician's oath to do no harm.

IV

Freud's approach to cocaine was by no means the only early instance of his penchant for contracting rash enthusiasms. A more
important if less spectacular example was his eagerness to believe
in Jean-Martin Charcot's "demonstrations" of hypnotic control
over hysterical symptoms (see Ellenberger 1970, 435–42; Sulloway,
28–49; Thornton, 43–85). Few historians today share that judgment, and even in 1886 Freud's colleagues in Vienna raised their
eyebrows at his gullibility. By 1893 Freud himself had developed
major reservations about Charcot's work (see S.E., 3:22–23). But
by then, fortified by the no less specious hypnotic "cures" of hys-

teria claimed by Hippolyte Bernheim in Nancy, he had committed himself to the debatable ideas that hysteria was an authentic syndrome and that the key to its conquest lay in some variant of mesmeric treatment. Though Freud deserves credit for having eventually abandoned hypnotism, in a sense he never recovered from his own "suggestibility" before Charcot—a condition, by the way, that may have been enhanced to some degree by his having braced himself with cocaine in order to act at ease with the venerated master in 1885 (Freud 1974, 161–66).

Another important step leading to Freud's invention of psychoanalysis proper was his elevation to paradigmatic status of his former friend and mentor Josef Breuer's long-abandoned "Anna O." case of 1881 to 1882. Anna, alias Bertha Pappenheim, had suffered from a variety of disorders, including paralysis of three limbs, severe coughing, and bizarre disturbances of speech, which most psychiatrists of the Vienna school would have taken as signs of brain injury or organic disease. But Breuer had considered Anna a typical hysteric—that is, a woman incapable of mastering her feelings—and Freud disputed that diagnosis only in placing even more emphasis than Breuer did on the contribution of sexual factors.

In Breuer's treatment of Anna, Freud had been smitten by a practice that Anna herself had proposed and had dubbed "the talking cure": inducing the patient to dredge up a memory that presumably lay behind a given symptom, which would then vanish. As Juan Dalma has pointed out, Anna probably got the idea from a popular book about Aristotelian catharsis written by Jacob Bernays, the uncle of Freud's future wife (cited by Ellenberger 1970, 484); but Breuer and Freud himself were eager to believe that in this parlor game "hysteria" had met its match at last. Since Anna's many symptoms were intermittent from the beginning, it was easy for both Breuer and Anna to be impressed for a while by the correlation between therapeutic talk and symptom relief. And Freud remained impressed by it—so he claimed, at any rate. As he later wrote in his *Autobiographical Study* (1925), "The state of things which [Breuer] had discovered seemed to me so fundamental that I could not believe it could fail to be present in any case of hysteria if it had been proved to occur in a single one" (S.E., 20:21).

Breuer himself—a modest and decent man who notably lacked Freud's Napoleonic ambition—had apparently idealized his memories of the Anna case in the thirteen-year interval before Freud cajoled him into writing it up for publication. Under Freud's pressure Breuer misled his medical audience into believing that he had lastingly cured Anna of many symptoms. The resultant collaborative book, *Studies on Hysteria* (1895), established Freud's own psychotherapeutic credentials as a colleague of the celebrated Breuer, though in fact the two men disagreed about most theoretical issues and were scarcely on speaking terms when the book appeared.

To dramatize his superiority to Breuer, whom he had come to despise with a passion that even Jones considered neurotic (Jones, 308), Freud told Jones and others a memorable tale about Breuer's having abruptly dropped Anna's treatment in a panic when he realized she had developed a transference love for him and was undergoing a hysterical pregnancy (Jones, 224–25). The burden of this story was that it would require a Freud, not a mere Breuer, to brave the tempests of transference and found a new therapeutic art upon them. Thanks to dogged research by Henri Ellenberger, however, we now know that Freud's tale was a fabrication (Ellenberger 1970, 480–484; 1972, *passim*). Far from having precipitously fled Anna's presence after making great progress on the case, Breuer had arranged well in advance for her commitment to a sanatarium. His letter of transfer characterized her condition as one of "hysterical insanity." And the surviving sanatarium notes, unearthed by Ellenberger, show that Anna retained the symptoms that Breuer claimed, thirteeen years later, to have "cathartically" removed (Ellenberger 1972).

Both Breuer and Freud knew of Anna's whereabouts and that her improvement—for she later became a famous philanthropist and social reformer—had begun only after she left Breuer's care. Indeed, Jones reports that "[a] year after discontinuing the treatment, Breuer confided to Freud that she was quite unhinged and that he wished she would die and so be released from her suffering" (Jones, 225). And Freud himself, according to Jung, told Jung that Anna had not been cured by Breuer (Jones, 225). It seems strange that neither Freud nor Breuer could recall that paramount fact when the time came to draw up *Studies on Hysteria*. Freud's career as a specialist in hysteria, it appears, was launched in an ethically shady atmosphere—and was then retrospectively adorned with a mischievous falsehood about Breuer, the chief benefactor of that career.

V

But did Freud perhaps become a more responsible scientist and physician once he was embarked on psychoanalysis itself? That would be surprising after his deplorable early record, especially since it was Freud the psychoanalyst who propagated the fictitious history of Breuer's dealings with Anna O. It is possible, however, that Freud no longer needed to cut corners once he had made a real breakthrough in knowledge. Did he, in his therapeutic practice and his subsequent system building, display a degree of prudence, open-mindedness, and concern for rival explanations that would justify our trust in his new doctrine?

We can begin addressing this question by looking at a typical case history: the highly regarded Dora case, which the patient terminated after three months in 1900 and which Freud wrote up shortly thereafter but published only in 1905 (S.E., 7:7–122). The document is generally considered important because it is Freud's first sustained effort to show in practice how his theory of neurosis meshed with his theory of dreams. But let us begin by thinking about Dora herself (Ida Bauer), a bright and attractive young woman with a tangled family history who was brought to Freud at age eighteen suffering from fainting fits with convulsions and delirium, catarrh, occasional loss of voice, shortness of breath, and a dragging leg. Here again, as with Anna O., we see a constellation of serious troubles crying out for attention to the possible relevance of an organic syndrome. Indeed, there was every reason to pursue that line of inquiry. Dora had grown up with a tubercular father who had contracted syphilis before her conception; father and daughter manifested virtually identical asthmatic troubles; and Dora herself urged Freud to consider the syphilitic basis of her case (7:75).

Interestingly enough, Freud readily agreed with her. As he explained, every neurosis finds a "somatic compliance" in some underlying condition (7:40), and in his clinical experience a father's syphilis is regularly "a very relevant factor in the aetiology of the neuropathic constitution of children" (7:21n.). This opinion, however, in no way dissuaded him from regarding Dora as yet another weak-willed woman exhibiting "intolerable behaviour" (7:75) and "a *taedium vitae* which was probably not entirely genuine" (7:24). Freud had pronounced Dora neurotic as soon as she had recounted her symptoms, and he already believed that in such a case the only hope of cure lay in undoing the patient's unconscious evasions. The organic aspect of Dora's coughing, he reasoned, was only its "lowest stratum," acting "like the grain of sand around which an oyster forms its pearl" (7:83). Why bother with it, then? Apparently Freud did not even take the trouble to put Dora through a routine physical examination. Instead, he subjected her to an extraordinary campaign of mental harassment.

In Janet Malcolm's apt words, "Freud treated Dora as a deadly adversary. He sparred with her, laid traps for her, pushed her into corners, bombarded her with interpretations, gave no quarter, was as unspeakable, in his way, as any of the people in her sinister family circle, went too far, and finally drove her away" (Malcolm 1981, 97). When Freud learned, for example, that Dora believed she had recently suffered an attack of appendicitis, he brushed aside such a shallow view of the matter and peremptorily decided that the appendicitis had really been a hysterical pregnancy expressing her unconscious sexual fantasies (7:103). Her shortness of breath, he decided, was indeed linked to her father's identical condition, but chiefly in the sense that she must have overheard him wheezing in an act of copulation (7:80). And her coughing, like Emma Eckstein's bleeding, was just another timid female love song (7:39). In Freud's now prurient mind, steamy erotic speculations were of greater diagnostic interest than manifest signs of disease.

Freud's novelistic case history, in which he plays Poe's infallible detective Dupin, is full of vindictive touches at Dora's expense. One of her complaints, evidently justified, was that her philandering father was tacitly encouraging advances made to her by the husband of her father's mistress—a state of affairs in which the least culpable party would surely have been the bewildered and frightened teenaged girl. But Freud set about to prove that Dora's troubles were produced chiefly by her own mind. When he learned, for example, that years earlier she had felt disgust at being sexually assailed by this "still quite young" and "prepossessing" man (7:29n.), he concluded, "In this scene . . . the behaviour of this child of fourteen was already entirely and completely hysterical. I should without question consider a person hysterical in whom an occasion for sexual excitement elicited feelings that were preponderantly or exclusively unpleasurable; and I should do so whether or no [*sic*] the person were capable of producing somatic symptoms" (7:28).

Freud's uppermost motive in the Dora case, it is clear, was to avoid being taken in by the shiftiness for which "hysterics" were notorious in the medical reports of his time. More specifically, his own diagnostic rule, borrowed from Fliess, told him that women with neurotic problems were almost certainly masturbators and that no progress could be expected until a confession on that point had been extracted. Believing, for example, the Fliessian law that recurrent enuresis is caused by masturbation (Sulloway 1979, 174n.), he forced Dora to admit that in childhood she had been a late bedwetter (7:72–76). Her catarrh, too, he informed her, "pointed primarily to masturbation" (7:76), and so did her stomach troubles. "It is well known," he observed, "that gastric pains occur especially often in those who masturbate. According to a personal communication made to me by Wilhelm Fliess, it is precisely gastralgias of this character which can be interrupted by an application of cocaine to the 'gastric spot' discovered by him in the nose, and which can be cured by cauterization of the same spot" (7:78).

Such flashes of outright quackery are easy to identify but also easy to discount as consequences of prevalent misinformation. Far more important for an assessment of psychoanalysis as an investigative method are the implicit rules by which Freud achieved closure in his diagnosis. Once embarked on a given path of reasoning, all he requried for confirmation was a suggestive detail or two, such as Dora's having dreamed about a jewel case (her genitals) and having brought a small purse to an analytic session and fiddled with it (7:69, 76)—in other words, the genitals once again. And wherever Dora's associations seemed wanting he simply supplied his own. He remarked, for example, that her dragging leg must indicate a worry that her fantasized pregnancy—fantasized only by Freud under Dora's strenuous protest—was a "false step" (7:103).

When Dora reported a dream about a *Bahnhof* (station) and a *Friedhof* (cemetery), moreover, the genitally obsessed Freud thought at once of a homonym, *Vorhof* (forecourt), "an anatomical term for a particular region of the female genitals" (7:99). Was not this term suspiciously connected to *nymphs* that Dora had seen in a painting the day before? Now "no further doubts could be entertained" (7:99) that Dora had been sneaking peeks at anatomy books—for how else could she have known the sexual meaning of *Vorhof* and of *Nymphen*, an arcane medical name for the labia minora? Yet Freud never states that Dora spoke the word *Nymphen* at all; he himself, having probably seen the famous Secessionist exhibit, is the one who tells us that the painting in question contained nymphs in the background (7:99). As for *Vorhof*, it is confessedly Freud's personal contribution. Does not his ingenuity here border on the delusional? By diligently sifting the contents of his own mind and ascribing them to Dora, Freud had indeed placed himself on a trail of sexually disordered thinking.

VI

The Dora case, then—and there was nothing atypical about its technique—cannot dispel the widespread suspicion that Freud's way with "free associations" was altogether too free. That suspicion haunted his entire psychoanalytic career, beginning with Fliess's cutting allegation in 1901 that Freud (as Freud himself summarized the point in a letter to Fliess) "perceives nothing in others but merely projects his own thoughts into them" (Freud 1954, 337). How could Freud defend himself against that charge? Certainly not by citing the rigor of his interpretive method, for that method allowed him, if other signs were supportive, to regard a patient's dissent as confirmatory, to consider irrelevancies as "displacements," and even, if he wished, to claim as "conclusive proof" of reconstructed memories the fact that patients "have no feeling of remembering the scenes" (S.E., 3:204).

To the end of his life Freud maintained that since his first recourse to psychoanalysis he had never persuaded a single patient "to accept things which [I myself] believe but which he ought not to" (S.E., 23:262). He rested this remarkable claim on three considerations (S.E., 23:262–65). In some cases, he reported, he and other analysts could tell when they were on the right track by their patients' emotional turmoil in the face of correct interpretations. Second, Freud pointed to the chances an analyst gets to reassess a hypothesis in the further course of the analysis; any false construction, he argued, would simply drop out of the picture after a while. And third, Freud maintained that the brilliant success of his treatment was itself proof of correct constructions, since the only explanation for his patients' eventual freedom from neurosis was that they must have "worked through" genuinely pathogenic repressed memories.

Of these three arguments, the least imposing ones are those based on patients' signs of turmoil in analysis and on the analyst's opportunities to double check his hunches. One can readily imagine why a patient of Freud's—Dora, for example—might have shown considerable agitation in the face of proposals that were zany and insulting rather than penetratingly correct. And there can be little probative value in a therapist's waiting to see whether a hypothesis is confirmed by the rest of the analysis, for everything that subsequently occurs can be colored and even shaped by that very hypothesis as it is seized upon by both parties. Thus we are left with the stronger-looking argument from cure. But as the philosopher of science Adolf Grünbaum has demonstrated, that argument too is fatally vulnerable (Grünbaum, 1979, 1982, 1983). For, in the first place, even genuine cures, to say nothing of the palliations Freud often took for cures, could have occurred for reasons other than veridical "Freudian insight"—just as faith healing has been known to "work" without validating the specific content of the healer's beliefs. And more ominously, even at their best Freud's cures do not appear to have been such in any accepted sense of the term.

If Freud had permanently removed a single neurosis, no doubt he would have told us about the case in detail. But the pro-Freudian researchers Seymour Fisher and Roger P. Greenberg have regretfully concluded that nearly all of Freud's substantially described cases were manifest failures (Fisher and Greenberg, 281–85). And often Freud simply misrepresented therapeutic outcomes—as, for example, in reporting the eighteen successfully completed cases that underlay "The Aetiology of Hysteria" (1896). In other papers of the period he never mentioned more than thirteen cases, and shortly after delivering that paper he complained to Fliess, "I get no new cases for treatment, and . . . not one of the old ones is finished yet" (Freud 1954, 162–63). Even two years later he had yet to mention a successful termination; on the contrary, he confided that his cases were still "doing rather badly" (Freud 1954, 245).

In 1906 Freud confided to Jung that "It is not possible to explain anything to a hostile public; accordingly I have kept certain things that might be said concerning the limits of the therapy and its mechanism to myself . . ." (Freud/Jung, 12). Only toward the end of his career, when his undeserved reputation as a healer was secure, did he begin confessing from time to time that he had "never been a therapeutic enthusiast" (S.E., 21:151) and that he had not found a reliable remedy for neurosis at all (see especially S.E., 23:216–253). Yet he did not feel prompted by that momentous admission to withdraw any of the theoretical claims he had rested on his previous untruths about therapeutic triumph. Indeed, he kept right on asserting that triumph whenever he found himself addressing the credulous public (e.g., S.E., 23:179). The total record leads to no other conclusion than that Freud's argument from success was a bluff from the beginning.

Freud, we recall, was fond of comparing the psychoanalytic revolution to those achieved by Copernicus and Darwin. But think for a moment of the contrast between Darwin's scientific stance and Freud's. The theory of evolution was complete in outline by the late 1830s, yet Darwin delayed publication for twenty years while gathering corroborative data that would display the cogency of his theory to any disinterested observer.[3] Freud, however, not only rushed into print with wild claims, misrepresented his therapeutic results, and recast interpretive rules in his favor, he also bent his rhetorical efforts to denying that skeptics were eligible to criticize him. His case histories and theoretical papers consist in large part of self-serving anecdotes, disarming literary parallels, artful fendings-off of objections, promises that the evidence will come later or false assurances that it was given earlier, declarations that his alleged cures and objective observations are proof of his theory, and attributions of his critics' doubts to unconscious resistance and repression. In brief, Freud, while continuing to profess that psychoanalysis was a rigorous natural science, had simply resigned from the wider scientific community and founded a cult of his personal authority.

VII

As that cult developed in the early years of our century, it gradually took shape around what Frank Sulloway, in a brilliant and indispensable study (1979), has called the psychoanalytic legend. Through Freud's personal sway over his disciples and the specific mechanism of the training analysis, which Hanns Sachs once approvingly likened to the novitiate of the Church (Sulloway, 486), the legend became focused on one event, Freud's *mysterium tre-mendum*, his self-analysis. That "most heroic" and "Herculean" feat (Jones, 319, 320), begun and climaxed in 1897, supposedly gave Freud the oedipal clue to his own psychoneurosis and, as a handsome bonus, to all others as well. The self-analysis stands functionally in the place of a conventional scientific defense; rather than being offered the evidence itself to examine, we are asked to embrace a set of intuitions that were revealed to the Master in an access of personal transcendence.

Needless to say, this obscure experience raises some questions for the laity. In the first place, if Freud's doctrine of repression is correct, he probably could not have cracked his own case merely through introspection; the myth of the self-analysis credits him with superhuman powers. Second, according to Jones the immediate motive for the self-analysis was a crisis of remorse caused by the death of Freud's father, whom he had hitherto felt obliged by his theory to hold guilty of having molested him and his siblings, all of whom he considered hysterics. Freud emerged from his self-analysis with a happy exoneration of his late father but a not so fortunate attribution of murderous and incestuous wishes to all children—even children who had actually been molested. (And henceforth parental seducers of children could protest, if they were good Freudians, that they had responded to infantile sexual wishes directed *toward them*.) Non-Freudians might think this a steep price to pay for clearing the elder Freud of a charge that had been generated by a half-baked and soon abandoned theoretical notion. And third, since the self-analysis apparently proceeded chiefly through Freud's study of his dreams, any arbitrariness in his method of dream interpretation would cast doubt on the "knowledge" thus obtained. If, for example, Freud merely assumed rather than proved that every dream is powered by an infantile wish—and that is just what he did—then his "discovery" of his own infantile fantasy life by means of dream interpretation was circular.

Freud supposedly laid to rest any doubts about his own case in two ways, by calling up infantile memories—for example, of his desire for his mother's naked body on a train when he was two years old—and by asking his mother to corroborate newly un-earthed recollections from infancy about a thieving nursemaid who was now to replace Freud's father in his mind as the family se-ducer. (Though Freud was in the process of deciding that most memories of early seduction were fantasies, he made an exception for his own case.) Yet he admitted that instead of having repressed his first memories of the wicked nanny, he could have learned about her thieving "in later childhood" and then have put her out of mind until 1897 (Freud 1954, 222). So much for that "proof" of the evidence that give us the Oedipus complex.

As for the train memory, its purport interestingly matched that of an observation Fliess had already confided about his own two-year-old son Robert, whose spontaneous erections he had been avidly monitoring (Freud 1954, 219; Sulloway, 190). The putative memory also dated from an age when the human brain is so undeveloped that long-term retention of any memories is dubious (Thornton, 175, 206). And the same objection applies a *fortiori* to still another of Freud's self-analytic treasures, his recollection of having felt jealous of a sibling who was born when he was *one* year old and who died just eight months later (Freud 1954, 219). Is not the whole self-analysis what Richard von Krafft-Ebing called Freud's seduction theory, a scientific fairy tale (Freud 1954, 167n.)?

Shaky though the self-analysis was, Freud appears to have leapt directly from it to his generalities about the panhuman condition. It was enough for him, seeking only confirmations as usual, that he now possessed a clue to the appeal of *Oedipus Rex* and *Hamlet* (Freud 1954, 223–24). And so he simply decreed that all children everywhere, at a stage of their lives when sexual enlightenment still lies ahead of them, literally desire to murder one parent and copulate with the other (as best they know how) and that those wishes, permanently enshrined in the repressed unconscious, play a key part in the formation of every psychoneurosis. Would we allow a less ingratiating rhetorician than Freud to sell us such an idea on his personal guarantee that it was true?

VIII

If we go along with the Freudian legend we find ourselves having to place total trust in Freud's genius as it was operating in 1897. The date is arresting: it marks not only Freud's anguish over his "seducing" father but also the height of his friendship with Fliess, the time when he began mentioning to Fliess that "sexual excitation [at age 41] is of no more use to a person like me" (Freud 1954, 227), and the most intense phase of what Jones called a "very considerable psychoneurosis" (Jones, 304), featuring extreme contentiousness and suspiciousness, wild mood swings between exhilaration and depression, cardiac arrhythmia, gastrointestinal disturbances, strangely vivid dreams, fainting fits, and episodes of what Jones characterized as "a twilight condition of mind" (Jones, 306). Ordinarily such facts would be of only peripheral interest within a scientist's intellectual biography, but Freud's case is different by virtue of his having supplied *no other* basis for his key discovery than a shamanlike revelation.

The truth is that much of Freud's conduct in the later Nineties was extraordinarily eccentric. Having contracted for no apparent reason "a violent antipathy" (Jones, 308) to Breuer, for example, he took elaborate precautions to keep himself away from Breuer's neighborhood, for the very thought of accidentally meeting his old friend and patron disgusted and unnerved him. His travel plans were circumscribed by special anxieties and taboos (Freud 1954, 214, 219, 237, 285, 306; Jones, 13, 181, 305, 307). He brooded constantly about the fated year of his death, passing one danger point only to see another looming (Jones, 310; Sulloway, 166). And he allowed his daily life to be haunted by dubious extensions of Fliess's already dubious numerological system. Thus he attached sinister meaning to telephone and hotel room numbers, always fearing they might contain a figure unpropitious for his destiny. Analytic apologists have tried to pin this dotty behavior on Fliess, but Fliess never intended his calculations to be applied to years, much less to phone numbers (Sulloway, 166).

Of greatest interest concerning Freud's degree of observational and reporting competence are his admitted hallucinations and his "twilight condition of mind." Was Freud, at the time he devised psychoanalysis, always capable of distinguishing between observation and fantasy or between having heard an idea and having originated it himself? Throughout this period and for a while thereafter he appropriated other thinkers' work as his own, expressing apparently sincere rage when challenged; he even charged the sexologist Albert Moll with plagiarism, whereas Freud was the one who probably lifted ideas from Moll (Sulloway, 254, 304, 311, 313+n., 315, 469). And Fliess's loss of confidence in him—for it was Fliess who became disillusioned with Freud's ethics and his science, not the other way around (Sulloway, 223)—dated from an episode, candidly recounted by Freud in *The Psychopathology of Everyday Life*, in which Freud suffered one of his several "priority amnesias." In their final meeting Freud proposed to Fliess that human bisexuality was the key to the neuroses, whereupon the startled Fliess reminded him that he, Fliess, had first tried that idea on Freud two and a half years earlier (S.E., 6:143–44). Freud was soon able to confirm Fliess's version of events, but here again his memory had betrayed him on a point of major importance to his Copernican ambitions.

Max Schur takes Freud's heart condition to have been his primary trouble in this period (Schur 1972, 40–62). In my opinion, however, E. M. Thornton makes fuller sense of the record by stressing Freud's continued or renewed recourse to cocaine. The known effects of that drug uncannily match every one of Freud's symptoms, from his first heightened and then extinguished libido and his various physical afflictions through his psychic bondage to Fliess and his flashes of paranoia—a condition he belatedly admitted, in a 1916 letter to Sándor Ferenczi, to be a typical consequence of prolonged cocaine use (Freud 1974, xix). We can now say with assurance that Freud's "cocaine period" did *not* end in 1887, the very year he met his fellow cocaine enthusiast Fliess. On the contrary, from at least 1892 through the end of the decade he was not only swallowing cocaine for relief of his head and stomach pains but applying it directly to his nasal membranes. Moreover, the emphasis of his published cocaine papers falls heavily on the drug's capacity to enhance stamina for work, especially in people who are prone, as he was, to depression (Freud 1974, 60, 61, 107–8). Thus it is plausible to think that Freud's research and writings at the time he founded psychoanalysis were influenced by the disorienting effects of the drug. And more broadly, cocaine probably had much to do with Freud's whole shift of attention from neurology to the underworld of contorted sexual fantasy (vom Scheidt).

In *The Interpretation of Dreams* Freud tells us that in 1895 he was not only administering cocaine to his patients but also "making frequent use of cocaine . . . to reduce some troublesome nasal swellings" and that he feared he had thereby damaged his nose (S.E., 4:11). Both Freud and Fliess, surely not by coincidence, suffered from chronic inflammation and infection of the nose, conditions probably caused by and certainly treated with cocaine (Schur 1972, 83–84). And again, both men took cocaine liberally to combat migraines (Jones, 309; Schur 1972, 99)—a paradoxical nostrum, for cocaine gives initial relief from headache through its vasoconstrictive effect but then redoubles the pain through a "rebound" dilatation, one that would of course cause the sufferer to reach for still more cocaine. Incidentally, since Freud appeared to his sympathetic friend as yet another nasal neurotic, he gratefully submitted to Fliessian cauterization of his own nose and even, according to Max Schur, to "surgery on the turbinate bone" (Jones, 309; Schur 1972, 81, 82). Bizarre as this information may appear, the cardinal point is a simple one: Freud had by no means done with cocaine at the time he withdrew into the mists of his self-analysis.[4]

To ascribe psychoanalysis entirely to cocaine, however, would be an act of reductionism comparable to Freud's own crude explanatory overreaching. Neither the origins nor the inadequacies of Freud's doctrine can be properly understood on that basis. His psychic troubles in the later 1890s, whether or not they were brought on by cocaine, did get hypostatized in his general theory of neurosis, but the greater part of that theory was demonstrably rooted in other sources—sources that have been coming to light only recently as scholars have challenged the Mosaic legend inscribed by Jones.

IX

Jones would have us believe that Freud at the time of his self-analysis was a tragically isolated man, surrounded by walls of anti-Semitism, prudery, and repression on the part of his medical colleagues. As Ellenberger (1970) and Sulloway have shown, this picture is totally false. Freud's elders treated their combative and bewildering colleague quite indulgently on the whole. They were not discernibly anti-Semitic, nor were they afraid to discuss sexual matters; one of their company was the great Krafft-Ebing, with whose classification of the perversions Freud is sometimes wrongly credited. And medical Vienna just then was full of the sexual theories of Albert Moll and Havelock Ellis, both of whom were far more advanced than Freud in their awareness and acceptance of unorthodox sexual practices. The myth of Freud's self-analysis has functioned chiefly as a means of extracting him from his milieu and crediting him with ideas that were already current.

But above all, that myth has served to set Freud apart from Wilhelm Fliess. It was Fliess, not Freud's self-analysis or his patients, who convinced him that infantile sexuality was prevalent and normal and thus that the belief in an early sexual grounding for neurosis could be sustained without recourse to a "seduction theory" (Sulloway, 192–93). It was Fliess again who bequeathed to psychoanalysis the idea of erotogenic zones and phases of development, the notion of a primary human bisexuality, the imputation of an unconscious homosexual component to all neurosis, and the conception of a latency period before puberty (Sulloway, 140, 174–89). The whole Freudian scheme of regression to "fixation points" in childhood development is Fliessian in origin, as Freud grudgingly acknowledged in 1913 (S.E., 12:318n.). Freud replaced the seduction theory, in Sulloway's words, with "Fliessian mechanisms of sexual latency, sublimation, reaction formation, and the pathological fixation of infantile, polymorphously perverse, sexual impulses" (Sulloway, 236).

Even Freud's grim proposal that girls at puberty must graduate from clitoral to vaginal sensitivity—a somewhat mystical project that has kept countless women in analysis while awaiting this neurological sign of grace—derived straight from Fliess's picture of normal development as the suppression of innate bisexuality. For Fliess and therefore for his disciple Freud, the clitoris, like libido and pleasure in general, was male, just as neurosis and unpleasure were female (Freud 1954; Sulloway, 163, 202+n.; Thornton, 206). To abandon the clitoris, in Freud's and Fliess's view as in that of less "scientific" authorities in other cultures, was therefore tantamount to becoming a real woman.

According to Sulloway, furthermore, what set psychoanalysis proper in motion in 1897 was not Freud's grasp of the Oedipus complex but his decision to adopt a totally Fliessian account of neurosis. Henceforward, he decided, not just the "actual neuroses" but also the "psychoneuroses" would be explained by disturbances in sexual development or functioning as understood by Fliess (Sulloway, 192). Thus Freud could continue to assert, with Fliess, that some mental disorders were caused by masturbation and coitus interruptus, but those relatively straightforward (if absurd) etiologies could now be joined by others that entailed the very nature of humankind as a species harboring a precariously attenuated sexuality.

Up till this juncture Freud's psychiatric colleagues had been only mildly puzzled by his one-track thinking, and even thereafter they saw nothing novel in his invoking of infantile sexuality, repression, sexual dream symbolism, resistance, transference, and sublimation. Those "discoveries" were commonplace notions that derived partly from popular belief, partly from Romantic *Naturphi-*

losophie, and partly from the discredited pseudoscience of mesmerism (Whyte; Ellenberger 1970). Though neurologists could see that there was something retrograde about Freud's humorlike "quantities of excitation" that build up within the organism and then seek a psychophysical discharge, no one seemed especially concerned about his reversion to that Greco-Roman medical idiom. No: insofar as psychoanalysis attracted notice at all in its early years, the persistently raised objection was to just one point, the *exclusively* sexual etiology of all neurosis. That was what put psychoanalysis on the map as a dogma to be reckoned with—and it was Fliess's idea.

Sulloway has shown, moreover, that Freud built his sexual etiologies on a foundation of erroneous genetic theory whose weakness undermines them far more drastically than even opponents of psychoanalysis usually realize. Everyone knows that Freud was a stubborn Lamarckian who never swerved from the idea that acquired characteristics are heritable. Students of his life, failing to notice his consistent record of premature generalization, have wondered why he would not back down on such a dispensable point. But Sulloway shows that the point was not dispensable at all. Freud needed Lamarckism because his relentlessly universal etiology of neurosis would never stand without it (Sulloway, 384–92). If a given case ever failed to yield the required sexual trauma, Freud was prepared to roll out his ultimate weapon, phylogenesis. The patient in such a case would be suffering from guilt produced by ancestral memory traces, perhaps even dating all the way back to the primal crime. Indeed, Freud's fully articulated psychology posited that "all the things that are told to us to-day in analysis as phantasy—the seduction of children, the inflaming of sexual excitement by observing parental intercourse, the threat of castration (or rather castration itself)—were once real occurrences in the primaeval times of the human family, and . . . children in their fantasies are simply filling in the gap in individual truth with prehistoric truth" (S.E., 16:371).

So, too, in the third edition of *The Interpretation of Dreams* (1911) Freud simultaneously extended his claims regarding the sexual basis of dreams and added to his interpretive arsenal a lexicon of universal, phylogenetically given sexual symbols (Sulloway, 350). It would be naïve to imagine that Freud empirically "discovered" these new rules—which were in any case lifted from popular dream books of an earlier time (Ellenberger 1970, 492–93; Sulloway, 323–

27)—and that he then found through exercising them that nearly all dreams requiring interpretation are sexually based. Rather, the ex post facto leap into phylogenetic explanation gave an appearance of justifying a long planned but tactically deferred extension of theoretical claims.

The other genetic doctrine Freud relied on—Haeckel's "biogenetic law" that ontogeny recapitulates phylogeny—has fared somewhat better over the years than Lamarckism, but not in the sense that Freud understood it. For Freud and many of his contemporaries, Haeckelian biogenetics applied not just to embryos but to the early years of life outside the womb. In this misguided extension of Darwinian thought, the human child supposedly recapitulated preceding evolutionary stages in their *adult* forms (Sulloway, 498). And since Freud shared the general late-nineteenth-century belief that *homo sapiens* had evolved upward from a primary sexuality which was being supplanted by "civilization," he therefore had to find adult manifestations of phylogenetically determined sexuality in childhood. Thus "Freud claimed that no one, looking at a nursing infant, could possibly dispute the sexual nature of oral gratification in infancy—a claim that indeed can be disputed if one does not equate infantile forms of pleasure, as he did on biogenetic grounds, with animallike sex" (Sulloway, 498). The voluptuousness that Freud ascribed not just to the infant's mouth but also to its anus was still another by-product of twisted evolutionism on his part. Freud apparently drew this inference not from actual babies he had observed but from the "invagination" of early multicellular organisms, which indeed combined the reproductive, alimentary, and cloacal functions within a single fold (Sulloway, 261–63).

In the same light we can understand why Freud was especially attracted to Fliess's universal latency period preceding adolescence. Of course there was no sense in which this could be considered a plausible inference from Freud's psychoanalytic interviews with adults. He believed in latency not just because Fliess already believed in it but because the idea introduced a certain tidiness into his vision of humankind as subject to two distinct sets of forces, one phylogenetic, the other experiential. The Freudian–Fliessian latency period formed a barrier between the realm of evolutionary recapitulation (from conception to age five) and that of sexual object choice (puberty and after). The very precariousness of "latency" constituted its appeal to Freud, for an organism that had to suppress a sexuality already rampant at birth would be ideally prone to neurosis—as Freud took our species to be (Sulloway, 378–79).

By today, however, it has become apparent that there is no such thing as a latency period. We now know that sex hormones, surely the chief physiological correlate of whatever Freud meant by sexuality, are secreted in negligible quantities before puberty and show no falling off after early childhood (Thornton, 208). But generations of deluded analysts, child care experts, and parents, unaware that they were subscribing to an arbitrary deductive construct rather than to an observed phenomenon, have allowed themselves to be saddled with Freud's lurid anxious-Victorian conception of the human infant as a tinderbox of sexual propensities.

X

The adjustment we must now make in our sense of Freud's intellectual style is dizzying in its implications, yet it should help us put his whole career into a coherent perspective at last. Previously we have thought of Freud as a clinical investigator and therapist who, though he speculated hobbyistically about a variety of extraclinical matters, drew the constructs of his theory from the startling and often distasteful discoveries he had stumbled across in his practice. But the consulting room was never a laboratory for Freud; it was only the arena in which he applied his prior deductions to specific cases, reassuring himself that his patients had repressed the kind of material he demanded from them. That is why he was undaunted by his continual therapeutic failures; his mind was on higher things. As he wrote to Fliess in 1896, "When I was young, the only thing I longed for was philosophical knowledge, and now that I am going over from medicine to psychology I am in the process of attaining it. I have become a therapist against my will . . ." (Freud 1954, 162).

Philosophical knowledge: that remained Freud's goal, and he gave himself to it with increasing indulgence as his circumstances became more secure. But unfortunately for his ultimate stature, his "philosophy" has turned out to be a tissue of retrograde second-hand notions and logically muddy inventions, combined with reckless leaps of gnostic intuition into the secrets of the mind, of history, and even of prehistory. It was the real Freud, not a Freud on holiday from his life's work, who solved with little effort such riddles as the race of Moses (an Egyptian), the reason for Woodrow Wilson's foreign policy ("little Tommy's" repressed infantile rivalries), the basis of social bonds (homosexuality), the cause of war (an innate death instinct), the source of female irrationality (penis envy and a biologically inevitable masochism), the ultimate fountainhead of guilt (the primal brothers had second thoughts after killing and eating the primal father), the earliest impulse toward wearing clothes (primitive women wove their pubic hair to hide their phallic deficit), and the subtlest puzzle of all, the origin of control over fire.

In prehistoric times, Freud divined, men went about dousing fires with urine, thus experiencing a homosexual gratification in vanquishing the phallic flames. (Women, with their second-rate fire extinguishers, were presumably *hors de combat* and thus destined for the hearth.) According to Freud, our first great benefactor was the man who could sufficiently master his homosexuality to save and nurture a fire instead of obeying his drive to pee on it (S.E., 22:185–93). Such was the anthropological wisdom of the discoverer of the Oedipus complex, itself allegedly a relic of that same fabulous epoch, the fall into culture and libidinal deprivation.

XI

Freud's legacy, it is clear, consists chiefly of pseudoscience that cannot be defended on any grounds. I predict, however, that many psychoanalysts, far from contesting this judgment, will take it in stride. By now they regard Freud as a liability to their own modern enterprise, and they would not be sorry to be disembarrassed of him altogether. For they think of themselves as having turned clinical interpretation and theoretical construction to much better account than he did "as [their] clinical findings," in Janet Malcolm's hearty words, "grow more precise and refined" (Malcolm 1981, 153).

Unfortunately, however, real as opposed to self-assumed progress in psychiatry depends upon means for testing hypotheses and weighing them against one another. This is just what cannot be accomplished for Freudian concepts in the "clinical" patient–therapist relationship. For, as Adolf Grünbaum has demonstrated, the inherent contamination of "clinical evidence" by a therapist's presuppositions is so inevitable, and the whimsicality of causal inferences drawn from free associations is so extreme, that no "clinically" derived theoretical conclusions can be considered dependable (Grün-baum 1979, 1982). And both Grünbaum and Morris Eagle have further shown that neo- and post-Freudian schools, while disputing this or that vulnerable postulate of orthodox Freudianism, invariably rest their own claims on the same epistemological quicksand that Freud did (Grünbaum 1983, 22–23; 1983a; Eagle).

Not surprisingly, then, no psychoanalytic or splinter school has produced cogent clinical support for any of its major developmental or therapeutic tenets, and the whole movement, as Malcolm herself has tellingly shown, is becoming ever more schismatic and doubt-ridden (Malcolm 1981). As for the handful of experimental corroborations of Freudian doctrine, they have invariably been naïvely designed, with the result that they have neglected to compare psychoanalytic explanations of a given phenomenon with rival ones (Eysenck and Wilson). And similarly, claims for the special efficacy of Freudian therapy have fallen quite flat, for outcome studies have consistently failed to credit psychoanalysis with better results than any number of briefer psychotherapies (see page 21 above), all of which, for that matter, show little or no advantage over placebo treatments (Prioleau et al.). Even Malcolm admits that " 'proof' of the efficacy of psychoanalytic cure has yet to be established . . ." (Malcolm 1981, 23). It is little wonder that people who are well informed about tangible advances in psychiatry tend increasingly not to quarrel with the Freudian tradition but simply to ignore it as unfruitful.

But why, then, finally, does psychoanalysis still flourish in pockets of our culture, most notably in the discourse of academic humanists and "soft" social scientists? A full answer would be complex—embracing, for example, such factors as religious yearnings, envy of mainstream science, a vogue for "hermeneutic" evasion of empirical tests, the indoctrinating effect of the therapy, the lure of deep certainties and ready-made interpretations, and the persistence of the spirit of unmasking that informs the works of Marx, Schopenhauer, Nietzsche, and Freud himself. In particular, Freud's "Fliessian" side, the one represented in his notions of innate bisexuality and polymorphous perversity, has proved irresistible to academic ideologues who crave a theory that will show the arbitrariness of bourgeois characterological norms. And on a more mundane level, it is a tribute to Freud's sheer gifts as a writer that he continues to charm so many otherwise skeptical people into granting him his Faustian dream.

People who fall under that spell, as I myself once did, find it hard to forsake their poetical science and return to the enigmatic, uncathartic world we actually inhabit. The analyzed in particular, as Malcolm has both remarked and exemplified, "are like members of a religious sect—people bound together by a mysterious experience yielding esoteric knowledge that no one outside the sect is privy to" (Malcolm 1983, 105). Arguments like the present one may well fail to move such an audience.

Yet I suspect that the fate of psychoanalysis will be sealed neither by acolytes nor by apostates but by a fresh generation lacking any cultural or personal stake in Freud's world view. When the Freud whom students first encounter is the one who accused Emma Eckstein of bleeding for love, who hounded Dora with monomaniacal accusations, who lied about his cures, and who enshrined crackpot doctrines in the heart of his explanatory system—and when, further, even intellectuals have grown wary of a therapy whose claims remain wholly unsubstantiated—psychoanalytic dogma will no longer seem esoteric but merely archaic. And when that judgment has become general, perhaps our successors will be able to understand more fully how, in the inebriate moral atmosphere of our century, we came to befuddle ourselves with the extraordinary and consequential delusion of Freudian thought.

Notes

1. As one sample of this deductiveness, consider Freud's assertion in "The Aetiology of Hysteria" that whereas traumatic sexual experiences before age eight result in deferred hysteria, the same experiences after age eight result in direct hysteria (S.E., 3:212). Freud cites a total of eighteen case histories in support of this dictum. Even if that figure were not inflated—and we will see that it was—how could a mere eighteen cases possibly yield such a universal law? The answer is that Freud was reasoning not from his cases but from his friend Wilhelm Fliess's rash speculations about "second dentition" and sexual development (Freud 1954, 159; Sulloway, 195).

2. Fliess derived many a fascinating conclusion from this theory—for example, that the day of a woman's death ought to coincide with the onset of her daughter's monthly period. Freud, right through his founding of psychoanalysis, was an avid devoté of Fliess's formulas for prediction, which, as Martin Gardner has shown, were so mathematically supple that they could generate any positive integer; in other words, Fliess's rules could never fail to "say why" any event had occurred, though by the same token all forecasts based on them would be spurious (Sulloway, 142).

3. Stephen Jay Gould (1979) suggests a more politic motive: Darwin

was reluctant to expose his secular materialism before a hostile world. Nonetheless, the contrast between Darwin's *scientific* prudence and Freud's impulsiveness remains striking.

4. As Swales (1983) cogently argues, cocaine may have figured thematically as well as inspirationally in the development of Freud's thought between his neurologic and psychoanalytic periods.

Works Cited

Cranefield, Paul F. 1958. "Josef Breuer's Evaluation of His Contribution to Psychoanalysis." *The International Journal of Psycho-Analysis*, 39: 319–22.

Eagle, Morris N. 1983. "The Epistemological Status of Recent Developments in Psychoanalytic Theory." In *Physics, Philosophy, and Psychoanalysis: Essays in Honor of Adolf Grünbaum*, ed. Robert S. Cohen et al. Hingham, Mass.: D. Reidel. Pp. 31–55.

Ellenberger, Henri F. 1970. *The Discovery of the Unconscious: The History and Evolution of Dynamic Psychiatry*. New York: Basic Books.

———. 1972. "The Story of 'Anna O': A Critical Review with New Data." *Journal of the History of the Behavioral Sciences*, 8: 267–79.

Eysenck, Hans J., and Glenn D. Wilson. 1973. *The Experimental Study of Freudian Theories*. London: Methuen.

Fisher, Seymour, and Roger P. Greenberg. 1977. *The Scientific Credibility of Freud's Theories and Therapy*. New York: Basic Books.

Freud, Sigmund. S.E. *The Standard Edition of the Complete Psychological Works of Sigmund Freud*, 24 vols. Trans. James Strachey. London: Hogarth Press, 1953–1974.

———. 1954. *The Origins of Psychoanalysis: Letters to Wilhelm Fliess, Drafts and Notes: 1887–1902*, ed. Marie Bonaparte, Anna Freud, and Ernst Kris. New York: Basic Books.

———. 1974. *Cocaine Papers*, ed. Robert Byck. New York: Stonehill.

———, and Jung, C. G. 1974. *The Freud/Jung Letters: The Correspondence between Sigmund Freud and C. G. Jung*, ed. William McGuire. Princeton: Princeton University Press.

Gould, Stephen Jay. 1979. "Darwin's Delay." In *Ever Since Darwin: Reflections in Natural History*. New York: Norton. Pp. 21–38.

Grünbaum, Adolf. 1979. "Epistemological Liabilities of the Clinical Appraisal of Psychoanalytic Theory." *Psychoanalysis and Contemporary Thought*, 2: 451–526.

———. 1982. "Can Psychoanalytic Theory Be Cogently Tested 'On the Couch'?" *Psychoanalysis and Contemporary Thought*, 5: 155–255, 311–436.

———. 1983a. "Freud's Theory: The Perspective of a Philosopher of Science." *Proceedings and Addresses of the American Philosophical Association*, 57: 5–31.

———. 1983b. "Is Object-Relations Theory Better Founded Than Orthodox Psychoanalysis? A Reply to Jane Flax." *Journal of Philosophy*, 80: 46–51.

Jones, Ernest. 1953. *The Life and Work of Sigmund Freud*. Vol. 1: *The Formative Years and the Great Discoveries: 1856–1900*. New York: Basic Books.

Malcolm, Janet. 1981. *Psychoanalysis: The Impossible Profession*. New York: Knopf.

———. 1983a. "Six Roses or Cirrhose?" *The New Yorker*, 24 January, pp. 96–106.

———. 1983b. "Trouble in the Archives." *The New Yorker*, 5 December, pp. 59–152; 12 December, pp. 60–119.

———. 1984. *In the Freud Archives*. New York: Knopf.

Masson, Jeffrey Moussaieff. 1984. *The Assault on Truth: Freud's Suppression of the Seduction Theory*. New York: Farrar, Straus & Giroux.

Prioleau, Leslie, Martha Murdock, and Nathan Brody. 1983. "An Analysis of Psychotherapy Versus Placebo Studies." With Open Peer Commentary. *The Behavioral and Brain Sciences*, 6: 275–310.

Schur, Max. 1966. "Some Additional 'Day Residues' of the Specimen Dream of Psychoanalysis." In Rudolf M. Loewenstein et al., *Psychoanalysis, A General Psychology: Essays in Honor of Heinz Hartmann*. New York: International Universities Press. Pp. 45–85.

———. 1972. *Freud: Living and Dying*. New York: International Universities Press.

Sulloway, Frank J. 1979. *Freud, Biologist of the Mind: Beyond the Psychoanalytic Legend*. New York: Basic Books.

Swales, Peter J. 1983. "Freud, Cocaine, and Sexual Chemistry: The Role of Cocaine in Freud's Conception of the Libido." Privately published by the author.

Thornton, E. M. 1984. *The Freudian Fallacy: An Alternative View of Freudian Theory*. New York: Dial Press.

vom Scheidt, Jürgen. 1973. "Sigmund Freud und das Kokain." *Psyche*, 27: 385–430.

Whyte, Lancelot Law. 1960. *The Unconscious Before Freud*. New York: Basic Books.

4

The Future of an Illusion

This essay-review, which appeared in **The New Republic** *in Janu-ary 1985, sets forth the importance and likely impact on Adolf Grünbaum's* **The Foundations of Psychoanalysis** *(1984). It is also a recapitulation, in other terms, of the argument I had presented five years earlier in "Analysis Terminable" (Chapter Two). Its re-ception in the pro-Freudian community, however, was significantly different. Critics of "Analysis Terminable" had flatly denied my charges, averring that psychoanalysis is good science and sound medicine. This time the letters of protest tended to concede the de-tails of my indictment, objecting only to the anxious prospect of having to forsake a comfortable doctrine that has become laden with cultural and even spiritual significance.*

My reply addressed this plaintive new mood:

The published letters objecting to my article "The Future of an Illusion" . . . are notable for the ground they collectively give away. Freud's trauma theory of neurosis, it is admitted, was wrong; many of his ideas were mere "products of his imagina-tion"; psychoanalytic clinical evidence is a circular artifact of the theory behind it; and analysts' claims of unique therapeutic effi-cacy are unfounded.

What, then, is left? Here my critics wax poetical. I have un-derrated the "mythic dynamism" of Freudian theory, which though untrue is surely "evocative of the truth." "Unconscious mean-ings," one writer chides, "will continue to move us in astounding and seemingly mysterious ways." Another writes that Freud's thought is "closer to philosophy than science," and still another invokes "religious truth . . . the reasons of the heart."

These apologetics, which Freud would have considered senti-mental nonsense, illustrate the ultimate survival strategy to which his followers have been reduced. Since specific Freudian claims are *indefensible, they must now be confused with the* domains of experience *that they touch upon. We are being asked to cling to psychoanalysis at the peril of forgetting that the mind is deep and dark. But as Ernest Nagel wrote in 1959, "the imaginative sweep of a set of ideas does not confer factual validity upon them." While honoring the reasons of the heart, let's also remember that erroneous psychological doctrines can be as harmful as they are evocative.*

I

Over the past several years Freudian psychoanalysis has been subjected to especially intense scrutiny from detractors and defenders. Was Freud right to abandon his "seduction theory"? Did he derive a good part of his supposedly original doctrine from misconstrued Evolutionism and from his overreaching friend Wilhelm Fliess? Is his movement on the way out, or have its early missteps been rectified by more recent Freudians and post-Freudians?

The charges and retorts have left many people confused, yet on the surface little appears to have changed. Though psychoanalysts now describe their therapeutic goals more nebulously than they once did, and though the public is coming to regard full-term analysis as a status symbol rather than a path to cure, apologists for that regimen are still heavily represented among the opinion makers of our culture. Moreover, the Freudian model of conflict and development still pervades conventional thought about psychiatric treatment, social work, and criminality. And academic literary pundits, who tend to think of themselves as experts in the world-historical vicissitudes of Desire, still feel free to pillage the Freudian system of its most "powerful" concepts, those that appear to explode bourgeois categories of thought.

Nonetheless, I venture to say that things *have* changed fundamentally—that, though the players are still on the field, the outcome of the game is no longer in doubt. With each passing year it has become more apparent that neither Freud's personal authority nor the institution he founded can satisfy or silence the one overriding question: *On what basis of observation and testing do psychoanalytic concepts and hypotheses lie?* And with the publication of a monumental new book, which I will discuss in the second half of this essay, people will now begin to comprehend that the entire

Freudian tradition—not just a dubious hypothesis here or an ambiguous concept there—rests on indefensible grounds.

By now the main obstacle to such understanding is not any fund of contrary evidence but simply the inertia of an entrenched tradition. A good many cultivated laymen as well as psychoanalysts take it as given that Freud, one of the founders of modern self-awareness, made some genuine discoveries about the mind. And they are encouraged in this belief by the currency of Freudian language in our everyday speech as well as our intellectual discourse. How could we possibly get along without such familiar notions as repression and the Oedipus complex?

But no one is challenging the watered-down, conversational apprehension of such terms. To do so would be no more useful than trying to sweep away such linguistic detritus of abandoned psychologies as "a magnetic personality" or "in a bad humor." In saying that Freudian notions will be found indefensible, I refer to their technical meaning within psychoanalysis as an articulated system. When we realize how ambitious and interlinked the claims of that system really are, we will hesitate to regard any of them as self-evident or commonsensical.

Take, for example, repression, which Freud rightly considered to be the cornerstone of his psychology. For psychoanalysis, repression is not a simple forgetting of unpleasant things but an unconsciously compelled and traumatic forgetting that alters one's mental economy in certain drastic ways. The concept takes its scope from boldly universal assertions about the oedipal strivings of infants, the meaning of dreams and errors, the mechanisms whereby character and sexual preference are formed, and the causation and cure of psychoneuroses. Those claims have not been warranted by independent research, and much has been tellingly said against them. Thus, though something like repression may yet be found to exist, its loss of scientific favor in all the domains to which Freud applied it deprives the idea of explanatory force.

Moreover, many of Freud's other major tenets were not derived from observation but extrapolated from his premise that repression is the mainspring of neurosis. It thus becomes imperative to ask whether that premise has ever been empirically justified. As I have argued elsewhere (Chapter Three), not a scrap of persuasive evidence for the repression etiology can be gleaned either from the record of Freud's mysterious self-analysis or from his therapeutic

accomplishments, which he brazenly exaggerated in order to intimidate his opponents. And thanks to the illuminating researches of
Frank J. Sulloway and others, it is now possible to trace his conclusions to their actual nonevidential sources in his reading, his remarkable subservience to Fliess, and his temperamental penchant
for what Joseph Breuer called "absolute and exclusive formulations."

A doctrine whose origins are this shady may nevertheless suit
the *Zeitgeist* well enough to impose itself on public credulity for
decades, especially if it is thought to have liberating implications.
Such was the good fortune of psychoanalysis in America from the
1920s until well after World War II. Sooner or later, however, the
Zeitgeist drifts elsewhere, leaving behind only the doubts that were
formerly dismissed as signs of cowardice before the "deep" and un-
palatable truth.

To show the plight of psychoanalysis in sharper outline, let
me refer to a document that is more eloquent than it was meant to
be—Dr. Arnold M. Cooper's recently published 1982 presidential
address to the American Psychoanalytic Association, wistfully entitled "Psychoanalysis at One Hundred: Beginnings of Maturity"
(Cooper 1984). Like many another semi-private exhortation to a
troubled body, this one is as revealing in its tactfully posed complaints as it is muddled in its vision of reform.

Dr. Cooper does not pretend, as most of his colleagues do, that
Freudianism is characterized by rigorous methods and tested results. He admits that Freud insisted on "establishing psychoanalysis as a movement of adherents to his ideas, rather than allowing . . . for free scientific interplay to determine, over time, the
correctness of his views" (252). No doubt, says Cooper, there were
compelling political considerations behind that dictatorial approach.
But now Freud's "cult of personality" (250) has evaporated, leaving
his American heirs with "a *mélange* of points of view—ego psychology, self psychology, object relations theory, revivals of inter-
personal theory, Lacanian derivatives, Kleinian views, and more"
(257). Having been founded more on ecclesiastic than on scientific
principles, Freud's movement has inevitably splintered into dogmatic sects, each scornful of the others' purported keys to definitive knowledge of the mind.

Though Cooper does his best to sound cheerful about this
Babel of analytic voices, his misgivings break through. How can
psychoanalysis call itself a science if, collectively, it has no clear
idea what its foundational theory should be? And how can its enor-

mously taxing therapeutic procedure be commended to potential patients if each school of thought has a different notion of what causes and cures neurosis? The problem, Cooper reminds his colleagues, is far from academic, for in this day of third-party payments "money, time, and freedom from scrutiny are no longer privileges, but are matters of negotiation with governmental and financial agencies" (261). More bluntly stated, "Even if we do not feel impelled by our scientific and theoretical curiosity, we might respond to the demands of a society that will not forever allow us to practice clinical psychoanalysis without evidence of its efficacy" (259).

Without evidence of its efficacy? That phrase will startle ex-patients who feel that they have validated both the truth *and* the efficacy of psychoanalysis through their own therapeutic experience. In ten years, say, of personal analysis—now the average span, according to the Freudian strict constructionist Janet Malcolm—have they not worked through their "transference" of primal feelings as reproduced in the patient–therapist dyad and rid themselves of certain neurotic traits? There is no arguing with such beneficiaries of the wisdom and healing power of psychoanalysis. But why won't the president of the American Psychoanalytic Association, of all people, credit their testimony?

The answer is that Dr. Cooper cannot afford to be as gullible as his clients. The third parties who tend increasingly to foot the bills, he knows, expect a therapy to yield results that (a) are proportional to the time and expense involved, (b) are demonstrably brought about by the designated curative factors, and (c) are appreciably superior to the results of placebo treatments—that is, of regimens in which the therapist, often for purposes of experimental control, tries to offer nothing but support or reassurance. On all three counts psychoanalysis has proved a fiasco. It is by far the most costly and time-consuming of all psychotherapies, yet it has not been shown to be more curative than a single one of its two hundred-plus rivals, even those that require only a few weeks of intervention. Indeed, it appears no better than regimens designed to *withhold* specific treatment factors or ingredients.

Since all psychotherapies, even placebos, apparently "work" to some extent, and since the nonplacebos propose divergent explanations of their effects, those nonplacebos all probably work by means other than the ones specified in their accompanying theories. It seems likely that the patient's positive feelings are occa-

sioned by a combination of hand-holding, suggestion, sensible practical advice, and authoritative-sounding mystification. If so, the only
psychotherapies that deserve public trust are those that perform
their task expeditiously and without leaving the patient emotionally bound to the therapist and intellectually addicted to his dubious theory. In this contest psychoanalysis appears to finish a poor
last.

If full-scale psychoanalysis thus lacks a clear practical jutifica-
tion, a medically conscientious analyst should probably transform
his practice, as many have already done, into some form of brief
treatment or counseling. As the leader of a still-prosperous guild,
however, Dr. Cooper cannot permit his presidential address to conjure up such a Dunkirk. According to him, what psychoanalysis
needs is more research, conducted by analysts themselves, to settle
the "exciting debates" raging within the field (259). His presuppo-
sition is that "new data" will resolve each controversy in favor of
some psychoanalytic idea or other (259).

But before Dr. Cooper's colleagues don their laboratory jack-
ets, they would do well to heed another eminent analyst who at
least partly understands what empirical rigor would entail. In *Hypothesis and Evidence in Psychoanalysis* (1984), Marshall Edelson
commendably embraces the "eliminative inductivism" that characterizes all science worthy of the name. "No conjecture about the
world," he writes, "is in and of itself confirmed by evidence. It is
always evaluated relative to some rival. The degree of its acceptance is simply the extent to which at any particular time it is
considered better than its comparable rivals" (17). And Edelson
recognizes that the worthiest rivals to any given psychoanalytic
hypothesis will be mostly nonpsychoanalytic. In a word, he sees
that the kind of in-house Freudian research envisioned by Cooper
would be scientifically inadequate.

To date, Edelson acknowledges, psychoanalysis has offered us
nothing but "enumerative inductivism"—the naïve quest for confirming instances of one's ideas, in the expectation that a certain
number of such instances will, as it were, send a hypothesis over
the top. "Enumerative inductivism is vacuous, because hypotheses
are underdetermined by data. That is, the same data can be explained by an infinite number of hypotheses, and therefore can be
held to 'support' any number of quite different hypotheses" (2).

Though this point is generally understood among scientists,
Edelson admits that Freudians have generally failed to grasp it.

They "still feel free to indulge in their delusion that their heaps of clinical observations, case reports, vignettes, and anecdotes do meet scientific requirements for empirical evidence" (2). Since there is scarcely a single piece of Freudian research that even attempts to go beyond enumerative inductivism, the inescapable conclusion—which Edelson tactfully leaves his fellow analysts to infer for themselves—is that not one Freudian concept or hypothesis has thus far received enough support to merit the belief of an independent-minded person. And while Edelson's discussion implies that he is personally willing to endorse psychoanalytic ideas before they have received proper validation, he offers no reason why anyone else should take such a reckless step.

II

Desperate as the condition of psychoanalysis is, until now its proponents have always been able to imagine a wonderful recuperation that could bring the Freudian tradition into the mainstream of science after all. That hope still flickers faintly in Marshall Edelson's book, which exhorts his fellow analysts to forsake enumerative inductivism and somehow introduce rigor into their "single subject research" on recumbent patients. Edelson's avowed purpose is to co-opt and mitigate the critique of psychoanalysis mounted in recent years by the eminent philosopher of science Adolf Grünbaum, whose reasoning (and whose friendship, I must add) I myself have found invaluable. But with the appearance of Grünbaum's epoch-making *The Foundations of Psychoanalysis: A Philosophical Critique* (1984), psychoanalysis now stands irremediably exposed as a speculative cult.

Hitherto, critics of psychoanalysis have tended to challenge specific notions that appear implausible or unnecessary, and loyalists have suavely replied that the heart of the doctrine lies elsewhere. In this endgame there has always been an empty square to sidle into. But after Grünbaum the wholesale debunking of Freudian claims, both therapeutic and theoretic, will be not just thinkable but inescapable. The power of Grünbaum's enterprise lies in the fact that he directs his main attention not to items of belief but to *grounds* of belief—that is, to the warrants that Freudians produce in justification of any particular hypothesis. Those warrants, he shows, are insubstantial; no outsider need ever be swayed by them.

Readers who are looking forward to a lively polemic, however, should be forewarned that nothing could be farther from Grünbaum's intention. What most distinguishes his work, here and elsewhere, is its combination of fairness and exhaustive rigor. To review the foundations of psychoanalysis once and for all, he finds it essential to represent them at their best. Thus he is no less concerned to clear away superficial and unjust attacks on psychoanalysis—Karl Popper's is notorious, thanks to Grünbaum's own critiques of it—than he is to see if the weightiest Freudian arguments have staying power. Rather than aim at the fat target of Freudian metapsychology (the Wagnerian theory of warring instincts and the evocative but gratuitous division of the mind into id, ego, and superego), Grünbaum examines the strongest justifications for the "clinical theory"—the concepts and hypotheses that Freud and others have regarded as indispensable. And though his critique of those concepts and hypotheses is shattering, he scrupulously declines to assert that he has refuted them; instead, he allows for the infinitesimal chance that they may yet find some justification after ninety years of existence as gratuitous dogma.

With a patience that borders on the excruciating, moreover, Grünbaum postpones his main argument until, in a 94-page introduction, he has laid to rest the "hermeneutic" construal of psychoanalytic theory. For readers unacquainted with the hermeneutic philosophers Jürgen Habermas and Paul Ricoeur or the hermeneutic psychoanalysts George Klein and Roy Schafer, that discussion will be heavy going. But Grünbaum's logic, if not his mercy toward the common reader, is impeccable; the muddle of the hermeneutic position must indeed be exposed if the case against Freudian "science" is to carry its deserved weight.

According to the hermeneutic school, psychoanalysis should not be held accountable to the validation of its causal assertions by received scientific standards of testing; it is just a means of arriving at particular interpretive insights which are self-certifying. That view is now fashionable among academic humanists, many of whom have little use for science to begin with. They would rather not be bothered by logical and empirical constraints when they apply their favorite cross-disciplinary doctrines to history, biography, and works of art. Grünbaum, however, demonstrates that "besides resting on a mythic exegesis of Freud's writings, the theses of these hermeneuticians are based on profound misunderstandings of the very content and methods of the natural sciences" (1). Psychoanalysis, he shows, is nothing if not a theory of motives for action and feeling, and the hermeneutic attempt to demote motives to mere "meanings" empties the theory of its only explanatory content.

Most analysts are only dimly aware of hermeneutics, but they too are unconcerned about the failure of their movement to establish any of its claims through adequately designed studies. Even some of the most enlightened spokesmen seem to think of research outside the treatment setting as desirable only for answering critics, not for determining fundamental points. This complacency goes straight back to Freud, who scoffed at the very suggestion that his ideas might require formal testing. They were already underwritten, he claimed, by "clinical experience"—the daily proofs of correctness that analysts encounter in their work. And later analysts, though they cannot agree on just what "clinical experience" proves, have adopted the same position.

In the main body of his book, however, Grünbaum demolishes this claim several times over. The hermetic clinical situation, he reveals, inevitably encourages a Freudian investigator to mistake arbitrary presuppositions for empirical findings. By citing the Freudians' own descriptions of their principles and procedures, Grünbaum shows that neither the *supposed data* nor the *causal constructions* they extract from that situation deserve the trust of a reasonably skeptical person.

In the official view, data gathered by analysts are considered adequately uncontaminated because they are largely products of "free association," a process that supposedly allows the patient's unconscious to express itself without the therapist's interference. But as Grünbaum has little difficulty in showing, such interference pervades the clinical relationship. Usually, patients who opt for psychoanalysis already know what kind of "free" material will be considered significant. If they do not, they soon pick up the appropriate cues from the therapist, who tends to break his silence only when an opportunity emerges to press toward a suitably Freudian conclusion. Nor can the defects of free association be shored up by appeal to such "consilient" data as the patient's dreams, slips, and conduct toward the analyst, for each of those sources is tainted in the same ways that free associations are. All are subject either to extraneous influence or to baseless causal interpretation or to both.

In this connection Grünbaum cites the candid admission of Judd Marmor, a noted analyst, that a "free-associating" patient invariably produces "data" that corroborate his therapist's particular school of thought, be it classic Freudian, Jungian, Kleinian, or whatever. Thus, in Marmor's words, "each theory tends to be self-validating" (quoted by Grünbaum, 211). Of course Marmor, after making such a damning admission, has gone right on endorsing the psychoanalytic sect of his choice; like Cooper, Edelson, and the analytic community at large, he apparently cannot envision an epistemological dilemma that would actually impinge on his faith. Most outsiders, however, should be able to grasp that if a theory is "self-validated" by its question-begging data, it desperately needs some independent source of corroboration.

Now suppose, for argument's sake, that an analyst *could* glean uncontaminated data from the clinical situation—for example, newly unearthed memories of scenes and conflicts from childhood. How would the analyst know, Grünbaum asks, that those scenes and conflicts were *causally relevant* to the adult patient's neurosis? Unless psychoanalysis can reliably establish such causal links, its entire justification for delving into the past is jeopardized and its theory dwindles to notes on an unequal, needlessly extended, and theoretically unilluminating conversation.

Even if an analyst could claim that a patient recalls the traumatic impact of a remote episode, he could hardly endow that patient with introspective knowledge of its specific pathogenic role for the "neurosis" at issue. Nor could he establish causality on the strength of its emergence through free associations. Whether or not those associations were unprompted, Grünbaum shows, their mere presence in the patient's contemporary thoughts would still tell us nothing about causation of recent symptoms by a hypothetical event in the distant past. Investigation "on the couch" thus proves to be a totally futile means of establishing the causal factors which lie at the heart of psychoanalytic doctrine and its therapeutic application.

In view of the collapse of both Freudian data and Freudian causal reasoning, we have here the epistemic equivalent of a black hole. Everything peculiar to psychoanalysis that Freudians purport to know from clinical experience is sucked into the abyss of baselessness. When they think they have perceived, say, the deferred effects of penis envy or of a maternal fixation or of aggression against the castrating father, Freudians have merely applied a psychoanalytic grid to utterances and behavior that could admit of less debatable explanations. It would scarcely be excessive to conclude—though Grünbaum characteristically refrains from doing so—that psychoanalysis is little more than a collective and contagious delusional system.

Most psychoanalysts, we can assume, will be slow to perceive the full import of Grünbaum's indictment. After all, for decades now they have touted the "clinically validated" modifications that they themselves have made to Freud's pioneering theory. Grünbaum, however, devastatingly shows that the stated grounds for the new versions are the same ones that fail to survive scrutiny in Freud's own example. In maintaining that *his* patients' free associations have taught him more believable tenets than Freud's, the analytic heretic or revisionist steps into the very epistemic quicksand that swallows up orthodoxy.

One unexpected finding of Grünbaum's study, indeed, is that until very recently it was Freud himself, among all Freudians and post-Freudians, who most clearly recognized the perilous standing of analytic knowledge. Precisely because he had no preexisting psychoanalytic tradition to render him complacent, Freud was more sensitive to the "suggestion" issue than his successors have been. As he put it, "[t]here is a risk that the influencing of our patient may make the objective certainty of our findings doubtful. What is advantageous to our therapy is damaging to our researches" (Freud, S.E., 16: 452).

So Freud felt obliged, however belatedly, to fashion what Grünbaum calls the Tally Argument, the only substantial reply to the charge of epistemic contamination that psychoanalysis has ever bothered to propose. According to the Tally Argument, the analyst does put words in the patient's mouth, but the patient's "conflicts will only be successfully solved and his resistances overcome if the anticipatory ideas he is given tally with what is real in him" (S.E., 16: 452). Presumably, then, any mistaken constructions will drop away in the course of treatment, and the patient's eventual cure will validate the correctness of those constructions that were allegedly crucial in bringing it about.

But after crediting Freud with having devised at least some defense of psychoanalytic knowledge, Grünbaum shows that the Tally Argument collapses in the face of two unanswerable considerations. First, as we have already seen, patients can get well for reasons having nothing to do with the specific content of what they "remember" or are told. A key premise of the Tally Argument is thus ill-founded. And second, psychoanalysis never did, and still does not, effect the regular and permanent cures Freud usually claimed for it. Thus if therapeutic success did validate one's theory of mental functioning (and it does not), psychoanalysis would still fail to earn such validation.

The demise of psychoanalysis—we are witnessing nothing less dramatic than that—raises a host of questions for clinicians, psychological theorists, experts in child development, lawyers and judges, social workers, historians, biographers, critics, and the educated public at large. Many of us must try to assess what, if anything, is salvageable from our earlier applications of a doctrine that once seemed uncannily true. And analysts themselves, insofar as they can bear to recognize that they have been caught up in a medical and intellectual charade, face the most awkward reappraisal of all.

As for Freud, we can now come to know him as he was, not as he was portrayed by his hagiographer Ernest Jones. Though he went through enough scientific-looking motions to lull the unwary, Freud was a Promethean visionary who disdained empirical prudence. He declared himself the peer of Copernicus and Darwin, but his real kinship lay with Nature Philosophers, mesmerists, and Late Romantic poets and novelists—authors whom he knew quite well, but whose insights he pretended to have accidentally and reluctantly corroborated through his "clinical evidence." The so-called evidence, consisting entirely of anecdotes and unsubstantiated claims, was always camouflage for his imperious will.

Taken as a Nietzschean transvaluator and acknowledged as one of the initiators of our modern assault on sexual hypocrisy, altruism, and supernatural belief, Freud will continue to repay study. But after what we have learned first from intellectual historians and now from the epistemologist Grünbaum, we can no longer suppose that he discovered a cure for neurosis or unlocked the secrets of the unconscious. So far as we can tell, the only mind he laid bare for us was his own. Once we have fully grasped that point, we can begin inquiring how such a mind—rich in perverse imagining and in the multiplying of shadowy concepts, grandiose in its dynastic ambition, atavistic in its affinities with outmoded science, and fiercely stubborn in its resistance to rational criticism—could ever have commanded our blind assent.

Works Cited

Cooper, Arnold M. 1984. "Psychoanalysis at One Hundred: Beginnings of Maturity." *Journal of the American Psychoanalytic Association*, 32: 245–267.

Edelson, Marshall. 1984. *Hypothesis and Evidence in Psychoanalysis*. Chicago: University of Chicago Press.

Freud, Sigmund. S.E. *The Standard Edition of the Complete Psychological Works of Sigmund Freud*. 24 vols. Trans. James Strachey. London: Hogarth Press, 1953–1974.

Grünbaum, Adolf. 1984. *The Foundations of Psychoanalysis: A Philosophical Critique*. Berkeley: University of California Press.

5

Beyond Sulloway's Freud: Psychoanalysis Minus the Myth of the Hero

In the spring of 1985, following Adolf Grünbaum's Gifford Lectures at the University of St. Andrews, Scotland, I traveled to the same campus to join a "Conference on Psychoanalysis and the Philosophy of Mind." The relevance of the following paper to "philosophy of mind" may not be immediately apparent. My message to the philosophers, however, was cautionary: "Don't weave theories of mentation around the Freudian unconscious until you have been given some reason to believe that it exists."

The St. Andrews papers can be found in Clark and Wright (1986).

I

In the wake of Professor Grünbaum's Gifford Lectures, we are assembled at St. Andrews to continue debating how seriously psychoanalysis should be regarded as knowledge. For some of us, however, Grünbaum's previously published work already portends the correct answer. Ingenious though Freud was in system building, Grünbaum (1984) has shown that neither Freud nor any of his followers have supplied one cogent reason for adhering to any distinctively Freudian tenet. To be sure, Grünbaum as an inductivist feels compelled to add that support for this or that Freudian notion may yet be forthcoming. But readers who understand the restraints of Grünbaum's argumentative tact can readily, and justifiably, infer that after nine decades of question begging and wanton conceptual embroidery, we might as well be waiting for Godot.

One advantage that Grünbaum reaps from his formal stance of patience is that he can maintain cordial rapport with the most methodologically alert analysts, those who still hope to bring the Freudian tradition into alignment with his high standards of verification. Whether such hopes are worth entertaining at all is, however, another matter—one that I will address directly before I am through today. Though it seems obvious at first that the most "reachable" Freudians deserve encouragement, surely there ought to be a statute of limitations on the postponing of judgment against a system of allegedly scientific thought for which no credible support has been mustered and whose proponents, more damningly, have consistently ducked the risk of falsification. In this paper I will try to show, through the "case history" of a rich and important book whose author as well as whose reviewers were reluctant to contemplate the insubstantiality of psychoanalysis, why we would be well advised to cease temporizing and acknowledge the scientific bad faith of the entire Freudian enterprise. Psychoanalysis, I will maintain, does not consist of a sum of hypotheses each of which remains as yet uncorroborated. Rather, it is in its heart of hearts a pseudoscience trafficking in dogma.

As someone who spent a decade inching his way from a pro-psychoanalytic stance to an opposite one, I am more than usually aware that Freudianism is internally resilient against exposure of its implausibility. The resilience lies not in intellectual virtues possessed by the theory but in the nature of its appeal to its adherents, most of whom have undergone an unnerving and cathartic experience of thought reform that has no counterpart outside the realms of religious and political indoctrination. Indeed, as many observers have noted, psychoanalysis shows every sign of being not just a method and a psychology but also a faith, with all that this implies about psychic immunity from rationally based criticism. Like other faiths, Freudianism readily rebounds when confronted with seemingly fatal objections, for it is inseparable from its believers' private sense of spiritual vitality and worth.[1]

Arguing directly with Freudians is thus a futile exercise if one expects to provoke deconversion experiences. But if one recognizes that the real audience for such discourse consists of uncommitted and increasingly wary bystanders, things begin to look brighter. In particular, epistemological and empirical critiques such as Grünbaum's *Foundations* and Eysenck and Wilson's *The Experimental Study of Freudian Theories* (1973) can produce a properly cautionary effect by showing that Freudian claims have not been adequately supported by evidence, are regularly defended in a circular manner, and are inherently unlikely because they invariably brush aside explanatory possibilities that place less strain on our credulity about cause and effect relations and the known properties of the human organism. Eventually, such unanswerable demonstrations are sure to prevail.

Even so, the long hegemony of psychoanalysis has lent it an air of "givenness" that leaves people inclined to regard any thoroughgoing critique as ipso facto extremist. The impression persists that at a certain moment Sigmund Freud must surely have achieved a great breakthrough in the understanding of mental illness and the dynamics of motivation. Otherwise, what has all the fuss been about for the greater part of a century? Rather than attend to the logic of a Grünbaum or an Eysenck and Wilson, many well-intentioned people will draw back and say, "Even while acknowledging Freud's errors, we must be careful not to discard the core of precious insight that he bequeathed us."[2]

To address such understandable recalcitrance we need to accompany the epistemological and empirical critique of psychoanalysis with a historical and biographical one, reconstructing, insofar as possible, the actual circumstances surrounding the birth and growth of Freud's movement. For people who are not already totally immersed in depth-psychological folklore, the "givenness" of psychoanalysis can be combated by an understanding of the influences, intuitive leaps, evaded questions, and extra-rational means of persuasion that went into the founding of the Freudian era. Before 1897, after all, there was no tradition of "Freudian insight" to lend psychoanalytic generalities an air of a priori plausibility. Were they warranted in the hour of their birth? Historical investigation can show, first, that Freudianism was far less original and forward-looking than most people realize; second, that its claimed basis in observation was more rhetorical than real; third, that its actual inspiration came from sources that merit our hearty distrust; and fourth, that its method of coping with apparent counterexamples was, from the outset, characteristically pseudoscientific.

Evidence to establish those conclusions already lies at hand, no thanks to the high priests of psychoanalysis who watch over the top-secret Freud Archives in Washington, D.C. Though much about the origins of psychoanalysis remains obscure, we have an ample basis for determining whether Freud actually stumbled across a *terra incognita* or was misled by his drive toward heroic fame. Indeed, we already possess book-length studies which put that question largely beyond doubt. Among them, preeminent in rigor and doggedness of research, stands Henri F. Ellenberger's *The Discovery of the Unconscious* (1970), a work whose long chapter on Freud only dramatizes what the total volume makes plain, namely, the derivative and curiously atavistic position of psychoanalysis in nineteenth-century psychiatry. No one who ponders the entirety of Ellenberger's subtly ironic narrative can fail to come away with a sense that psychoanalysis was a high-handed improvisation on Freud's part.

Here, however, I want to concentrate on a successor volume to *The Discovery of the Unconscious*, a book that duly cites Ellenberger's key findings while breaking crucially important new ground of its own. Everyone who follows Freud studies is aware of Frank J. Sulloway's *Freud, Biologist of the Mind: Beyond the Psychoanalytic Legend* (1979; the slightly revised 1983 edition will be cited here). Yet my own perusal of that book and of its reviews leaves me convinced that few early readers, or for that matter even Sulloway himself, correctly perceived either the book's limitations or its revolutionary implications.[3] I hope to show you not only that Sulloway was right about the distortions that constitute "the psychoanalytic legend," but also that his own failure to achieve sufficient distance from that same legend left his study ambiguous in fundamental respects. This outcome is not just instructive in its own right. It deserves to be repaired in detail, for Sulloway's work, once stripped of its contradictions, offers a treasurehouse of information about the empirical groundlessness of psychoanalysis in its earliest phases.

Sulloway's presentation builds upon Ellenberger's by completing the account of the issues and developments that actually shaped Freud's thought. I have in mind, for example, the prevalence of premature attempts to unify evolutionary theory, neurophysiology, and psychology along biogenetic lines; the flourishing of sexological theory with particular emphasis on infantile libido; the lingering but somewhat disreputable appeal of *Naturphilosophie*, with its proto-Freudian vitalism and instinctual polarities; and the comparable lingering of popular and Romantic notions of represssion, the unconscious, sublimation, and dream interpretation. Sulloway makes it clear, as Ellenberger did in smaller compass, why some of Freud's colleagues regarded him not as a shocking innovator but as a throwback to the heyday of mesmerism.

The thesis of Sulloway's study is adumbrated in the two parts of its title. Freud, Sulloway maintains, was a "biologist of the mind," and as such he was guided by principles that have been obscured by the psychoanalytic legend. According to the canonical account, Freud severed his intellectual roots in neuroanatomy when he founded psychoanalysis, an observational "pure psychology" that was meant to be autonomous from, though ultimately compatible with, physical knowledge about the human brain and nervous system. The legend has credited Freud with heroic powers of introspection, of penetration into the minds of his patients, and of courage in defying the prudish timidity of his colleagues and a hostile public. We have been told in effect that without Freud we would have had no concept of the unconscious or repression or infantile sexuality, no theory of hidden meaning in dreams and myths and errors, and no hope for the cure of neurotic suffering. But Sulloway maintains that this picture constitutes a willful "nihilation" of Freud's actual intellectual milieu. Freud was indeed original, says Sulloway, but chiefly in synthesizing ideas from disparate sources and in stating as universal laws what others had either entertained more tentatively or long since rejected as "old wives' psychiatry."

This argument has many strands, only a few of which I will be able to trace below. Its core, however, is the contention that Freud, after the debacle of his early, creakily mechanistic "Project for a Scientific Psychology," never did cease resting his mental system on premises borrowed from the physical sciences of his day. Instead, he made two moves that look initially paradoxical but bespeak considerable cunning. First, he temporarily suppressed explicit reference to his organic reasoning and maintained that he had derived psychoanalysis entirely from self-observation and from study of his patients. And second, he *expanded* his physical premises, allowing himself to be guided, after about 1895, less by energic-physiological considerations than by what Sulloway calls directional-historical ones. The early Freud focused on proximate causes within the individual organism, inquiring how the psyche and soma were interlinked. The later Freud largely replaced such causes with ultimate evolutionary ones, which he openly embraced only after psychoanalysis had gained a secure (though misleading) reputation as a clinically based psychology.

Freud broke off his "Project," Sulloway shows, because he was defeated in his attempt to account physiologically for the far-fetched mechanism of repression, whereby a trauma suffered at, say, age three would suddenly begin producing symptoms at, say, age thirty-five. With characteristic impetuousness, Freud retained the threatened doctrine and merely shifted his grounds for believing in it. At the time he established psychoanalysis, Sulloway claims, Freud's overriding question had already become not how but *why*—for example, why sexuality should be the domain requiring massive repression and why we must endure a latency period before the recrudescence of our libido at puberty.

If Sulloway is right, in founding psychoanalysis Freud passed from being an overtly neuroanatomical speculator about mind to being a "cryptobiologist"—someone who put forward mentalistic hypotheses but whose hidden grounds for doing so were taken from neo-Darwinian theory about the emergence of the species. According to Sulloway the biogenetic and Lamarckian assumptions that finally surfaced in works like *Totem and Taboo* (1912–13) were already, by 1897, decisive for Freud in underwriting his leading ideas about innate bisexuality, repression, and regression to developmental "fixation points."

Sulloway's argument may be wrong in certain particulars, but it possesses the immediate advantage of not straining our credulity in the ways required by the psychoanalytic legend. As Grünbaum reminds us, it was quite impossible for Freud to have gleaned his arcane developmental concepts from the consulting room, much less from introspection about his own infancy. Those concepts obviously came from other available sources—and *Freud, Biologist of the Mind* shows what those sources probably were.

Sulloway demonstrates plausible continuities in Freud's career where the psychoanalytic legend has posited only inexplicable leaps. The legend tells us that Freud suddenly ceased being influenced by evolutionary and neuroanatomical science at the moment he conceived of psychoanalysis and found that it cured his patients' neuroses; that his openly Lamarckian whimsies stood completely apart from his metapsychology; and that notions like the death instinct were detachable philosophical speculations that just showed up in his texts one day, unbidden by the "clinical evidence" which allegedly governed his more sober theorizing. Sulloway, by contrast, shows us a single Freud who kept brooding about the same fundamental problems, and he proves that the death instinct makes a kind of sense only if one adopts a "psycho-Lamarckian" perspective—that is, if one "sees as the major agent of evolutionary change the organism's reactions to its physiological needs" (Sulloway 1983a, 408). Freud adhered to exactly that perspective, and it was indispensable not just to a few peculiarly vulnerable ideas but to his entire conception of the human species and its vicissitudes.

As Sulloway convincingly argues, Freud was not only encouraged but also decisively influenced by his friend and fellow psycho-Lamarckian Wilhelm Fliess, whom the psychoanalytic legend has stigmatized as a psychotic crank. According to the legend, Freud passed through an "oedipal" but intellectually inert dependence on Fliess prior to the great breakthrough of his self-analysis. But Sulloway reveals Freud to have been a loyal Fliessian in the very act of formulating such "Freudian" notions as sexual aims dating from birth, erotogenic zones whose dominance and supersession constitute the path of normal development, fixation upon those zones when development goes awry, the mechanisms of sublimation and reaction formation, and an innate bisexuality that must be stifled with especial "organically repressive" force in women, whose clitorises Freud took to be literally male organs. And this is to pass over more sensational but less fundamental ways in which Freud emulated Fliess—for example, in recklessly extrapolating from Fliess's numerological system and in diagnosing and gruesomely treating "nasal reflex neuroses' in such unfortunates as the now celebrated Emma Eckstein.

A further merit of Sulloway's argument is that, once we have put aside the fiction that Freud reasoned directly from "clinical evidence," we can nevertheless perceive that he had *some* basis for his gnostic inferences about infancy and prehistory. That is, we need not join the most intemperate critics of psychoanalysis who dismiss the entire system as a cocaine vision or an articulation of Freud's admittedly flagrant misogyny. To be sure, psychoanalytic theory does bear the morbid imprint of its author's prurient and clouded state of mind in the later 1890s. But Sulloway reminds us that Freud's thinking, though heedless in consequential ways, was at least responsive to a scientific tradition that still had many respectable adherents.

By taking due note of Freud's psycho-Lamarckian reasoning, for instance, we can absolve him of total arbitrariness in having declared *ex cathedra* that every dream vents a wish that was repressed in infancy and ultimately inherited from the phylogeny of the race. Sulloway's exposition shows us that such tenets were as logically necessary to Freud, the devoted believer in accumulated "racial" memory and recapitulation, as they were unfounded in evidence that would count as such today. Similarly, Freud's curious optimism at the moment he felt obliged to renounce his "seduction theory" no longer seems deranged if we bear in mind, as Sulloway urges us to, that this was the very period in which he was giving himself over to Fliess's developmental laws. Freud claimed in a letter that he had been left with nothing, but before long he had in hand a more breathtakingly speculative scheme of early repression than the one he had forsaken. Only when we have appreciated the overwhelmingly deductive nature of his suppressed reasoning can we understand why, in the absence of striking clinical success with the new oedipal etiology, Freud felt serenely confident that he had solved the riddle of human susceptibility to psychoneurosis.

II

My summary makes clear, I trust, that *Freud, Biologist of the Mind* constitutes a major challenge to the heroic Freud myth and thereby to psychoanalysis itself as a doctrine allegedly rooted in observation and therapeutic results. Yet the short-term fate of all such challenges seems to be a blend of misconstrual and peremptory rejection. It is true, to be sure, that Sulloway's book was immediately hailed as a classic by such diverse judges as Hans Eysenck, Rosemary Dinnage, Robert R. Holt, Arnold Bernstein, Marie Jahoda, and M. Gerard Fromm; that it won the Pfizer Award in 1979 for the best American or Canadian work on the history of science; and that Sulloway has recently been granted a MacArthur Fellowship, presumably because of what he accomplished in this, his only book to date. Nevertheless, given the continuing strength of the psychoanalytic legend, we cannot be surprised to learn that many reviewers rejected Sulloway's argument out of hand while nearly all others accepted it only in a drastically weakened sense—a sense that, ironically, Sulloway himself was half inclined to approve.[4] Regarded together, the book and its reviews show how "legendary" expectations can take precedence over plausibly marshaled facts that point in an opposite direction.

Insofar as Sulloway's reviewers perceived his exposition to be in conflict with Freudian pretensions, they tended either to misrepresent it or to rebut it with allegations drawn from the very psychoanalytic legend that Sulloway was calling into question. Thus a good many reviewers chose to interpret Sulloway as claiming that Freud was scarcely a psychologist at all but rather, as Richard Wollheim put it in a singularly haughty dismissal in *The New York Review of Books*, "a biologist who passed as a psychologist" (Wollheim, 25; see also Brooks, Chessick, Hopkins, Khan, Lothane, Wallace). That was not Sulloway's point at all.[5] Again, Mark Kanzer spoke for many orthodox Freudian reviewers when he lamented, "what Sulloway misses is that [Freud's] ultimate criterion was the clinical usefulness and validation of [his] postulates" (Kanzer, 522; see also Chessick, Hopkins, Lothane, Pollock, Wallace). After Grünbaum's unmasking of the contaminated data and spurious causal reasoning behind Freud's clinical inferences, not to mention Freud's own belated confessions that his therapy was largely unsuccessful, one can only smile at such piety toward the image of Freud as the empirically scrupulous healer. Yet that same piety pervaded the negative reviews, which conveyed near-shock at Sulloway's presumption in seeking to demean what George Steiner called "a dominant presence in the spirit of the age" (Steiner, 40). One reviewer after another adduced Freud's greatness as evidence against the plausibility of Sulloway's argument, as if it were unimaginable that our psychological Copernicus could be demoted to a fallible representative of his age.

To me, however, the outstanding feature of the reviews is that nearly all of them *overlooked* the most glaring weakness of *Freud, Biologist of the Mind*.[6] For, relentless though he is in tracing Freud's sources, Sulloway is inconsistent and misleading in evaluating the success with which Freud transformed those sources into adequate scientific hypotheses. At times he clearly acknowledges that a system dependent at its core on spurious doctrines cannot also be an accurate empirical science; yet elsewhere he appears to make exactly that quixotic claim. The result, I am afraid, is that even relatively unprejudiced readers have missed the revolutionary purport of Sulloway's findings.

Near the end of the book Sulloway voices the following important judgment, which appalled some of his reviewers:

> Acceptance of Freud's historical debt to biology requires a rather uncongenial conclusion for most psychoanalytic practitioners, namely, that Freud's theories reflect the faulty logic of outmoded nineteenth-century biological assumptions, particularly those of a psychophysicalist, Lamarckian, and biogenetic nature. As we have seen, these assumptions were eminently plausible in Freud's day. Indeed, so plausible were they that Freud was not always aware of how much faith he placed in them or of how much his clinical observations absorbed from them "empirical" meaning. Yet because he pursued such a bold and relentless logic in the world of scientific ideas, his thinking illuminates the power of his theoretical preconceptions in a particularly dramatic fashion. . . . [S]uch "clinical" discoveries as the abreaction of trauma seemed to Freud a direct corroboration of the bioenergetic principles that pervaded his theory of mind. Similarly, the child does appear to recapitulate the history of the race in many essential respects, but it recapitulates the embryonic, not the adult stages, as Freud and other biogeneticists had mistakenly thought. . . . [M]uch that is wrong with orthodox psychoanalysis may be traced directly back to [such assumptions]. To cite a prime example, Freud claimed that no one, looking at a nursing infant, could possibly dispute the sexual nature of oral gratification in infancy—a claim that indeed can be disputed if one does not equate infantile forms of pleasure, as he did on biogenetic grounds, with animallike sex. Time and time again, Freud saw in his patients what psychoanalytic theory led him to look for and then to interpret the way he did; and when the theory changed, so did the clinical findings. (Sulloway 1983a, 498)

Here, I submit, we feel the full weight of Sulloway's implicit brief against Freud: psychoanalysis was founded not on observation but on deductions from erroneous dogma, and as a result the entire system can make no claim on our credence. Yet in the few remaining pages that follow this admirable summary, Sulloway writes repeatedly of Freud's "fruitful insights" and even of his "scientific greatness," and he concludes by saying, "After all, Freud really was a hero" (Sulloway 1983a, p. 503)—a sentence that allowed many a reviewer to reassure the public that Freud's ghost had nothing to fear from Sulloway (e.g., "Did Freud . . . ," Gifford, Glazer, Harvey, Leonard, Pruyser, Robinson, Strouse).[7]

There is of course a sense in which Freud can be considered both erroneous and heroic. In his own self-conception he was always destined for fame, and the very fact that he was able to satisfy what Sulloway calls his "obsessional need for intellectual immortality" (Sulloway 1983a, 217) *without* having found either a viable therapy or an accurate psychology does compel a certain awe. Yet Sulloway, while he supplies a rich fund of data and even a theoretical overview that will help future investigators understand how the Freud legend took hold, must finally be judged to have given that legend far too much credit. For throughout his book, not just in its closing pages, he heads off his own provocative insights by referring magnanimously to Freud's "discoveries" and "recognitions" and "scientific gains." And oddly, in every instance the "discovery" at issue is thrown into doubt by Sulloway's own account of its genesis.

Take, for example, Freud's dream theory, which Sulloway shows to have been a wholly deductive construct inferred from the faulty repression etiology of neurosis and indebted to the wildest psycho-Lamarckism. Yet here is Sulloway's summation: "Freud's mature theory of dreaming is virtually unparalleled, even today, for the remarkable insight that it brought to bear upon the psychological mechanisms of dreaming" (334). Though Freud is revealed to have derived his universal dream symbols from books like Karl Albert Scherner's *Das Leben des Traums* of 1861, Sulloway writes of "his understanding of the frequency and the importance of symbols" (337) in the universal language of dreaming. Freud is said to have "discovered the specific *wish-fulfillment* meaning of dreams in 1895" (322); later he "came to see" the true role of dream censorship (330). And having shown that the "findings" gleaned from Freud's case histories always tagged along behind his latest theoretical passion, Sulloway nonetheless awards those same case histories "considerable importance . . . in confirming his theory of dream interpretation" (344). Freud's "specific dream interpretations," Sulloway opines, "seem more acceptable to us than they once did to his colleagues" (344).

Likewise, in the very paragraphs where he shows that Freud's notion of the id was extrapolated from his questionable dream theory (329) and from the now discredited tenets of Lamarckian biogenetics (365), Sulloway alludes to the "discovery" of the id, as if that amorphous and ambiguous concept were a natural phenomenon that Freud had brought to light. Again, Freud is said to have "grasped" and "recognized" the meaning of slips (351)—a meaning which, far from having been independently apprehended in a fresh investigation, was a mere by-product of the equally vulnerable repression etiology. And though Sulloway's reconstruction of Freud's self-analysis plainly shows that Freud was already hunting among his memories for confirmation of Fliessian infantile sexuality, once again Sulloway writes of what Freud "recognized," "was able to recall," "discovered," and "was able to confirm" (209). "Self-analysis," Sulloway concludes, "finally allowed him to confirm from his own experience just how remarkably widespread the opportunities were in every *normal* childhood for both traumatic and spontaneous sexual activity" (209). On the contrary, a reasonably skeptical reading of Sulloway's narrative "confirms" only that Freud was, as usual, grasping at any pretext to turn his hunches into laws.

Which Sulloway are we to believe, the one who has shown us a Freud habitually given to intellectual *ejaculatio praecox* or the one who calls Freud's major works "a magnificent achievement, which certainly places Freud among the most creative scientific minds of all time . . ." (358)? The answer is obvious. Not only does Sulloway's accumulated evidence speak more persuasively than his praise, but in later published comments he has characterized psychoanalysis as "a highly problematic theoretical system" (Sulloway 1982, 247) and remarked that the history of this "narcissistic" movement "is a fascinating example of the power that ideology can have when it becomes institutionalized within the educational mechanisms of science" (Sulloway 1983b, 36). As he wrote to me in 1985, "there is nothing more dangerous than people who think they are right (and scientific) when they are not, especially after they have had eighty or ninety years to prove themselves."[8]

Sulloway's current view of his book nevertheless differs significantly from my own. He tells me that much of the seemingly pro-Freudian language I have cited above merely characterizes Freud's own perception of what he was "discovering" and "recognizing." No doubt that was the intent behind many individual passages of narrative. Yet we could be forgiven for inferring that Sulloway's explicit references to "scientific greatness" mean what they say and provide a warrant for ascribing substance to Freud's "recognitions" and "discoveries." Otherwise we are left with the paradox of a "greatness" consisting entirely of error.

I suspect that Sulloway's confusion arose from three sources. First, he harbored the well-trained intellectual historian's awareness that scientific innovators often proceed in highly unorthodox ways and are given to loose speculation on any number of nonessential topics; thus he was determined not to be scandalized by Freud's departures from textbook inductivism. Second, in the absence of later critiques such as Grünbaum's he was inclined to lend some credence to the analysts' clamorous arguments from "clinical evidence." And third, he admired Freud's synthetic vision for its sheer intricacy and scope, quite apart from its degree of empirical adequacy. Whatever his reasons may have been, however, the unfortunate result was that Sulloway failed to draw conclusions from the evidence of outright and egregious scientific malfeasance that runs through his account of Freud's conduct. We must attend to that evidence, segregated from its setting of palliative rhetoric, if we are to grasp the pseudoscientific essence of Freud's intellectual tradition.

III

Of all Sulloway's reviewers only one, Frank Cioffi, fully understood that *Freud, Biologist of the Mind* not only exposes psychoanalytic myths but also exemplifies "how difficult it is, even for an aspiring iconoclast, to stand upright in the presence of the Freud legend . . ." (Cioffi 1979, 504). And it was Cioffi again who posed the following important challenge, which carries us even beyond Sulloway's present assessment of Freud's standing:

> Although much of what he recounts undermines it, Sulloway does not directly address the most potent and strategically necessary myth of all—the myth of Freud's superlative integrity. For the Freud myths were not devised by Freud's followers; they are no more than reiterations of accounts Freud himself had given. To depart from these would have been to impugn Freud's veracity and who, with the exception of one or two noble spirits, has been willing to do that? Certainly not Sulloway, who mealy-mouthedly concludes: "The myths were merely [Freud's] historical due and they shall continue to live on protecting his brilliant legacy to mankind."
>
> Carry on lying. (Cioffi 1979, 504)[9]

Cioffi's impugning of Freud's honesty sounds indecorous, but it is entirely justified by the biographical record that Sulloway and others have uncovered. Though Freud loved to sermonize about courageously opposing the human penchant for self-deception, it is no exaggeration to say that his psychoanalytic career was both launched and maintained by systematic mendacity. Sulloway's unwillingness, in 1979, to face that fact squarely rendered his argument inconclusive and even self-defeating. It is time to remedy that defect and, specifically, to understand the necessary relation between Freud's cavalier ethics and the scientific failings of his movement.

Freud's guile was truly chronic. For many years before and after he conceived of psychoanalysis, for example, he tried to erase from history his phase of fervent and destructive cocaine evangelism (see above, pages 51–52). In the pivotal Anna O. case he lied about Bertha Pappenheim's alleged cure by Breuer and lied again, in a maliciously self-serving story, about Breuer's flight from Pappenheim's supposed advances (Ellenberger 1970, 1972). One can add that he must also have lied to Breuer about his own fictitious cures of hysteria, for only on that basis, it appears, could Breuer have been coaxed into dusting off the thirteen-year old Pappenheim case, about which he retained understandable misgivings, and reluctantly agreeing to collaborate with Freud in *Studies on Hysteria*.

Throughout his psychoanalytic career Freud lied about his therapeutic success, meanwhile privately confiding that such duplicity was necessary to keep his critics at bay (see above, page 59). Again, having lifted key ideas from Albert Moll, Freud not only suppressed acknowledgment of his indebtedness but had the effrontery to accuse Moll of plagiarizing *him* (Sulloway 1983a, 313+n., 315, 469). He lied to Fliess and then to the public in denying that he had "leaked" Fliess's theory of bisexuality to Otto Weininger (Sulloway 1983a, 223–29). And he employed a blatant strategy of historical falsification in omitting from his *Autobiography* any mention of Fliess, without whose thirteen years of support and guidance psychoanalysis as we know it would never have come into existence.

Let us put together such conduct with the fetching tale Freud told about his titanic self-analysis and his persecution by fearful and prudish colleagues; with his seven-year silence before he could admit his privately recognized mistake about the seduction theory; with his recourse to tendentiously edited anecdotes and dream reports that appeared to validate his conclusions instead of merely exemplifying them (Glymour); with his many dishonest references to his success as a clinician; with his anti-empirical insistence on absolute fidelity to his teachings; with his vendettas against former disciples who deviated from the prescribed line; with his denigration of opponents as sufferers from repression and resistance; and with the coercive rhetorical tactics that pervade his apologetics. We can then begin to grasp that Freud's greatest creation was not a scientific discovery but a seductive work of art, namely, the story he devised about a mythic Sigismund who had returned from the frightening psychic underworld with precious gifts for humankind.

My point, however, is not that Freud was by nature a congenital liar. It is rather that, given his determination to advance a doctrine that had nothing to be said in its scientific favor, he had no alternative to resorting to legend building. We cannot make adequate sense of the record, including the details that Sulloway so deftly recounts, unless we see that the arbitrariness of psychoanalysis itself dictated much of Freud's shifty behavior.

Take, for example, Freud's Orwellian decision to obliterate Fliess's role in the formation of psychoanalytic theory. Sulloway, still inhibited by the remaining force of the psychoanalytic legend, explained that decision as a general wish on Freud's part to disguise his biological premises so that psychoanalysis would appear to be an autonomous science. As some reviewers (e.g., Goldstein, Himmelstein, Holt) noticed, such a motive does not in itself appear sufficiently pressing to have warranted a drastic falsification of the record. Yet the falsification assuredly did occur. It becomes understandable if we look more closely at the evidence that Sulloway himself provides regarding the flimsiness of Freud's "science" at the time of his definitive quarrel and break with Fliess.

Sulloway makes it clear that Freud had to repudiate Fliess because in moving from the seduction theory to psychoanalysis proper he was bringing his thought into nearly total compatibility with Fliess's. That is, locating neurotic etiology in the traumatic repression of "normal" childhood sexuality rather than in repressed sexual abuse constituted a surrender to Fliess's account of the infant as a recapitulator of early man's adult sexual experience. Once Freud had taken that step, the pressing question was whether he had any right to put forward his exclusive authorship of psychoanalysis. As Sulloway shows, Fliess repudiated Freud because he came to believe that Freud intended to steal his ideas, only crediting Fliess with the subtheory of bisexuality which Freud had already tried unsuccessfully to appropriate as his own. If the world were ever to hear of Freud's real debt to Fliess, psychoanalysis would be revealed to have been generated by something other than Freud's genius as a diagnostician of himself and others.

The specific bone of contention at the Freud–Fliess breakup in 1900 was Fliess's theory of periodicity, which Freud had hitherto embraced with amazing credulousness (amazing, that is, to anyone who persists in regarding Freud as a prudent thinker). Even in later years Freud expressed grudging admiration for that side of Fliess's thought (Sulloway 1983a, 183). Why, then, was periodicity a sore point in 1900? The answer is that Fliess, as he himself recalled, adduced periodic processes to show Freud why "neither sudden deteriorations nor sudden improvements were to be attributed to the analysis and its influence alone . . ." (quoted by Sulloway 1983a, 221). Fliess's argument was an explanation for Freud's therapeutic failure, and it must have incensed Freud precisely because, having told Fliess all along how badly his treatments were going, he had no effective rejoinder to propose. When Fliess refused Freud's peace offer of a collaborative book on bisexuality, Freud felt he had no choice but to turn Fliess into a nonperson—a task he accomplished with an effectiveness that even Stalin might have envied.[10]

What concerns me here, I must repeat, is not Freud's desperate conduct per se but the necessary symbiosis between the unfoundedness of psychoanalytic claims and the manner in which they were—and still are—propounded. A doctrine like psychoanalysis can make its way in the world only by surrounding itself with rhetorical barbed wire, obscuring its unflattering origins and neutralizing objections through extrascientific means, either by direct slander (as in the continuing stigmatization of Fliess) or by generic diagnosis (all critics are suffering from repression) or by establishing special epistemic barriers (only the analyzed are entitled to criticize) or by multiplying escape clauses to forestall possible falsification. Psychoanalytic history is a rich data base for the study of all these restrictions upon intellectual give-and-take. In my opinion this is not an unhappy accident, the sign of a collective behavioral lapse that can be corrected once it has been pointed out. Nor is it, as Sulloway appears to believe, a corruption of Freud's legacy. It is rather a native feature of psychoanalysis as a pseudoscience.

Here I diverge in emphasis from Grünbaum, whose well-merited polemic against Popper leads him to highlight the testability of some Freudian hypotheses. As Cioffi has urged in a trenchant and illuminating article (Cioffi 1970), it is not finally very interesting that certain psychoanalytic propositions, extracted from their context of vague auxiliary claims, can be treated as authentic hypotheses. What matters is that "this is not the role which they have played in the lives of those who originated and transmitted them, nor of those who have since repeated, adapted or merely silently rehearsed them" (Cioffi 1970, 498). An emphasis on the potential falsifiability of some Freudian tenets obscures the more telling fact that everything about the actual propagation of psychoanalysis, from the inherent cloudiness of its concepts (Nagel) through its safety nets against falsification and its cliquish means of repelling criticism, bespeaks divergence from the empirical attitude. What marks psychoanalysis as a pseudoscience is not the unfoundedness of its propositions—a condition that could in principle be altered by events—but precisely that perennial reluctance to submit itself to the sink-or-swim ordeal of scientific evaluation.

Cioffi shows, and many other observers have confirmed, that Freud habitually buttressed his dubious hypotheses with ex post facto provisos instead of asking himself whether they might be wrong. In part those provisos consisted of new theoretical entities and catch-all excuses, such as "the hereditary factor" and "the quantitative factor," which could be invoked whenever a given prediction went unfulfilled. Again, Freud coped with potential disconfirmation by brashly redefining his terms and stretching the scope of his concepts—as, for example, in his riposte to the proposal that shell shock constitutes a challenge to the sexual etiology of the neuroses: "mechanical agitation [e.g., concussion in battle] must be recognized as one of the sources of sexual excitation" (S.E., 18:33). And when all else failed, Freud simply invented a new mental law to cover the case at hand, blithely overlooking his own previous adherence to an opposite law or cynically calculating that no one would recall the earlier pronouncement.

Thus, as Cioffi (1970) shows, by putting disparate texts together we can infer that, according to Freud, humanitarianism stems from repressed homosexuality but is also compatible with open homosexuality; childhood trauma both is and is not a necessary condition for neurosogenesis, which also comes about either from repressed perversion or in conjunction with active perverted practices; recall of specific sexual material from infancy is both necessary and unnecessary to the undoing of a neurosis; a strict superego is produced by the misfortune of having either a hard, cruel father or, alternatively, an indulgent one; explicit castration threats are both required and not required for the generation of castration anxiety; the unconscious contains no contradictions but is perpetually engaged in coping with them; and Little Hans at age four owed his mental health to the sexually enlightened attitude of his parents, whose prudish falsehoods about sex brought on the same Little Hans's animal phobia at age five. Quintessential pseudo-scientist that he was, Freud could not be bothered to notice that his conflicting claims, taken together, free us from each of those claims singly; he was too busy extricating himself from one potential embarrassment after another.

Freud was already a pseudoscientist from the hour that he published *The Interpretation of Dreams*, disingenuously invoking therapeutic success as proof of his repression etiology and employing sheer allegorical ingenuity to paper over outrageous methodological liberties (Glymour).[11] As he progressed in his career, increasingly averting his gaze from the disheartening realm of observation and fixing it instead on suppositions about instinct and prehistory, things only got worse. And here—in tracing Freud's increasingly reckless invocation of "the hereditary factor"—is where we can return to Sulloway's book as an especially rich repository of evidence. Sulloway shows not only that the "mature" Freud held genetic excuses at the ready for any case in which the predicted sexual noxae might not be forthcoming, but also that even an unpropitious-looking short-term line of inheritance could be trumped by reference to "the antiquities of human development," which had allegedly "stored up" erotic trouble in modern Europeans through Lamarckian memory traces of primeval traumas (S.E., 16:371).

The late appearance of this ultimate explanatory wild card is a sign of the mounting trouble Freud was having in justifying the relatively straightforward but no less fanciful oedipal repression etiology of 1897. The same reason helps to account for his theoretical turn toward fixed and universal dream symbols (which could redirect any interpretation that threatened to be nonsexual), toward masochism (which could account for a dream that seemed not to convey a wish), and toward the death instinct and the repetition compulsion (which ascribed to the organism powerful inherent tendencies justifying, among other salient phenomena, the failure of neurotics to respond dramatically to psychoanalytic treatment). Freud's eventually explicit appeal to Lamarckism at a time when that doctrine was in very broad retreat is only the most spectacular instance of his willingness to pay any price to spare his pet ideas.[12]

Freud's heirs, whom Sulloway is inclined to disprize as "ideologizers" of psychoanalytic insight, think they have significantly improved on this lamentable record—but have they? Both the defenders and the critics of ego psychology in its multiple exfoliated forms have scanted the fundamental continuity of pseudoscientific method throughout the Freudian tradition. Even in the act of altering some of Freud's notions, modern analysts have faithfully perpetuated his habits of supporting claims with question-begging anecdotes and further claims, of looking only for confirming rather than disconfirming signs, and of appeasing doubts by alluding to decisive factors accessible only to the anointed investigator and his peers. And when contemporary Freudians pride themselves on doing without the phylogenetic line of reasoning, as if the rest of the system were adequately determinate in its specifying of claims and consequences, they appear to be doing their best to illustrate the Freudian mechanism of denial. Apparently they feel that psychoanalysis can now survive by gradually dismantling some of its excrescent theoretical knobs and pulleys, just as it formerly survived by superadding them. Both stratagems are reprehensible dodges from longstanding and unanswerable doubts about Freud's original scientific romance. Despite some expressions of misgiving and halfway attempts at reform (e.g., Edelson), the entire Freudian record from the 1890s until now is eloquently self-consistent.

I believe that the future study of psychoanalysis will be most fruitfully concentrated on the phenomenon that Sulloway, to his permanent credit, first brought to our attention: the propagation of a legend which has carried its own antiscientific and authoritarian means of inducing belief, rejecting criticism, and coping with deviation. If I am right, *Freud, Biologist of the Mind* will remain indispensable—provided, however, it is read with the precautions I have detailed above.

When Sulloway praises the sophistication of Freud's brainchild, noting that "Freud recognized every possible combination of hereditary predisposition with environmental determinism" (319), we must insist that the perceived sophistication was that of an overreaching system builder, not of a scrupulous empiricist or even of an error-prone one. True, Freud showed considerable imagination and subtlety in being at once genetic and environmentalist, psychological and biological in outlook. But Sulloway, I think, does not adequately recognize that this grand inclusiveness of causal reference, whereby each cited factor served in practice to safeguard the others from refutation, was already pseudoscientific in Freud's hands before Freud himself became a sainted authority figure. Psychoanalysis did not go astray by allowing "ideology" to become "institutionalized within the educational mechanisms of science." It went astray because it never adhered to the scientific spirit in the first place. If we can finally face that fact without equivocation, we will find ourselves readier not just to answer Freudian sophistries, but to greet with appropriate skepticism whatever opiate of the intellectuals awaits us next.

Notes

1. The "religious" apprehension of psychoanalysis was epitomized in a published letter objecting to "The Future of an Illusion" (Chapter Four). "Surely Crews . . . would agree that there are ways of discovering truth other than the strictly objective and scientific. What of aesthetic and intuitive, personal and relational, and religious truth—of all the 'reasons of the heart'? It is in the realms of the personal and 'existential,' the relational and 'intersubjective,' that the truth of psychoanalysis may be found" (Rogers).

This view is so widely shared, especially among my humanist colleagues, that it deserves a careful reply. In the first place, there is no uniquely scientific way of *discovering* truth; any means will do, including being hit on the head with an apple or dreaming of snakes arrayed in rings. Let us by all means leave room for intuition. Scientific rigor properly enters the picture only when we try to ascertain whether purported laws of nature, however derived, merit our belief.

Universal propositions about mental functioning constitute such purported laws. For example, Freud's assertion that a neurosis is always the "negative" of a perversion aspires to the status of a reliable generalization about the world we commonly experience, and as such it risks falsification— or would do so if psychoanalysts behaved less dogmatically—in exactly the same sense as a proposition about the mating habits of bees or the orbits of the planets. If, on the other hand, people like my dissatisfied reader mean to assert that "religious truth" resides in the therapeutic experience rather than the propositional content of psychoanalysis, then their position is simply incoherent. Even the most intense experience asserts nothing and thus cannot meaningfully be characterized as "true."

2. See, for example, Jonathan Lieberson's review of Grünbaum's *Foundations* in *The New York Review of Books*. Finding no cogent way to weaken Grünbaum's case, Lieberson simply decrees in conclusion, "Nevertheless,

there is something to psychoanalysis . . . ," and he chides Grünbaum for not making due allowance for *future* improvements in the theory (Lieberson, 28). Does it make sense to award a psychological doctrine a special "something" that is exempt from all requirements of demonstration or to take as yet unattempted corrections of psychoanalytic theory to be reassurance that the theory itself is fundamentally sound? According to the same logic we could spare astrology from debunking by imagining a day when the ancient charts will have been brought into more exact alignment with the modern conformation of the heavens.

3. I owe thanks to Jennifer Snodgrass and to Dr. Sulloway himself for supplying me with seventy-nine reviews and other discussions in English, French, German, and Italian. Dr. Sulloway has also kindly offered comments on a draft of this paper.

4. I do not maintain that all negative comments on Sulloway's book have been motivated by prejudice. Some reviewers correctly noted that Sulloway gives short shrift to Freud's later career and to his nonscientific sources of inspiration, and many complained, not without reason, that he pays too little heed to the internally systemic traits of psychoanalysis as opposed to its borrowings from other fields. Still others objected to a certain grandiosity of tone, to Sulloway's favoritism toward a questionable-looking theory of birth order and creativity, and to signs of excessive reverence toward his Harvard mentor Edward O. Wilson and the controversial field of sociobiology. Of course none of these reservations diminish the importance of Sulloway's research—largely accomplished, it should be pointed out, when the author was still in his twenties.

5. As Sulloway protested in his preface to the paperback edition, Wollheim and others had chosen to attack a straw man; the actual thesis of the book is that "Freudian psychoanalysis is a sophisticated 'psychobiology'" focused squarely on the mind but drawing inspiration from evolutionary and embryological theory as well as from extant conceptions of physiology, anthropology, and psychology proper (Sulloway 1983a, xv).

6. For notable exceptions see Cioffi 1979 and Hopkins.

7. One can see from the sprinkling of favorable reviews by psychoanalysts why Sulloway must have been tempted to accentuate the positive in this manner. One reviewer even suggested that *Freud, Biologist of the Mind* "be advocated as the work with which psychoanalytic candidates . . . will have to start from now on" (Pruyser, 401). If this should come to pass, I hope the institutes will have the foresight to collect their students' fees in advance.

8. Letter of 21 January 1985; quoted with permission.

9. Sulloway's actual concluding sentence reads: "The myths are merely his historical due, and they shall continue to live on, protecting his brilliant legacy to mankind, as long as this legacy remains a powerful part of human consciousness" (Sulloway 1983a, 503; the myths in question are listed, explained, and challenged on pages 489–95).

10. While Stalin made up lies about his former associates in order to justify destroying them, there is no evidence that he actually came to believe those lies. Freud, by contrast, convinced himself that Fliess was Exhibit A of the rule that repressed homosexuality can bring on paranoia; indeed,

he told Abraham that this etiology had been revealed to him precisely through his effort to understand Fliess's case (Sulloway 1983a, 234–35). Here is a paradigmatic instance of the still prevalent tendency among Freudians to declare their opponents mentally disturbed—a tactic that, interestingly enough, was to become standard practice in Soviet psychiatry. For a challenging perspective on the Freud–Fliess relationship, see Swales.

11. "Faced with the evidence that the methods on which almost all of his work relied were in fact unreliable, Freud had many scientifically honorable courses of action available to him. He could have published his doubts and continued to use the same methods, reporting his results in company with caveats. He could have published his doubts and abandoned the subject. He could have attempted experimental inquiries into the effects of suggestion in his therapeutic sessions. He did none of these things. . . . Instead he published *The Interpretation of Dreams* to justify by rhetorical devices the very methods he had every reason to distrust" (Glymour, 70). In Glymour's keen estimation *The Interpretation of Dreams* "formed a turning point in Freud's life and work: half a rotation from scientist towards mountebank" (Glymour, 69).

12. See Sulloway 1983a, 440, and the classic discussion by Nagel, who remarks: ". . . Freud did not think that his conclusion, though regarded by all competent biologists as false, refuted *any* of his premises. It is therefore pertinent to ask what could refute those premises and whether they are at all refutable" (Nagel, 44). Nagel here construes "refutable" in Cioffi's sense, not Grünbaum's; that is, he sees no *disposition* on Freud's part to be dissuaded by any consideration.

Works Cited

Bernstein, Arnold. 1980. Review in *Modern Psychoanalysis*, 5: 97–99.

Brooks, Peter. 1980. "The Crypto-Biologist." *New York Times Book Review*, 10 February, pp. 9, 26.

Chessick, Richard D. 1980. Review in *American Journal of Psychotherapy*, 34: 446–47.

Cioffi, Frank. 1970. "Freud and the Idea of a Pseudo-Science." In *Explanation in the Behavioural Sciences*, ed. Robert Borger and Frank Cioffi. Cambridge: Cambridge University Press. Pp. 471–499.

———. 1979. "Freud—New Myths to Replace the Old." *New Society*, 50: 503–504.

"Did Freud Build His Own Legend?" 1979. *Time*, 30 July, p. 51.

Clark, Peter J., and Crispin Wright. 1986. *Philosophy, Science and Psychoanalysis*. London: Basil Blackwell.

Dinnage, Rosemary. 1979. "The Genius of Freud." *Observer*, 9 December, pp. 41–43.

Edelson, Marshall. 1984. *Hypothesis and Evidence in Psychoanalysis*. Chicago: University of Chicago Press.

Ellenberger, Henri F. 1970. *The Discovery of the Unconscious: The History and Evolution of Dynamic Psychiatry*. New York: Basic Books.

————. 1972. "The Story of 'Anna O': A Critical Review with New Data." *Journal of the History of the Behavioral Sciences*, 8: 267–79.

Eysenck, H. J. 1980. "Freudian Myths." *Books and Bookmen*, 25 February, p. 38.

————, and Glenn D. Wilson. 1973. *The Experimental Study of Freudian Theories*. London: Methuen.

Freud, Sigmund. S.E. *The Standard Edition of the Complete Psychological Works of Sigmund Freud*. 24 vols. Trans. James Strachey. London: Hogarth Press, 1953–1974.

Fromm, Gerard. 1980. "Freud Rescued from Psychoanalysis." *Commonweal*, 107: 251–52.

Gifford, George E. 1980. Review in *Journal of the History of the Behavioral Sciences*, 16: 388–89.

Glazer, Michael. 1980. Review in *Group*, 4: 60–61.

Glymour, Clark. 1983. "The Theory of Your Dreams." In *Physics, Philosophy and Psychoanalysis: Essays in Honor of Adolf Grünbaum*, ed. R. S. Cohen and L. Laudan. Dordrecht, Holland: D. Reidel. Pp. 57–71.

Goldstein, Jan. 1981. Review in *Journal of Modern History*, 53:304–6.

Grünbaum, Adolf. 1984. *The Foundations of Psychoanalysis: A Philosophical Critique*. Berkeley: University of California Press.

Habermas, Jürgen. 1971. *Knowledge and Human Interests*. Trans. Jeremy J. Shapiro. Boston: Beacon Press.

Harvey, Joy. 1982. Review in *Journal of the History of Biology*, 15: 317–18.

Himmelstein, Jerome L. 1981. Review in *Theory and Society*, 10: 463–467.

Holt, Robert H. 1981. "The Great Analyst Reanalyzed." *Contemporary Psychology*, 26: 95–96.

Hopkins, Jim. 1979. "Killing and Eating Father." *New Statesman*, 98: 900.

Jahoda, Marie. 1979. "From the Bench to the Couch." *New Scientist*, 84: 792.

Khan, M. Masud R. 1981. Review in *International Review of Psycho-Analysis*, 8: 125.

Kanzer, Mark. 1980. Review in *Psychoanalytic Quarterly*, 49: 517–523.

Leonard, John. 1979. "Freud, Biologist of the Mind." *Books of the Times*, October, pp. 491–92.

Lieberson, Jonathan. 1985. "Putting Freud to the Test." *New York Review of Books*, 31 January, pp. 24–28.

Lothane, Zvi. 1981. Review in *Psychoanalytic Review*, 68: 348–61.

Nagel, Ernest. 1959. "Methodological Issues in Psychoanalytic Theory." In *Psychoanalysis, Scientific Method and Philosophy*, ed. Sidney Hook. New York: New York University Press. Pp. 38–56.

Pollock, George H. 1981. Review in *Journal of Interdisciplinary History*, 11: 517–20.

Pruyser, Paul W. 1980. Review in *Bulletin of the Menninger Clinic*, 44: 400–402.

Ricoeur, Paul. 1970. *Freud and Philosophy*. Trans. Dennis Savage. New Haven: Yale University Press.

Robinson, Paul. 1979. "Freud as Sociobiologist." *Psychology Today*, September, pp. 97–99.

Rogers, Marc. 1985. Letter to *The New Republic*, 11 February, p. 2.

Storr, Anthony. 1979. "The Super Ego of Sigmund Freud." *Book World* (*Washington Post*), 23 September, pp. 4–5.

Strouse, Jean. 1979. "Freud without Myths." *Newsweek*, 29 October, pp. 97–98.

Sulloway, Frank J. 1982a. "Profeta? No, Biologo. Intervista con Frank J. Sulloway." *Panorama*, 13 December, pp. 239–52.

———. 1982b. "Freud and Biology: The Hidden Legacy." *Psychology in Nineteenth-Century Thought*, ed. William R. Woodward and Mitchell G. Ash. New York: Praeger. Pp. 198–227.

———. 1983a. *Freud, Biologist of the Mind: Beyond the Psychoanalytic Legend*, revised ed. (1st ed. 1979.) New York: Basic Books.

———. 1983b. "Ideology and the Control of Scientific Knowledge: The Case of Freud and His Psychoanalytic Legend." *Psicoanalisi e Storia delle Scienze*, ed. M. Ranchetti. Florence: Leo S. Olschki.

Swales, Peter J. 1982. "Freud, Fliess, and Fratricide: The Role of Fliess in Freud's Conception of Paranoia." Privately published by the author.

Wallace, Edwin R. 1982. Review in *Bulletin of the History of Medicine*, 56: 602–04.

Wollheim, Richard. 1979. "Was Freud a Crypto-Biologist?" *New York Review of Books*, 8 November, pp. 25–28.

II

The Theorized Academy

6

Deconstructing a Discipline

Here is the text of a talk I delivered in 1979 at a Modern Language Association forum on "The Sociology of Literary Theory." It represents my first attempt to come to grips publicly with the avant-garde spirit that was already beginning to transform American literary study in ways that have continued to preoccupy me. The talk, which had to be compressed into fifteen minutes, now seems to me too cavalier in skimming over manifest deconstructionist claims and in neglecting differences between various parties who identify themselves as poststructuralist, but it isolated what I still believe to be a key issue, the poststructuralist challenge to the idea of rationally mediated critical discourse.

When I was first asked to contribute to a panel on the sociology of literary theory, I experienced an access of humility. Could I really consider myself a sociologist? What did I know about the august science practiced by Karl Mannheim, Talcott Parsons, and Lewis Feuer? As often happens, however, upon reflection I was able to bring my humility under control. After all, I told myself, what is sociology but the systematic explanation of the behavior of groups other than one's own—and more often than not, groups to which one feels superior? In particular, the sociology of knowledge—that branch of the discipline which we are practicing today—is well known for its efforts to show that all ideas other than the sociologist's are determined by such variables as class and status. Say, I thought—this sociology could be fun! I gradually became conscious of an upwelling sense of vocation.

Even now, however, I feel that some methodological caution is required. To be sure, class and status decidedly play a role in the incidence of belief in this or that literary theory. Yet the connections, as I will try to indicate, are often ironic rather than straightforward. Furthermore, it is impossible to infer from the known class and status of a literary theorist what the content of his theory is likely to be. It would take a very keen sociologist, for example, to detect major differences of class and status between literary professors at Harvard and those at Yale. Yet from the standpoint of literary theory, a brief trip between Cambridge and New Haven would be like a journey to the moon. Discouraging as it may be to the aspiring sociologist of knowledge, there seems to be a certain amount of voluntary association in these matters. The question, then, cannot be whether there is such a thing as the literary theory held by the upper middle class or the literary theory of the untenured. As sociologists, all we can do is begin at the other end, with a school of thought that we dislike, and try to say some objectively unpleasant things about the reasons for its popularity.

In this spirit, I call your attention to a body of ideas that is variously named poststructuralist or deconstructionist. Since I don't wish to focus on individual theorists, let me offer a composite sketch of this position. Anyone may feel free to dissociate himself from my account of it. Indeed, I would hope that before long, no one will wish to call himself a poststructuralist or a deconstructionist, and we can all maintain that we have recovered from a virus that was just passing through our community.

Deconstructionism, I gather, holds that knowledge about literature is strictly unattainable. Perceptions of meaning cannot be made apart from the critic's expectations and world view, and so-called evidence for an interpretation is simply further speculation within a perceptual set. Literature and critical discourse about literature are equally problematic—equally "literary," if you will. We must therefore abandon the old-fashioned quest to discover what a given author was trying to communicate. We needn't fall silent, however; rest assured of that! Criticism can resume business in an expansive new mode as literature, as a form of activity rather than a body of propositions. It even has a useful task to perform, namely, the dismantling or deconstructing of our prior understanding of texts—including the understanding held by authors.

This doctrine as it has been practiced thus far displays several puzzling features. Deconstructionism denies that propositions can be true, but it graciously makes an exception for the propositions of its own theory. It scorns the idea of extrinsic standards of value, but it elevates the subversion of conventional opinions into exactly such an extrinsic standard—one that is luckily met by every single text that the deconstructionist critic examines. In denying the primacy of authorial intentions, furthermore, deconstructionism behaves as if those elusive intentions were knowable after all; the program of decentering implies recognition of a center. And in asserting that no form of discourse is more privileged than another, deconstructionism lays claim to knowledge of the ultimate order or equality of things—a knowledge, once again, for which the theory makes no provision. These anomalies suggest to me that we are dealing here, not with a fully considered epistemology, but with a polemical posture or a current of ideological enthusiasm.

This hypothesis receives corroboration from many statements by American partisans of deconstructionism, who tell us that their style of reading is in fact an instrument of liberation. Liberation from what? That depends on the individual crusader. For some, the enemy is the traditional literary establishment, with its stuffy ideas about historical periods, its gossipy approach to the question of who influenced whom, and its pretensions to certain knowledge. For others, the enemy is capitalism or patriarchy or enforced sexual conformism—principles that appear to pervade the classic literary texts, but which can be undermined by the critic who knows in advance that authorial intentions count for nothing. And some deconstructionists, aligning themselves with a self-styled postmodernism, believe they are helping to free language itself from hierarchies of patterning that have been imposed by an oppressive, centuries-old social order.

Now, an uninitiated sociologist of knowledge, hearing of these vague yet sweeping plans for liberation, might well imagine that their agents came from the lowest circles of the dispossessed. Someone who feels that syntax itself is repressive and exploitative must surely be an abject victim of the authorities he is challenging. We know, however, that in this case our sociologist would be quite wrong. The chief American adherents of deconstructionism do not resemble Spartacus in any degree. They congregate in some of the most prestigious universities; some of them are department chairmen; others give foreign lectures under government sponsorship and serve on powerful fellowship committees, dispensing the largesse of corporations. Some of them, it is true, are politically engaged as that term is usually understood; but some others feel that they are doing their part merely by amusing themselves at the peripheries of texts.

Taken at face value as efforts to found a new social order, the critical maneuvers of the more politically minded deconstructionists would appear to border on the delusional. They fail the first test of any revolutionary utterance, that it be understandable to people outside the revolutionary's immediate circle; and there is something distinctly odd about attacking a system of oppression by altering the rules of its literary criticism. But of course we needn't take these efforts at face value. They are made by people who, to a significant extent, are members in good standing of the academic establishment from which they claim to be freeing us. And in at least three respects, the benefits they seek are conferred, not upon the huddled masses, but upon themselves, at the expense of others.

In the first place, the deconstructionist denial that there are standards of evidence by which one critical judgment might be found more adequate than another effectively turns criticism into a mystery exclusively controlled by its high priests. To be sure, such exclusivism has always thrived in the academic world. It has been moderated, however, by a shared willingness to acknowledge that young critic A has said something new and important about Shakespeare or that young critic B has forced us to revise our understanding of *The Red Badge of Courage*. In other words, a consensus on the point that authors do indeed write books and wish their manifest emphases to be respected has enabled critical authority to be earned, not just seized or sequestered. All of the deconstructionist spokesmen beyond a certain age acquired their own reputations in that traditional and relatively democratic way. In now declaring that there are no standards of evidence, no intentions worth deciphering, nothing but more or less creative misreadings, these same spokesmen are anticipating a day when there would be only one access route to the inner sanctum. It would be the path of currying favor with *them*—imitating their mannerisms, praising their cleverness, using their favorite code words from the latest Parisian sources. As we ought to have learned by now from the larger political realm, a scorn for independent criteria of judgment is ultimately a means, not of fostering spontaneity and liberation, but of guaranteeing that entrenched leaders will not be contradicted by upstarts possessing uncongenial ideas.

Secondly, the deconstructionist position frees the critic himself from an obligation to make reasonable inferences. As Gerald Graff has pointed out, the debatable assertion that critics cannot arrive at true statements becomes a program whereby the critic should *try not* to make such statements. Thus we see the novelty of critics explicitly saying their one remaining responsibility is to be interesting. Interesting to whom, we may ask? The answer is all too clear: interesting to their fellow deconstructionists and to apprentices in search of the password to employment and tenure. Once again, the elevation to primacy of a totally subjective idea of value would tend to consolidate power in the hands of those subjectivists already holding it. Since there is no way of arbitrating disputes about who is interesting, the deconstructionists sitting in the chairs of literature would win the contest by default.

Thirdly, the inquisitive sociologist cannot avoid noticing that the deconstructionist program promises to allay one of the besetting self-doubts of academic critics, a fear that the things worth saying about the finite number of authors in one's field have already been said. Every literary scholar, I suspect, experiences that worry—an anxiety not of influence but of surplus or surfeit. The only remedy against it is to immerse oneself in historical materials and to discover how little, on a given issue, has been settled once and for all; but that remedy is available only to people who believe in knowledge and who have been taught how to define a problem and to go about investigating it. Deconstructionism appears to offer another way out—an abolition of all constraints upon interpretation. I find it hard to imagine that such a fashion will last for very long. In departments where it prevails, however, it will deprive a good number of students of the mental discipline that the older deconstructionists themselves received in an earlier phase of our profession. Weariness of rational standards in one generation becomes a pathetic ignorance of them in the next.

There is, of course, a socially progressive role to be played by professors of literature. We can help to make our students more capable of independent judgment by teaching them to read accurately and to write scrupulously, in a comprehensible idiom. Our own prose can set an example in this regard. We can also mediate between relatively uninformed readers and great works of imagination, holding out alternatives to a life of passive consumption and manipulation. It is the promise of these benefits that has thus far induced our fellow citizens to subsidize the peculiar industry of academic literary criticism. If, instead, we write for a hermetic community of fellow critics; if we take the banal fact that readers never entirely agree about the meanings of texts and derive from it the non sequitur that misreading is a virtue; if we answer the larger society's doubts about our seriousness by explicitly reducing criticism to a supposedly revolutionary act of self-display—then we can hardly expect to continue being supported.

A parting word. My remarks about deconstructionism will, I know, identify me in some circles as a defender of outmoded critical schools and as an opponent of all innovation along structuralist lines. The shortest answer I can think of is that real innovation in any field requires commitment to the goal of accurate knowledge. If we had time today, we could debate whether the structuralist movement has significantly added to our knowledge of literature. Perhaps it has. My subject, however, has been an ideological postscript to structuralism—a current of thought that purports to leave behind the entire realm in which propositions can be checked for their adequacy to fact. I am taking exception, not to every effort to break free from the known intentions and values of authors, but to the claim that those intentions and values are of no account. To oppose such a claim is simply to reaffirm that knowledge, even knowledge about something as elusive as literature, continues to call us—even if it has to call over a rising chorus of irrationalism.

7

Criticism Without Constraint

This essay, published early in 1982, expands and illustrates the argument of Chapter Six. Readers unfamiliar with recent critical trends will be able to catch the flavor of "indeterminism" and to see why I hold that its more developed forms constitute a dubious program of liberation from traditional intellectual goals.

Even to a superficial observer, it must be apparent by now that the academic study of literature has fallen upon anxious times. The outward symptoms are unmistakable: tenure track openings for new Ph.D.'s have all but disappeared, graduate programs have been trimmed, and undergraduates have been deserting the English major for more vocationally oriented programs. And these palpable setbacks have intensified soul-searching among those who remain within the profession or who hope that it will somehow find room for them. Is literary criticism really needed? Does it constitute a legitimate discipline or only a pastime? And can there be any justification for the old faith—now professed only with apology or irony—in the historical study of authors and periods, when the only student enthusiasm we can rely on is borrowed from such topical domains as feminism, science fiction, and popular culture?

There is, to be sure, one conspicuous sign of vitality in "English," namely, an unprecedented excitement over literary theory emanating from the continent. The glow of cosmopolitanism, however, may prove after all to be mere hectic on the patient's cheek. The terms that now cause pulses to race—deconstruction, dissemination, epistemes, the mirror stage, and the like—are so undescriptive of literary detail that they tend not so much to explain literature as to replace it. And whether or not the theories of the hour are warranted, they scarcely offer a lasting antidote to the prevailing mood of restlessness and doubt. Either by design or by consequence, they are directed *against* the main task of criticism as it is still widely conceived—that is, as the pursuit of meaning that authors presumably impart to their works in creating them.

There can be no mistaking the fact that the study of meaning has now been vigorously contested. Some theorists hold that such study is always marred by a simplistic equation of meaning with the mental states of authors before or during the act of composition. A preoccupation with meaning, they say, leads to an undervaluing of conventional elements that are crucial to the way literature is perceived. But that cogent point is in itself no menace to academic business as usual. The real challenge comes from theorists—let me call them *indeterminists*—who argue that meaning is conferred not by authors but by readers, and that a work's meaning is therefore constantly subject to change. If that position is accepted, meaning ceases to be a stable object of inquiry and one interpretation is as lacking in persuasiveness as any other. The inevitable corollary is that debates among critics are entirely pointless. Such is the conclusion urged by the most influential of contemporary schools, Jacques Derrida's "deconstructionists," who claim that the "evidence" marshaled for any given interpretation is simply an artifact of that interpretation. If the deconstructionists are right, the greater part of our criticism has consisted of exercises in self-delusion.

But *are* they right? Indeterminist arguments are often so hard to follow that their arbitrariness goes unnoticed. Who has demonstrated that meaning originates with readers? The decision to say that texts do or don't bear authorially determined meaning is not an empirical matter but one of methodological and even temperamental convenience. If we want to believe that a work's meaning became fixed forever in the act of its creation, all we need to do is say so. Then, following E. D. Hirsch, Jr. (1967, 1976), we can distinguish between meaning and "significance"—the coloration that literature acquires by assimilation into each reader's unique consciousness. In this light, indeterminists have shown only that *significance* is volatile, a fact that everyone already knows.

Despite its elusiveness and potential tediousness, there is much to be said for retaining the idea of determinate meaning. For one thing, it agrees with the intuitively plausible notion that authors write in a purposive spirit. For another, it gives us invariant objects of investigation and an impersonal criterion of interpretive adequacy. That is, we can prefer one reading to another if we are shown that it is more compatible with what the author could have possibly wanted to communicate. Around such a standard we can gather (or preserve) an intellectual community devoted to accurate knowledge of important texts and of the cultural past. In a word, we hold onto criticism as a relatively orderly institution that shares the goals and findings of historical scholarship.

But institutions, precisely because they impose constraints on their members, can inspire subtle forms of rebellion. Theorists who effectively deny the existence of meaning would seem to be expressing such rebellion. In some cases, perhaps, they object on ideological grounds to the cultural tradition that gets treated so reverently by "normal" critics. Or perhaps they want to write more expressively than rationally, and would like to hold up some liberating doctrine against their would-be judges. Whatever the grievance, by embracing indeterminism they cry for more freedom, even at the expense of removing literary works from authorial control.

Let us be careful to note the difference between *denying the privileged character* of created meaning and merely *studying something else*. A good many legitimate issues—regarding genre, convention, influence, structure, and style—can be addressed without direct reference to meaning, and an indeterminist can write usefully about such issues if he decides (however inconsistently) to exempt them from his relativistic outlook. Yet the record of theorizing by critics who hope to *break the authority* of meaning is singularly unimpressive, for reasons I would like to explore. It seems that the dismissal of authorial purpose tends also to be a dismissal of scholarly prudence. For, if the author's inferable intentions are to be put out of mind, the only remaining guide is the theorist himself, now awash in literary data that will be compliant to even an eccentric and ill-considered idea.

Insofar as indeterminists entertain a "scientific" purpose, it is to learn exactly how literature is registered by "the reader," without whose mental activity a text would be considered only black squiggles on a page. But what in fact is known about this reader, and who is he really? Is he an experimental subject hooked up to electrodes as he sweats his way through "Dover Beach"? Is he the individual critic writ large? Or is he perhaps a composite of all the critics whose views about a certain work have been taken seriously? "The reader" fails to provide the slightest actual guidance.

For, if he is not conceived as an everyman whose mind is unavailable to inspection, then he is only a precipitate of one or more interpretations that have been arrived at in the usual way—not through some pristine encounter with the text but through rereading, reflection, immersion in previous criticism, and trial and error. That halting, irreplaceable process is necessarily oriented to a norm—congruence with discernible intention—lying outside any reader's psychology.

If anyone could argue his way past the difficulties besetting anti-intentional theory, it would be Stanley Fish of Johns Hopkins. An indeterminist who departs from the pack by being consistently clear, logical, and devoid of Left Bank affectation, Fish has earned a name as the shrewdest and most rhetorically brilliant of "reader-response" theorists. In fact, however, he has ended by quarreling chiefly with his own unsustainable ideas. His several theoretical retreats—all presented as bold discoveries—constitute eloquent testimony to the speciousness of supposing that one has been initiated into the confidence of "the reader."

Fish's odyssey began not with a direct challenge to authorial control, but with an ingenious variant of it. In *Surprised by Sin: The Reader in Paradise Lost* (1971), he claimed that Milton *wanted* us to misread his elaborately suspended sentences—forming premature conclusions as we struggled from phrase to phrase—so that he could repeatedly "surprise" us and thereby remind us of our fallen state. But if this was indeed Milton's aim, the real surprise is that it went unnoticed for three hundred years, until one reader happened upon it. As Fish explains in a book (1981) containing his influential essays of the past decade, his original contention had to be covered by an even more implausible one: that all other readers had "really" experienced *Paradise Lost* just as he did, "even though they may not (consciously) know it, and . . . if they will only listen to me they will learn how to recognize the configurations of the experience they have always had."

Though Fish's theory was clever to a fault, the reader it invoked was a dunce—a Charlie Brown who, having had the syntactic football yanked away a hundred times, would keep right on charging it with perfect innocence, never learning to suspend judgment until he arrived at the poet's verb. Of course the author of *Surprised by Sin* could never have been such a dysfunctional reader of Milton or anyone else. It could only be a matter of time before Fish, a man who takes objections seriously even as he makes a show of refuting them, would have to abandon the whole project of masquerading as "the reader." Yet meanwhile he found himself launched on a paradigmatic career as an "advanced" theorist. There could be no collapse into historically tempered interpretation after he had been perceived, with a gratitude and an outrage that were equally flattering, as the bearer of an exciting anti-traditionalist methodology.

A record of Fish's progress through the Seventies would show, first, how he felt compelled to replace "the reader" with any number of readers, none of whom could be counted on to share any of the others' literary experience; second, how he gradually, with understandable misgivings, recognized that this conception undermined all sense of the text as a fixed entity; and finally, how his discomfort with the resultant subjectivism issued in yet another doctrine, that "interpretive communities," not individuals or texts, confer meaning, and that within one such (wholly undefined) community the meaning of a work is stable and certain.

Thus Fish, the student of line-by-line reader response, no longer even pretends to know how people behave in the presence of literature. In his flight both from authorially sanctioned meaning and from the dubieties of his own "affective stylistics," he has arrived at a total determinism whereby the individual reader or critic is merely a "product" of his community; every text now has a (deceptive) "structure of meanings that is obvious and inescapable from the perspective of whatever interpretive assumptions happen to be in force." Starting as a maverick, Fish has become a Pangloss; you can't go wrong because you are always within a community that tells you exactly what to think.[1]

This contention slanders every critic who has ever altered his views on a controversy out of regard for a superior argument. And if meanings are obvious and inescapable, how does Fish account for the drawn-out interpretive disputes in which he once took such emphatic delight? Could anyone believe that members of the same interpretive community never disagree? Fish's last-ditch theory is falsified by the entire history of criticism, including his own history of skipping from theory to theory without detectably changing "communities."

But of course Fish is only one "scientific" indeterminist among many. To get some idea of whether others are faring better, we may look briefly at a new book by a sympathetic commentator, Jonathan Culler's *The Pursuit of Signs: Semiotics, Literature, De-*

construction (1981). The same author's *Structuralist Poetics* (1975) has for some years been the most circumspect introduction to the critical uses of French linguistic structuralism, a mode of thought whose paramount strategy is to bypass "the subject," alias the meaning-conferring author. Culler hopes that structuralist discipline will enable us to grasp each literary genre as a semiotic system—as a network of signs that take their significance not from authorial purpose or from any reference to the outside world, but from their unconsciously registered relations with each other. And now he has expanded his survey of semiotic theories, meanwhile trying to make room for Jacques Derrida's "poststructuralist" critique, which threatens to "deconstruct" any laws or patterns that the critic might want to regard as irreducible.

One minor symptom of the times is that Culler has become more adamantly "theoretical" in the period between *Structuralist Poetics* and his latest statement. While in the first book he claimed that structuralism offers both "a theory of literature and a mode of interpretation," by now he is determined to pass, as his first chapter insists, "Beyond Interpretation." The idea that critics should spend their time delving into the meaning of individual works, he says, has been the cardinal impediment to "a comprehensive theory of fictions." Such a theory, Culler leads us to believe, cannot remain out of reach if we only shift our attention from thematic questions to the deepest laws of reading.

When he considers what the opponents of traditional literary meaning have accomplished thus far, however, Culler is repeatedly disappointed, even vexed. Norman Holland's effort to affix all responsibility for meaning onto the invariant "identity themes" of readers, for example, strikes him as nothing more than "a vulgarized and sentimentalized version of the New Criticism, with organic unity transferred from the work of art to the entire 'text' of a person's life." According to Culler, Harold Bloom's oedipal version of textuality is diminished by an assumption that each work of art can have only one "precursor" text with which it conducts an anxious dialogue. Roman Jakobson's system of linguistic analysis founders on its lack of any criterion for determining which features are significant for readers. Hans Robert Jauss's "reception aesthetics" fails to transcend the forbidden ambition of supplying "historically authorized interpretation," and Michael Riffaterre's search for "the word or sentence from which [each poem] is generated and of which its every element is a variant" is "much too crude and reductive." Riffaterre's enterprise too "is continually deflected by the temptations of interpretation," as is that of another theorist we have already met, Stanley Fish. Culler begins by extravagantly praising Fish, but he ends by indicting him as timid, "bathetic," and guilty of "duplicity" for having "faked" the experience to which his theory of reader response pertains. One begins to wonder if what Culler calls "the general collapse and self-destruction of [Fish's] theory" isn't a prognosis for anti-intentional criticism in general.

Although Culler himself would resist such a prognosis, the least we can say is that something appears to be fundamentally amiss here. Note the pattern: according to Culler, the theorist typically goes wrong either by regressing to interpretation—that is, seeking historically determinate meaning—or by allowing himself to be carried away by a pet idea. When the critic is guided by intentionality he forgets to be a structuralist, but when he liberates himself from intentionality he seems to become a crackpot. There appears to be no middle ground on which the star witness of semiotics, the reader, can take the stand. But we already know why not: "the reader" is simply the critic's marionette.

Even though Culler fails to see why structuralist thought about literature never fulfills its promise, *The Pursuit of Signs* deserves praise for its candor. Yet Culler himself betrays a defect that runs through nearly the entire range of indeterminist discourse: a dependence on empirically dubious sources of authority. Again and again he shows himself ideologically disposed to favor any celebrated thinker who maintains, in Lévi-Strauss's quoted words, "that understanding consists in reducing one type of reality to another; that the true reality is never the most obvious; and that the nature of truth is already indicated by the care it takes to remain elusive." Nietzsche, Marx, Freud, Durkheim, Saussure, Derrida, Althusser, Barthes, and Foucault appear in Culler's pages, not as proponents of ideas that bear testing, but as tutelary figures deserving of automatic honor. Culler seems unaware of the extent to which he is endorsing, not a science of signs, but a narrow "school of suspicion" with an iconoclastic *parti pris*.[2]

The trouble with embracing thinkers largely on the basis of their doctrinal radicalism is that one becomes less concerned with cogency and accuracy of statement than with keeping up in the rush to discard "reactionary" assumptions. Thus Culler, who has always been devoted to what he calls the "sober, unambiguous metalanguage" of semiotics, now finds himself saddled with the later Derrida, who requires that criticism be regarded as "*a pastime or activity that is in and of the sign*" (emphasis added). As Culler reports, this means that we eventually reach "not a discipline, not another mode of analysis, but acts of writing, acts of displacement, *play which violates language and reality*" (emphasis added).[3] New rules are suddenly in effect: even one's own analytic system must be deconstructed if one is not to be thought an intellectual rightist. Can Culler meet the challenge? Surely, he hazards, the contemporary critic need not "deem himself a poet or seize every opportunity to pun." But is he really sure? One can already hear the scandalized whispers that Culler is too incorrigibly earnest and rational, too "Anglo-Saxon," to be a trustworthy message bearer from Paris to the New World. It will be interesting to see if his forthcoming book, *On Deconstruction,* manages to display a sufficient degree of the impishness which has now become *de rigueur.*

If, as seems apparent, the refusal to acknowledge authorial meaning rarely yields more than trifling results—if it even leads, in one manifestation, to a program of reducing criticism to a sandbox amusement for the ultrasophisticated—we must wonder why it attracts such fervor. To address that question we must leave behind such relatively scrupulous theorists as Culler and Fish and attend to the ideological flavor of indeterminism as a movement. The main bogey of that movement, though it sometimes appears to be bourgeois consciousness or American provincialism or empirical prudence or authority in general, is clearly conventional literary study. Evidently we are witnessing an internal wave of protest whose activists, by decreeing meaning to be null and void, seek to cancel the gains in literary knowledge achieved by their less agitated colleagues and predecessors. Somehow they feel sullied and embarrassed by the humdrum business of literary research; they want us to know that they have washed their hands of it.

It is not difficult to see how such a movement could take hold, especially in an academic population whose affinities lie at least as much with the artist's Romantic liberty as with the scientist's control. Once it has been established that the normal task of criticism is to interpret texts and that we must prefer those interpretations which are most consistent with authorial intention, the scene has been prepared for claustrophobia. What will remain to be said about a finite number of works that are becoming better and better understood? That question—or better, that groundless fear, for it ignores the way changes in methodology generate new issues to be addressed—haunts a critical industry whose reckless growth in the quarter-century after World War II has now been succeeded by a painful stagnation; the sense that "everything has been done" turns to panic as opportunities for appointment and promotion disappear. Such a climate is ideally suited to nurturing a mania for theories, however poorly supported, that promise to multiply the number of allowable remarks one can make about literature.

Yet this cannot be the whole story, for indeterminism arrives at our shores by first-class passage, in the hands of renowned American critics whose future is hardly in jeopardy. They are not supplicants but dictators of academic style. Although they appear, in championing indeterminism, to be turning away from their own impressive achievements as interpreters, only a fool would take them for revolutionaries. We may guess that for them at least, the "freedom" I mentioned earlier has less to do with anti-academic feeling than with a wish to fend off certain potential intrusions upon elite sensibility.

In order to explore this hunch, let me turn finally to two recent books by Geoffrey H. Hartman, the Karl Young Professor of English and Comparative Literature at Yale. The more recent work, *Saving the Text: Literature/Derrida/Philosophy* (1981), strikingly exemplifies the frothiness of "theory" in the Derridean mode. But the earlier one, *Criticism in the Wilderness: The Study of Literature Today* (1980), is even more telling, for, as a highly defensive reply to opponents of "the hermeneutical Mafia," it places on view all the hostilities and confusions that go to make up the full-blown indeterminist spirit. These books, moreover, invite study because their author—a senior fellow of the School of Criticism and Theory, a trustee of the English Institute, and a member of the executive council of the Modern Language Association—has long been recognized as a preeminent American critic. His own progress, which I will not pause to recount, from historically informed interpretation to vapid attitudinizing could stand for the fate of much "advanced" academic discourse over the past two decades.

Hartman is quite aware of belonging to a movement of resistance to a continued concern for meaning. He even gives the movement a name, *revisionism*, which points to its essentially oppositional purpose. In championing the revisionists, he has in mind chiefly himself and his Yale colleagues Paul de Man, J. Hillis Miller, Harold Bloom, and Jacques Derrida, who shuttles between Paris and New Haven. But lest he be thought parochial, Hartman admits as tentative members such further enemies of "objective" reading as Stanley Fish (a Yale Ph.D.), Fredric Jameson (now at Yale), Hans-Georg Gadamer, H. R. Jauss, Wolfgang Iser, and Norman Holland. If he is only lukewarmly supportive of this secondary group, it is not because he specifically disputes their ideas, but because he fears they have not altogether forsworn the quest to discover what literary works are about. Through precept and example Hartman urges us not to "methodize indeterminacy" by merely shifting the source of meaning from authors to readers. As he says in an untypically straightforward sentence, "contemporary criticism aims at a hermeneutics of indeterminacy."

Hartman thus stakes out a critical turf somewhat to the left of Jonathan Culler's. Instead of hoping to uncover universal laws of literary response (and then to assure us that they are offered just in fun), he strives unabashedly to keep conclusions at bay. The critics he admires are those whose language is "curiously unprogressive or exitless." Their work "reveals contradictions and equivocations, and so makes fiction interpretable by making it less readable. The fluency of the reader is affected by a kind of stutter: the critic's response becomes deliberately hesitant." And the prince of stutterers is the later Derrida, whose "exhibitionistic" and "interminable"— these are terms of forgiving fondness—treatise called *Glas* supplies us, not with anything so vulgar as ideas, but with "a chain of secondary elaborations stretching to infinity."

Hartman himself is never more at home than when recapitulating the "sense of débris" that pervades *Glas* or in trying his own hand at the recommended form of verbal doodling:

> That the word "knot" may echo in the mind as "not" is one of those small changes that analyst or exegete are [sic] trained to hear. "When thou hast done, thou hast not done." There are so many knots: Donnean, Penelopean, Lacanian, Borromean, Derridean. At the beginning of *Glas*, the similarity in sound of *Sa* (acronym for "savoir absolu") and *Sa* ("signifiant") is such a knot with a positive philosophic yield. Yet because of the equivocal, echo-nature of language, even identities or homophonies sound on: the sound of *Sa* is knotted with that of *ça*, as if the text were signaling its intention to bring Hegel, Saussure, and Freud together. *Ça* corresponds to the Freudian Id ("Es"); and it may be that our only "savoir absolu" is that of a *ça* structured

like the *Sa*-signifiant: a bacchic or Lacanian "primal process" where only signifier-signifying-signifiers exist. . . .

Enough, you say. But Derrida adds: "Reste ici ou glas qu'on ne peut arrêter." In his pamphlet on Adami, Derrida plays further on IC, which now reappears in the form of ICH ("I" or "Je"), the abbreviated ICH(TOS) symbol for Christ (see the fish of Adami's picture), and by chiastic reversal both the chiasmus itself (X) transliterated as CHI, and the querulous pronoun QUI. Freeplay reaches here a methodical craziness that parallels Christopher Smart's. But taken altogether a series of slippery signifiers has now established itself on the basis of the problematics of the subject, its construction and subversion. Though this verbal gematria is no more, no less, persuasive than Lacan's diagrammatia, it has the same treacherously memorable effect, as if Lacan's imaginary and symbolic realms had finally come together in a sort of *specular script*.

   Let me try to formulate this basic mirror-writing as

IC(ICH / CHI)INRI

I have added the last term, the acronym of Christ on the Cross, to that crossing or chiasmic middle term, which stands for the problematics of subject or ego, and to the first term, which evokes, together with the initials of Christ and the first syllable of ICarus (as in "la voie/voix d'Icare"), the Immaculate Conception.

I quote at such length because, as can be seen, Hartman's most indulgent mode departs so sharply from ordinary critical writing as to beggar description. Here is a self-congratulatory hermeticism whose purpose seems to lie somewhere between the dropping of names, the displaying of tidbits of esoterica, and the muddling of agency. In this ghostly prose, sounds echo, similarities appear, a text is almost signalling its intention, the Lacanian primal process hums along, and a series of slippery signifiers establishes itself—as if neither Hartman nor Derrida had anything to do with these stage effects.

   Given Hartman's aspirations toward inconclusiveness, it may seem anomalous that in *Saving the Text* he also puts forward a general theory of literature. But there is little danger of his being too easily understood. At times he appears to be proposing that literature originates in "a primal word-wound" which, conveniently for the theorist, has undergone such transformation that its traces are no longer available for study. Elsewhere he hints that literary form "saves the text" from the maddening openness, the impossibility of closure, that Derrida ascribes to language. But then again, the main idea of his book, "inspired," as he confides, "by French reflections," may be that "literature is the elaboration of a specular name"—whatever *that* means. It would be tacky to ask for specifics from a writer who disarmingly announces, "I cannot find it in myself to worry the question of the relation of empirical evidence to theory. . . ." According to revisionist etiquette, theory "should not impose or lacerate but *allow in others—in the world itself—an unconstrained response*" (emphasis added). One must cultivate an exquisite vagueness if such a response is to be achieved.

Thus Hartman goes well beyond Culler and Fish in reconciling himself to the continental view that criticism is less a body of propositions than a branch of literature to be cherished for its affective power. In *Criticism in the Wilderness* he sets out to repeal "[t]he automatic valuing of works of art over works of commentary," to lift criticism from its "second-class status in the world of letters." As opposed to Matthew Arnold, who called the epochs of Aeschylus and Shakespeare "the promised land, toward which criticism can only beckon," Hartman suggests that perhaps "we are forerunners to ourselves"—that is, that criticism is already our outstanding literary genre.

In order to match "the primacy of art," Hartman believes, critics must marshal a "near-daemonic" force, an extravagance or "brilliance" which "liberates the critical activity from its positive or reviewing function." The criticism he admires is therefore that which deserves to be called "digressive," "outrageous," "freakish," even "ridiculous," for that way lies the Sublime. And if Hartman's own prose, with its indefinite musing, its cautious good manners, and its superabundant allusiveness, seems deficient in the required frenzy, we need only recall that language in general, according to the latest Gallic conception, is already "mad," "treacherous," "insidious," "vertiginous," and so forth. Do we not all experience "the fear (a thrilling fear) of the abyss in all words whose resonance haunts us and must be appeased"? If readers fail to appreciate the steely courage of critics who dare to navigate this void, it must be because they find "a possible loss of boundaries" to be just "too threatening." Even boredom, it seems, is a form of defensive homage to the extremity of revisionist heroics.

What readers may think, however, is of less moment to Hartman than what critics require for themselves. On that subject he is cryptic but suggestive. "The revisionists," he tell us, "challenge the attitude that condemns the writer of criticism or commentary to nonliterary status and a service function. To that extent they are a political movement that attacks the isolation of the critic: isolation within the university and from broader, more public issues, but isolation also from inwardness and philosophical concerns." We have already explored one of the key terms in this revealing statement, *nonliterary status*, and we may be sure that by *philosophical concerns* Hartman intends the standard Nietzschean line: "the drive of the interpretive mind to revise or reverse, to unmask itself as well as its object, to penetrate so deeply that everything human is alien to it. . . ." But what about the other terms: *political movement, service function, isolation from inwardness*? To see what Hartman means by those phrases is to locate the little eddy of American academic culture within which his exhortations might be considered meaningful and even welcome.

Our problem today, Hartman opines, lies with those who would "separate out, *bureaucratically*, the functions of critic and artist" (emphasis added). The idea of acquiring definite knowledge of literature conjures to his mind the specter of "technocratic, predictive, or authoritarian formulas," of a "monumental, totalizing system," even of "a managerial society full of technicians, operators, language therapists, a department of discourse control and emendation." A national emergency! And closer to home, our favorite books "are in danger of being routinized or contaminated by endless readings forced out of industrious hordes of students." To forestall such an outcome, Hartman implies, elite critics must become Luddites in the factories of meaning production. By staunchly refusing to reach conclusions about literature, they will help to preserve "inwardness" from the ravages of middle-class rationality and homogeneity.

Not least among the questions raised by such a "politics" is whether its intended beneficiaries include anyone besides the revisionist critics themselves. What, for example, about those "industrious hordes of students" whose parents are paying the critics' salaries? Does Hartman wish to instruct them in techniques of meaning-avoidance, and if so, does he think they will thereby become keener thinkers, more humane readers, better citizens? The answer, so far as one can tell, is that he disprizes those students and has no interest in addressing their educational needs. The critic, says Hartman in another anti-technocratic sally, "if he practices in an English department, . . . carves and trims and patches and binds the prose of future leaders destined to build or destroy the economy"; he is nothing more than "a retainer to those in our society who want not the difficult reality but merely the illusion of literacy." Even the purest revisionists are regrettably "tainted by the odor of academic life: secure, yes, but also *service-ridden. For the university has opened its doors*" (emphasis added).

Here, I think, we arrive at the core of the problem as Hartman sees it: colleges are no longer the finishing schools of yore. Yet revisionists with power can at least decline to be "hired grammarians" for those semi-literates who have been, as Hartman puts it none too delicately, "dislocated into institutes of Higher Education." And they can keep 'em guessing about the mysteries of criticism. If "[t]he 'service function' imposed on English departments . . . contributes to dividing literary studies into the grind of 'communication' or 'rhetoric' courses as against high-stepping intellectual entertainment"—why, Hartman simply opts for the entertainment.

Despite its arrogance, however, *Criticism in the Wilderness* is a distinctly melancholy collection of statements. It abounds in references to "resentful and lonely" critics whose colleagues misunderstand them and who are paid too little for undergoing "a routine that can seriously hamper self-development." Although Hartman repeatedly disparages what he elsewhere calls "academic-rotarian" professors who crave definite ideas, he complains bitterly against critics who "carp at critics" and who "bite or bark at their own kind." And his concluding proposal that students of law and medicine be required to study literary interpretation, presumably along the lines of the "hermeneutic highjinks" that he favors, is as wistful as it is devoid of a rationale.

Thus Hartman's campaign against isolation does not as yet appear to be a notable success. Nor could it be, given his renunciation of rationally based choice between competing theories, hypotheses, and interpretations. The vision of a community of investigators, whether within or between disciplines, is a phantom unless the parties involved acknowledge grounds of evidential appeal. And the fact that Hartman hasn't quite decided what he wants— is it fraternity, recognition, or mere exemption from the "service" that underlings will still be required to perform?—only renders his situation more pathetic. His tentative brief for boldness, his decorous critique of decorum, his politics of educational disdain—what are they, if not the marks of a mandarinism whose intellectual pretexts have dropped away?

Obviously, Hartman's attitude cannot be taken to stand for those of all critics who advocate indeterminism. Even Stanley Fish, though he appears farther than ever from a believable conception of how critics arrive at their views, has repented of once having written that his dismissal of objectivity "relieves me of the obligation to be right . . . and demands only that I be interesting. . . ." And Jonathan Culler may remind us that some indeterminists sincerely believe they are being "scientific" in trying to dispense with intentionality.

Yet by now it should be clear that despite the variety of its moods, indeterminism as a movement bears implications that are both irrationalist and undemocratic. To be sure, not every indeterminist matches Hartman's sarcasm in speaking of the deteriorating "varnish" and "veneer" of "this ideal of a freemasonry or grand democratic concourse of polyphonic yet pacific persons." But in disparaging the evidential grounds on which scholars and critics can address one another's ideas, indeterminists create a vacuum that can only be filled by cliquish power. A whole department or university operating without regard for independent rules of judgment would be barbaric in principle if not in outward demeanor.

I do not mean to suggest, however, that indeterminists amount to some sinister public force. Even when they write of terror and revolt, it is only in order to strike a modern attitude; no one appears headed from Yale Station to the Finland Station. On the contrary, the indeterminists are for the most part mild-mannered professors who are trying to fend off discouraging thoughts about the waning importance of criticism. They have much in common with those colleagues who greet their movement not with eagerness to test its cogency but with bland, incomprehending gratitude that *something* is still happening within a comatose field. For on one side and the other—that of "philosophical" affectation and that of routine exegesis—assumptions remain largely unexamined. If shopworn ideas about nothingness and meaninglessness are still allowed to pass for breakthroughs in theory, the fault may lie less in our superstars than in ourselves.

Notes

1. How can an indeterminist be a determinist as well? There is no contradiction. Precisely because Fish is dizzied by the consequences of his *authorial* indeterminism, he seeks anchorage in a rigid conception of interpretive communities, whose supposedly lockstep thought patterns—unsupported by a single example—counterbalance the total unknowability he now ascribes to literature. In short, an authoritarian notion comes to the rescue of an anarchic one that has turned unruly.

2. "Although [the "human sciences"] begin by making man an object of knowledge," Culler writes, "these disciplines find, as their work advances, that the self is dissolved as its various functions are ascribed to impersonal systems which operate through it." One would infer from such a sentence that the abolition of the human subject in structuralist thought is effected through empirical discovery rather than by fiat. Yet Culler himself cites testimony to the contrary by Foucault and Lévi-Strauss, who announce, respectively, that man "is only a recent invention . . . a simple fold in our knowledge" and that "The goal of the human sciences is not to constitute man but to dissolve him."

3. Cf. *Structuralist Poetics*, where Culler could still assert that "the range of meanings which a line of verse can bear depends on the fact that numerous other meanings are manifestly impossible." By more recent standards, such a remark reveals a deplorable want of "playfulness."

Works Cited

Culler, Jonathan. 1975. *Structuralist Poetics: Structuralism, Linguistics, and the Study of Literature*. Ithaca: Cornell University Press.

———. 1981. *The Pursuit of Signs: Semiotics, Literature, Deconstruction*. Ithaca: Cornell University Press.

Fish, Stanley E. 1971. *Surprised by Sin: The Reader in* Paradise Lost. New York: St. Martin's.

———. 1981. *Is There a Text in This Class?* Cambridge: Harvard University Press.

Hartman, Geoffrey H. 1980. *Criticism in the Wilderness: The Study of Literature Today*. New Haven: Yale University Press.

———. 1981. *Saving the Text: Literature/Derrida/Philosophy*. Baltimore: Johns Hopkins University Press.

Hirsch, E. D., Jr. 1967. *Validity in Interpretation*. New Haven: Yale University Press.

———. 1976. *The Aims of Interpretation*. Chicago: University of Chicago Press.

8

Dialectical Immaterialism

This essay appeared in The American Scholar *in September 1985. In addition to registering the odd situation of a doctrine that is thriving in the universities and collapsing nearly everywhere else, it makes a serious if preliminary effort to explain both the "survival mechanism" and the evolutionary contours of Marxist theory. Though psychoanalysis enters the argument only tangentially, I conceive of Marxism and Freudianism in parallel terms; see also this book's Introduction (pages xii–xiii) and Chapters Five and Nine, which develop the applicable idea of pseudoscience.*

I

If we ask ourselves which doctrine, since the time of the French Revolution, has proved most consequential for the reshaping of human existence, only one answer is conceivable: it is Marxism. The much-noted decline of that doctrine's appeal in recent decades is equally beyond doubt, as is the principal cause: Marxism retains its hold on the imagination only where it has not yet been put into effect. As Marxist movements have seized power across the world, fundamentally altering both civic and private life and shedding unprecedented quantities of blood,[1] well-informed people who suffer under non-Communist regimes have found it steadily harder to believe in the Marxist promise. For the most part, only disaffected Western intellectuals appear capable of maintaining the faith, and even they are now largely demoralized.

Though it is precisely "intellectual Marxism" that will concern us here, a nonacademic reader might wonder if the phenomenon is still sufficiently common to be worth examining. France, for example, which had been the seedbed of the subtlest and most passionate Marxist thought since the Forties, has turned with a vengeance toward an anti-Marxist mood. By 1979 Vincent Descombes could write of a "complete disappearance [of philosophical Marxism] from the French scene" (Descombes, 129). Germany has its Jürgen Habermas, but by now Habermas has made so many compromises with non-Marxist sociology that it is hard to say just what is Marxist about his thought. As for England, no one can read the recent polemics of E. P. Thompson (1978) and Perry Anderson (1984) without gathering that a terminal exasperation with vanguard Marxism lies at hand. And according to Martin Jay in his monumental *Marxism and Totality* (1984), a book I will draw upon at length,[2] the American "generation of 1968" has largely lost its initial enthusiasm for the Marxist vision (Jay, 19+n.). Another sympathetic and knowledgeable observer, Walter L. Adamson, now flatly declares that "Marxism as a political ideology is dead" (Adamson, 1).

Yet when we turn to the Anglo-American academy and take note of prevailing approaches to cultural study, we find a completely different picture—in Herbert Lindenberger's words, a "general resurgence of Marxist thought during the last two decades" (Lindenberger, 19). In part this revival has consisted of explicit methodological theorizing, whereby principles of historical materialism are recommended for essential understanding of movements and works of art. Such theory, as we will see in a representative example, has adapted itself to an "advanced" philosophical climate and is now considered subtle and profound by many academic readers, who tend on the whole to be less demanding than modern Marxist intellectuals themselves have been.

Further, influential departments in several fields of study have begun to practice what I will call Left Eclecticism, a welcoming of many styles of anti-establishment analysis—not just orthodox Marxist but also structuralist, deconstructionist, feminist, gay, Lacanian, Foucauldian, and assorted combinations of these. The heart of Left Eclecticism is an understanding, ultimately borrowed from the Marxist ethos, that analytic and theoretic discourse is to be judged primarily by the evident radicalism of its stance. The schools of thought thus favored make sharply divergent claims, yet all of them set themselves against allegedly repressive Western institutions and practices. In dealing with a given painting, novel, or piece of architecture, especially one dating from the capitalist era, they do not aim primarily to show the work's character or governing idea. The goal is rather to subdue the work through aggressive demystification—for example, by positing its socioeconomic determinants and ideological implications, scanning it for any encouraging signs of subversion, and then judging the result against an ideal of total freedom. That, in essence, is the Marxist path. Thus we could say that the adversary Marxist animus, which long predated the other schools that make up Left Eclecticism, has perpetuated itself within them.

On one level it is easy enough to guess why academic Marxism has been flourishing. Thanks to the "post-Vietnam" sentiment that continues to flood the universities and is now the conventional wisdom of the younger professoriate, academics have felt reluctant to question too closely any program that appears to "side with the people"; and though Marxism itself may be tainted by its record, Marxists have always known how to borrow energy and legitimacy from fresher movements than their own. But if we want to understand "methodological Marxism" more critically—to see why it takes the form that it does and how seriously its claims deserve to be regarded—we need to situate it both philosophically and, as it were, emotionally within the evolution of Marxist thought. To do so will require some disorienting leaps between very general reflections, biography, and a necessarily sketchy introduction to Marxist academicism. My aim will not be to prove anything but rather to propose a framework for making sense of discourse that most uninitiated readers would otherwise find impenetrable.

Marxism, I will argue, has been beset from the beginning by unfruitful and intractable contradictions, and its modern adherents have felt obliged to keep diluting and occluding their claims in response to objections and untoward events. The result is that the doctrine has arrived in the universities by political default yet, through the very process of forced etherealization, has acquired a labyrinthine quality that suits a certain academic cast of mind. At the same time, the political inertness of "methodological" Marxism virtually guarantees that its vogue will be short-lived. To comprehend this phenomenon in relation to its antecedents, then, is also necessarily to begin speculating about its probable aftermath.

II

The first thing to be understood about Marxism as a total system is that, in order to inspire passionate belief, it does not have to be even approximately correct in its assertions about the world. This is because Marxism constitutes the supreme example of what Michael Polanyi defined as a *dynamo-objective coupling*—that is, a quasi-religious doctrine purporting to be at once scientifically accurate and morally urgent. In Polanyi's words, "Alleged scientific assertions, which are accepted as such because they satisfy moral passions, will excite these passions further, and thus lend increased convincing power to the scientific affirmations in question—and so on, indefinitely" (Polanyi, 230). The fact that no coherent intellectual link can be established between the moral and scientific kinds of appeal is awkward for Marxist philosophers but ideal for survival of the doctrine. Any refutation of its scientific pretensions can be parried with a moral thrust: "Yes, but we cannot turn our backs on the exploited masses." And any debunking of the moral record can be checked through further recourse to science: "Yes, but we are dealing with impersonal laws of history here." Such doubleness enhances Marxism's ability to weather unpropitious decades, busying itself with analytic niceties and internal housekeeping, and then to emerge with fresh zeal when the international Left is once again visibly on the march. Thus a Marxist intellectual can grant nearly every defect in his tradition and yet cling to it tenuously for its apparent wholeness as a *Weltanschauung*.

The negative side of this picture is that Marxism, precisely because it is emotionally resistant to disconfirmation, can never shake itself free of the wishful thinking that vitiated Marx's own ingenious feats of analysis. We know, of course, that every one of Marx's major prophecies—the spread of the northern European model of production throughout the world, the progressive immiseration and radicalization of the proletariat, the decline of nationalism and religious zeal as potent historical factors, the inability of capitalism to swerve from a suicidal course, the aptitude of Communism for improving upon market mechanisms for efficient production and distribution of goods, and the gradual disappearance of the state in collectivist societies—has by now been confuted. What is less well appreciated, at least by modern Marxists, is that such failure was virtually guaranteed by Marx's insistence on regarding history in morally polarized terms—a tendency that time and disappointment have done nothing to diminish within his movement.

Simply to say that Marxism has had trouble characterizing the world with adequate objectivity, however, is to miss the theory's own impact on events. Marx's historical determinism both over-looked *and abetted* the freedom of leftist dictators to put their ide-ology and their whims into immediate and momentous action, quite irrespective of "means of production" or "evolution of class con-sciousness." By propagating a "scientific" eschatological romance—the destined final victory of the proletariat—Marx saddled his movement with an enduring bloody-mindedness about the rela-tion of means to ends. Since history was headed toward the prom-ised goal, custodians of the revolutionary state could conceive of their task as the helpful clearing away of human impediments ("class enemies"). In addition, the idea of bringing about not only distributive justice but also a correct form of consciousness that must be manifested by all survivors of the revolution has opened the citizen's mind as well as his conduct to inspection, punishment, and reconstruction.

Judging from the course of Marxist controversy, one suspects that it is too much to expect of Left theorists that they will purge Marx's claims of such incitements to savagery. Theorists who have seriously tried to do so—for example, Max Horkheimer, Mau-rice Merleau-Ponty, and Lucio Colletti—have ended by renouncing Marxism itself, for they came to see that Marx's Manichean anni-hilationism was not an accidental by-product of his "science" but rather was its very engine. But the loyal Marxist is precisely some-one who identifies *himself* with an ordained class of people to whom "history" has granted extra liberties, and thus he will be unlikely to recognize that the theory is undemocratic and mischie-vous in its essence. Instead, he will appease his conscience by blaming "the capitalists" for thwarting history's wishes and goad-ing the international Left into regrettable overreactions.

It is important to recognize, however, that the Western Marx-ist tradition has had its own version of intellectual scrupulousness, consisting of efforts to render the doctrine better able to withstand historical surprises. If, for example, a proletarian revolution—the very centerpiece of Marxism as originally conceived—now appears chimerical, Marxists will feel compelled to cast about for a new "proletariat" (blacks, women, indigenous tribes) or to relocate the revolutionary principle in a domain that will be less accessible to prying doubters—for example, in the persecuted but irrepressible libido. Such was the influential direction chosen by Herbert Mar-cuse. Again, if Marxist theory is shown to be internally contradic-tory, a theorist can riposte by calling logic itself into question, stigmatizing the nondialectical choice between exclusive alternatives as an instrument of the abominated ruling class. And similarly, if a theorist finds himself on the brink of admitting that his doctrine is flatly contrary to available evidence, as a last resort he can even deny that "evidence" and "truth" are epistemologically applicable notions. This in brief is how Marxism has come to be entangled, through Habermas and others, with the hermeneutic school of philosophy.

It would be a gross simplification, however, to depict the Marxist tradition as proceeding in a straight line from Marx's epistemological assurance to such a fragile state. As we will now observe in narrowing our focus to two quintessentially representative Western Marxists, the emotional commitments that require "Marxism"—whatever it is—to survive the theorist's exercises in recrimination and autocritique impart a pendulumlike motion to Left debate. If one theorist gives us a "humanist" Marxism, another, detecting a suspiciously bourgeois flavor in such a concoction, will be sure to declare it inauthentic and call instead for a dry "scientific" Marxism, one that restores the seeming rigor of dialectical materialism. And both parties will be able to cite Marx himself as their ally, for Marx's career passed from one extreme to the other and was rich in ambiguities at every period. It is only when the potential Marxes have been completely actualized—when there is little further to be said in the quarrel between Marxist humanism and Marxist scientism, and both traditions appear equally futile—that theorists feel tempted to retain their doctrine at the extreme price of dropping its reference to a solid world. The only setting in which such ghostly Marxism can flourish is the academy, a kind of heaven for concepts that have slipped their earthly moorings.

III

If Western Marxism can be identified as the tradition of theory that attempts to make adjustments between Marx's vision and the disappointments of actual history, then the paradigmatic Western Marxist was unquestionably the Hungarian Georg Lukács. In *History and Class Consciousness* (1923) Lukács made a fatefully ingenious attempt to abolish, through metaphysical prestidigitation, the newly apparent chasm between Marx's historical laws and the triumph of Bolshevism. Lukács realized that Lenin had achieved his spectacular results through opportunistic feats of will that were nowhere anticipated in *Capital*—feats that appeared in fact to refute the mature Marx's whole necessitarian outlook. Moreover, in the years when *History and Class Consciousness* was being composed, the model of government by workers' soviets, to which Lukács among other Marxist intellectuals was passionately committed, was rapidly giving way to a brutal centralism. In these awkward circumstances, Lukács's way of trying to be constructive was to accord the newly omnipotent Party a philosophical warrant for its caretaker role. To do so without a sense of self-betrayal, he felt compelled to invoke as his explanatory framework the quasi-mystical Hegelian voluntarism that Marx himself had largely outgrown.

In this anti-scientific and utopian perspective, history was neither a sum of discrete events nor the operation through time of impersonal laws, but rather a process of self-realization, a coming-to-consciousness of a collective subject. Lukács identified that subject with just one class, the proletariat, which had been "objectified" through the capitalist fetishizing of social relations ("reification") but which would eventually arrive at full self-awareness. Such an awakening would not so much accompany the worldwide revolution as constitute it, and that revolution in turn would *be* history in its "totality"—that is, its complete realization. Meanwhile, since even in Russia large segments of the actual working class were far from understanding or desiring the completion of history, the proletariat's consciousness would have to be prompted and its agency temporarily supplanted by a knowing vanguard—the Communist party. The Party was to be a trustee for the proletariat while the latter was learning to deserve its destiny.

The enormous influence of this argument is not easy for an outsider to fathom. In the first place, Lukács's contentions about history and the proletariat were patent illusions. As Adamson asks, "How could it ever have been supposed that the proletariat was history's creator-subject when it has appeared only in the past one hundred years? How has Lukács, himself no proletarian, managed to gain knowledge of 'proletarian knowledge'? Or is Lukács's proletariat merely his personal fantasy, an abstract negation of the reified world?" (Adamson, 117). More ominously, we can now see that the tutelary role that Lukács granted the Communist party, not without agonized misgivings, amounted to a philosophical blank check for any future deeds the Party might see fit to perpetrate.

The biographical aftermath of *History and Class Conscious-*

ness is itself an important element in Lukács's legacy. Aided by the Comintern, which had no use for Hegelian speculators and which denounced his book as "idealist," Lukács himself realized that his argument had been cosmetic. Stalin's accession to power and withdrawal into the ruthlessly anti-revolutionary policy of "socialism in one country" brought Lukács to a crossroads. Instead of indulging in further messianic daydreams about the proletariat, he would simply have to choose between the Party and his ideals. Lukács picked the former and lived out a long career that was literally and spiritually "in the East," offering to his fellow Marxists in the West the spectacle of a gifted and cultivated thinker trying to stomach the literary bureaucrats' "socialist realism" and applauding Soviet power plays, only drawing the line at the invasion and reconquest of his own native Hungary in 1956.

Lukács, then, lent impetus to Western Marxism not only by reintroducing the Hegelian-idealist dimension but also by becoming in his own person a cautionary example. Clearly, new ways had to be found to shield Marxist theory not only against disconfirmation but also against the power of Communist parties to compel obedience from the theorists themselves. It was inevitable that Lukács would find an opposite number—someone who would stand the Lukácsian system on its head and call the result a purer Marxism, though in fact he was furthering Lukács's own work of hedging Marx's claims. This person proved to be the leading French structuralist Marxist, Louis Althusser, who doubly merits our attention because he happens to have decisively influenced present-day academic Marxist theory in England and America.

In the 1960s Althusser devised an exceptionally elaborate doctrine that was intended to rebuke both the independent Marxist humanists (Lukács, Gramsci, Korsch, Sartre) and the orthodox champions of "economism" (Engels, Plekhanov, Kautsky, Stalin) for having succumbed to the temptation of "expressive totality"— the idea that all social, economic, and political features under a given dispensation reflect a single controlling principle. Althusser insisted that ideology and political conduct, for example, could develop somewhat independently of one another and that the social formation as a whole therefore deserved to be understood piecemeal, according to the specific "nonsynchronous" structures that make it up. Those structures, though deeply related, were not the properties of individual subjects or of a Hegelian metasubject; on the contrary, "subjects" were virtual fictions constituted *by* structures and were therefore not to be considered primary historical agents.

In developing this emphasis Althusser had several aims in mind. First, he sought to explain Stalinism without discrediting Marxism itself. That is, Stalin's misdeeds, now that Khrushchev's revelations had made them notorious, could be treated as atavisms from an earlier stage of development—as "capitalist" or even "feudalist" crimes. That was a convenient (though hypocritical) vantage for continuing to assert the virtues of socialist man. Second, Althusser wanted to establish a degree of autonomy for theory itself. As an unwavering member of the French Communist party, which still retained the Zhdanovite mentality that had recently obliged French intellectuals to align their thought with Stalin's Lysenkoism, Althusser hoped to persuade Party leaders that the loyal intellectual should be left free to work out the deep implications of Marxist laws. And third, Althusser wanted to use that freedom to reground Marxism in a rigorous, scientifically precise understanding of Marx's most important texts, which he taught his followers to read in a protostructuralist (nonsubjective and non-"expressive") spirit.

When Althusser invoked science, we must understand, he had in mind nothing so potentially unwieldy as inductivist empiricism. His conception echoed that of his teacher Gaston Bachelard, who had maintained that science is constituted precisely by its break with experience and that scientific concepts thus live out a life of their own, dictated by an internal logic. This view, far from uncommon in France, enabled Althusser to claim that a given science—dialectical materialism, for example—could be judged only by criteria already contained in its own theoretical discourses. And thus liberated from empirical scruples, he went on to draw extravagant parallels between the structure of ideology and that of the personal unconscious as it had been described by his sometime psychoanalyst and fellow anti-empiricist, Jacques Lacan. Indeed, he modeled his briefly famous "return to Marx" on Lacan's Saussurean "return to Freud," which purported to strip psychoanalysis of all bourgeois accommodationist elements while lending the most radical (and debatable) Freudian concepts a previously undreamt-of linguistic construction. In short, Althusser's alleged science of purified Marxism became an amalgam of uncorroborated notions from modish sources.

From our standpoint here, as we look ahead to a purely academic Marxism, the other crucial aspect of Althusser's doctrine was the high valuation it placed on theory itself. In Marxism generally, theory had always been tolerated as a necessary device for exposing the underlying nature and operation of capitalism; but theory was ultimately esteemed for its effects on practice, not for its own sake, and under classlessness it would be wholly subsumed within the communal organization of life. Althusser, however, laid emphasis on the permanent need for ideological propositions as means of generating social consent. Thus he not only pleaded for the relative autonomy of present-day theory but also envisioned the "scientific" theorist—the only truly knowing member of the polity— as retaining a cardinal role under Communism. Indeed, he saw fit to designate theory-making as a mode of production in its own right, and he implicitly accorded paramount status to that mode in the revolutionary state. What product, after all, could be more essential than social consent?

Althusser's many troubles, however, began with this very claim. Lukács, we recall, had replaced the authority of the proletariat with that of the Party—a dangerous exchange, but one that fitted nicely with brute realities. But here was Althusser implying that the best proxy for the ever-lagging proletariat was none other than the Marxist intellectual—in a word, himself. Fellow Marxists hotly charged Althusser not just with egocentrism but with the graver error of having merely inverted vulgar Marxism by collapsing the material base into the cultural superstructure. The charge was sufficiently plausible to force Althusser into making a craven "self-criticism" of his "theoreticist deviation" (Althusser 1976, 105–61). Class struggle, he now claimed to have realized, was after all a privileged referent, not just another signifier; in fact, it was the ultimate yardstick for gauging the correctness of theory.

What really doomed Althusser, however, was not his abortive heresies and unseemly apologies but a misfortune to which Marxist theorists are chronically susceptible. Precisely because they announce universal laws with evanescent political aims in mind, their whole system of thought can be made to look ridiculous by a sudden turn of events. Althusser was emboldened to attack the humanist line of de-Stalinization because it was already under attack from Mao Zedong, whose Cultural Revolution seemed to pose an attractively democratic alternative to the Soviet model of industrial development at any cost in suffering. When the Paris students took to the streets in 1968, many of them had both Mao and Althusser in mind. But Althusser hadn't had *them* in mind, and their scorn for the "conservative" Communist party and their defiance of its discipline mortified him. His subsequent silence led some of them (most notably Régis Debray) to denounce him from the Left, and others (the *nouveaux philosophes*) to turn sharply against Communism in its entirety—as Debray himself eventually did.

By the end of the Sixties scarcely anyone, including the ungrateful Party, was left to share Althusser's peculiar ideological niche. And in the Seventies the word began to leak out that Mao's Cultural Revolution had been an orgy of irrational persecution and a momentous setback for Chinese social development. In the whole Communist world no viable model remained for Althusser's pedantically fundamentalist yet fanciful "return to Marx." Well before he tragically lost his reason in 1980, Althusser's philosophy had become an embarrassment throughout the Western Left.

To a connoisseur of internecine Marxist disputation, Lukács and Althusser represent opposite ends of a spectrum that runs between "humanistic" and "scientific" extremes. Yet such a contrast is not finally very impressive. Lukács's humanism consisted in his invoking an early Hegelian Marx so as to make conceptual and ethical room for the Soviet Communist party, which even in 1923 was not noted for its humanistic bent. And Althuser's scientism was enlisted in a comparably gratuitous effort to find in Marx's writings an irrefutable basis for a scheme of analysis that was pseudoscientific at best. Both thinkers were involved in the same grim comedy of trying to justify theory itself—really, to justify a loyal-but-independent intellectual class—in the eyes of a Communist party which demanded conformity pure and simple. From a non- or anti-Communist perspective, the one truly significant difference between Lukács and Althusser would appear to be that the latter, forty years farther into the age of Left bureaucracy and terror, felt more at home with essentially static structures and apparatuses than with means of progressive change.

IV

If, as we are told, Western Marxism is now in general retreat, we might expect the Marxist theorizing that finds its way into the Anglo-American academy to be a humble and tentative affair. Among the more conscientious radical professoriate, that is indeed the case.

The atmosphere of Left Eclecticism, however, encourages wanton posturing. Under that dispensation, and more particularly in the absence of the passé assumption that theories are supposed to account for data more parsimoniously and cogently than their rivals, a Marxist academic need only skirt the classic dilemmas of his tradition—making sure, however, to identify his claims as avant-garde in provenance and affinity—to gain a place at the banquet table of radical pan-theoreticism.

Surprisingly, moreover, the confinement of Marxism within a methodological context turns out to be the perfect tonic for a doctrine whose combined implausibility and apocalyptic ferocity were earning it such a bad name in the larger world. In the United States at least, Marxism as a mere "hermeneutic" takes on a conservative function that everyone tacitly recognizes. Instead of being an incitement to insurrection, it is now just one of the work stations in the assembly line that produces articles, books, degrees, and promotions, thus ensuring the Marxist theorist's own continued livelihood and repute. And precisely because the methodological Marxist can be considered harmless, he can choose to reassert the heedless, inspiring utopianism that mortifies more troubled spokesmen of the Left.

To see such born-again yet anemic Marxism at close range and to grasp its place in the new academic order, let me turn now to my own field, literary study, and focus on a single manifesto that is often cited as a powerful overview and methodological guide: *The Political Unconscious: Narrative as a Socially Symbolic Act* (1981). There can be little doubt that its author, Fredric Jameson, is the most eminent Marxist literary theorist alive. After a cautious start in summarizing and explaining other Marxists' and structuralists' ideas (1971, 1972), Jameson, who has taught on three University of California campuses and at Yale and now holds a chair at Duke, made his greatest impact with *The Political Unconscious*, which one knowledgeable observer has dubbed "a *summa marxologica* for our time" (LaCapra, 83). Jameson is considered so weighty that, among other honors, a special issue of the methodologically rarefied journal *Diacritics* has addressed the import of his thought ("Fredric Jameson"); and one admirer, William C. Dowling, has devoted a whole book, *Jameson, Althusser, Marx* (1984), to unraveling the mysteries of *The Political Unconscious*.

The reason for all this acclaim cannot be found in the originality of Jameson's thought. As Dowling recognizes, the main idea behind *The Political Unconscious* "had been outlined by Terry Eagleton some five years before," and the book "turns to productive and, often, pyrotechnical use the systems of such thinkers as A. J. Greimas, Northrop Frye, Hans-Georg Gadamer, and Claude Lévi-Strauss" (Dowling, 14)—a list that could be considerably lengthened.[3] Above all, Jameson's interpretive framework—most obviously the neo-Lacanian idea of unconscious ideology and the invocation of "structural causality" to reconcile Marxist and post-Marxist perspectives—is largely borrowed from the Althusser who had not yet been induced by the Party to confess his ideological sins.[4]

From a Marxist standpoint Jameson has nothing to add to Eagleton's *Criticism and Ideology* (1976), a book whose argument foundered in the Althusserian maelstrom of jumbled determinism and autonomy.[5] Tonally, however, Jameson leaves his rival far behind. In the first place, he has mastered the Parisian manner of stating the most high-handed claims as if they were self-evident. Yet at the same time, his ceremonious prose reassures us that we are reading a fellow academic, someone who is preoccupied by complexities that will require the most exquisite adjudication. Unlike Eagleton, then, Jameson does not incur the risk of being too easily comprehended. As Dowling would have us acknowledge, for Jameson "the plain style is the limpid style of bourgeois ideology where there is no need for obscurity because all truths are known in advance. . . . A genuinely Marxist style, then, will be one that produces what Jameson calls . . . 'dialectical shock.' . . . As Jameson also says, a dialectical style is one that makes you hear the shifting of the world's gears as you read" (Dowling, 11–12).

Because his radical stance is only rhetorical, Jameson can wave aside all the misgivings that have nagged at Western Marxism from Lukács through Habermas. I gather that he adheres to Althusser not because he feels trapped in the same box as his hero—the Soviet tyranny and the intellectually backward Communist parties seem very distant from his mind—but because he regards Althusser as having forged the most appealing link between Marxism and the other strains of thought that he wishes to appropriate. Thus Jameson combines his own already eclectic Althusserianism with a full-blown Hegelian expressive causality—the very tendency that Althusser did his best to keep at arm's length. The "universal science" (38) of Marxism has revealed to Jameson that history (or, on occasion, "History") bears a simple meaning: the nightmarish yet ultimately triumphant "collective struggle to wrest a realm of Freedom from a realm of Necessity" (19). This meaning then becomes the unwobbling pivot of an otherwise rickety system of interpretation.

Like Marx, Jameson thinks that the realm of Freedom can be found not only in the future but also in the remote prehistoric past, into which he can apparently gaze without hindrance. What he finds there is a sensuous paradise from which we have "fallen" (25) into our present "increasingly dessicated [*sic*] and repressive reality" (237), but to which we will somehow return. In the prelapsarian dawn of the race, Jameson tells us, people lived in such ideal social harmony, without division of labor or distinction between old and young, that they did not even perceive themselves as individuals; in fact, they *weren't* individuals but participants in an unselfconscious oneness with nature. Their senses were exquisitely vivid yet undifferentiated—so that, for example, they were blessedly incapable of the modern "abstraction and rationalization which strips the experience of the concrete of such attributes as color, spatial depth, texture, and the like . . ." (63). Of course they felt no need to indulge in painting or other such protocapitalist arts. As for sex, that too was communal and devoid of stress; the male and female nonindividuals intermingled joyously without kinky repressed desires, possessiveness, or institutional complications.

Although only Marxists, according to Jameson, can fully grasp this blinding vision of plenitude, he asserts that it has been unconsciously intuited throughout the development of capitalism; it is in fact the chief repressed content of all capitalist art. Never mind whose "political unconscious" has been doing the actual psychic work of repressing; Jameson does not pause over such banal questions. The essential methodological point is that, in advance of reading any given narrative, he knows approximately what will be its most significant content—or, in many cases, its anti-content. The heart of the text will always be in some sense the Ur-meaning of History which cannot be directly manifested under capitalist false consciousness.

When no evidence for this ultimate expressive referent turns up, Jameson is more convinced than ever of its ubiquitousness as a repressed Althusserian "structural cause." Thus no possibility remains of his *not* reaching Marxist findings in every act of analysis. This is why he can coolly declare, as if he were remarking that tomorrow will be Thursday, that Marxism constitutes "something like an ultimate *semantic* precondition for the intelligibility of literary and cultural texts" (75). Quite simply, the Jamesonian Marxist perspective is "the absolute horizon of all reading and all interpretation" (17). In fact, Jameson tells us that since Marxist doctrine and final historical meaning are the same thing and since all non-Marxist critics have repressed that fact, every school of interpretation *except* his own is ideological in character.

As Jameson frankly states, he means to "rewrite" each examined novel or play as an allegory of its alleged determinants and of the "modes of production" that he will purport to find sedimented within its "archaic structures of alienation" (100). There is a revealing precedent for such allegory, and Jameson cordially associates himself with it. This is the method that the medieval Fathers of the Church devised for, as he puts it, "rewriting the Jewish textual and cultural heritage in a form usable for Gentiles" (29). Jameson is convinced that we could hardly improve upon this expedient for sweeping aside hermeneutic obstacles to a totalizing faith. Much of *The Political Unconscious* is therefore openly devoted to articulating a modern version of the fourfold patristic method of imperious Christianization, with just one major change: Marxist "History" now stands in Christ's anagogical place as the ultimate sacred referent.[6]

Jameson, then, is such a dogmatist that the entire trajectory of empiricism from Bacon until now would appear to have passed him by. Yet there is obviously something else going on here. If our theorist really expected the rest of the literary academy to lay down its arms and join his allegorical crusade, not even the latitudinarian ethos of Left Eclecticism could make room for him. As Dowling keeps observing appreciatively, however, beneath his surface bluster Jameson is an accommodationist—a "politic" master of the discreet "sidestep" and "flanking maneuver" who "treads lightly" whenever his readers' sensibilities might be wounded by forthrightness (Dowling, 54, 102, 103, 117). Jameson's mission is not to revolutionize but to reconcile by means of a unique *pax Jamesoniana*. To critics of whatever advanced persuasion and to Marxists who are still troubled by the perennial tug-of-war between base and superstructure, he brings a comforting message: we can all get along if we do so on my terms.

As Dowling explains, Jameson's project is to steer "a middle course" (Dowling, 122) between vulgar-Marxist reduction on the one hand and structuralist-poststructuralist decentering on the other. For Jameson, however, a middle course entails ecumenically incorporating extremes rather than avoiding them. His strategy, in Dowling's words, is "to swallow up the enterprises of Derrida, Foucault, et al. by showing that they are incomplete without a theory of history that only Marxism can provide . . ." (Dowling, 13). Such a "completing" of the anti-transcendental poststructuralist program is in actuality a flagrant negation of it. But we are not dealing with logic here—only with priestlike gestures of inclusion.

The Jamesonian interpretive process follows a two-stage recipe whereby potentially antagonistic methods of reduction are made to cooperate serially. First the critic sets about the business of a poststructuralist, catabolizing the superficially intentional-looking literary artifact; then he recycles the denatured remains for Marxist ends. Stage one, Jameson says, finds "its privileged content in rifts and discontinuities within the work, and ultimately in a conception of the former 'work of art' as a heterogeneous and (to use the most dramatic recent slogan) a schizophrenic text" (56). Thus the author, that potential troublemaker who thought he knew what he was doing, is safely bumped aside. Then comes the culminating Marxist stage, which consists of the critic's "rewriting of the literary text in such a way that the latter may be seen as the rewriting or re-structuration of a prior historical or ideological *subtext*" (81)—namely, some variant on the usual homily about History.

Stated so baldly, the process sounds like a job of mugging, but in practice Jameson impregnates it with mystery and drama. He does so by ascribing to the text itself the tensions, rumblings, and convulsions of "wondrous dialectical transfer" (280) whose all too mundane source is his own apparatus for scrambling literature and then retotalizing it on more congenial terms. Rather than just lie there inertly between its covers, the Jamesonian novel or play, somewhat like History itself, keeps suffering electric "moments" and "movements" in which it is seized first by a desire to repress its own latent content—to "demonstrate the impossibility of such representation" (280)—and then by a contrary desire to "tilt . . . powerfully into the underside or *impensé* or *non-dit*, in short, into the very political unconscious . . ." (49). In this performative critical discourse, each successive literary work is required as it were to try its hand at a Fredric Jameson impersonation, first "doing" his Gallic deconstructive voice and then his Teutonic Hegelian one.

In an earlier phase of academic history—say, three decades ago—Jameson's grandiose system would have struck nearly everyone as an eccentric curiosity, a Spruce Goose of theory that succeeds only in occupying inordinate hangar space. Sympathetic contemporary readers, however, understand that Jameson is not really trying and failing to account for commonly recognized features of literature and history. Rather, he is staking out the interpretive liberties he intends to exercise as he jostles with other contenders for Left-Eclectic turf. Thus no one takes offense when he announces that "everything is 'in the last analysis' political" (20), that his own politics are the only thinkable kind, and that he intends to "liberate . . . us from the empirical object . . ." (297)—that is, from the ideologically unsanitized work of literature itself. Other beneficiaries of Left Eclecticism aim to accomplish comparable feats of liberation through the practice of their own interpretive rules.

Ironically, then, the people who are best situated to register the speciousness of Jameson's system are not his fellow professors but rather those remaining Marxists who care about addressing the shortcomings of their moral and intellectual tradition. They know what Jameson chooses to conceal, that the Althusserian scaffolding of his theory had already collapsed well before he patched it back together to impress the gullible belletrists. And insofar as Marxists are troubled, as many are, by the bloody record of Left regimes, they can only take offense at Jameson's studied concentration on our prehistoric communist past and our blissful Communist future. In Dominick LaCapra's words, "the pathos of utopianism in blindingly eschatological form may be understandable coming from members of a destitute and desperate underclass; it is suspect when it emanates from intellectuals as a kind of strained, high-altitude messianism" (LaCapra, 104).

By placing *The Political Unconscious* alongside *History and Class Consciousness*—even the contrast in titles is suggestive—we can gauge how far Marxism has declined in certainty, clarity, and sincerity since Lukács's day. Instead of the anticipated triumph of a specific class which was alleged to be the unified subject-object of history, we now get the merest hints of a soporific Marcusean paradise for all—and no proposed means of arriving there. This is not just the difference between a work of political philosophy and one of literary theory, for Jameson too imagines that he is paving the way for "alliance politics" (54n.) on the American Left. But such politics are extremely remote from the vaporizing of *The Political Unconscious*. The truth is that Jameson has quietly abandoned the whole Western Marxist project of trying to render Marx either more humanistic or more scientific so as to chart a better political course. Since the antinomies lying at the heart of Marxism have been found to be irreducible, Jameson opts to resolve them through the only means yet untried, incantation.

V

Given the atmosphere of Left Eclecticism, the illogic of *The Political Unconscious* cannot be considered a serious handicap. On other grounds, though, Jameson's school and "methodological Marxism" in general may soon find themselves *déclassé*. With *The Political Unconscious* Jameson has completed the Althusserian transfer of focus from allegedly progressive historical forces to the theorist's private capacity to hold intricate structures in his mind—a mind which in Jameson's case has become dubiously fetishized as a collective world-psyche. Comparable feats of projection have long been tolerated in the academy, but not within its Left component. It seems inevitable that advocates of younger and less metaphysically encumbered "isms," particularly those that are tied to one-issue social movements, will find less and less to admire in such narcissistic Marxism.

   Even among those Left academics who prefer analysis to solidarity, the Marxist tradition may already be in grave trouble. Few potential recruits are now eager to be associated either with its blemished utopian ingredients or with the increasingly devious sophistries that are required to spare them from dismissal. Thus the same impatience that overwhelmed French Althusserian Marxism in the Seventies may now be ready to strike down its American academic counterpart. One need not be very observant, for example, to notice the beginnings of an exodus from the camp of Marx to that of the late Michel Foucault, who is also the clear favorite of a new academic generation that cares little for the tortuous history of Marxist apologetics.

   It is a nice question, however, whether Foucauldian analysis arose in order to thwart Marxism or, rather, to save its debunking spirit from its doomed propositional content. Foucault himself, significantly, began as a Marxist and a student of Althusser's; they were both Party members in the dreary Lysenko period and thus, unavoidably, were both questing to free Left discourse from Zhdanovite supervision. Certainly Foucault's ideological wariness—"to imagine another system," he once declared, "is to extend our participation in the present system" (Foucault, 230)—bespeaks a widely shared wish to flee from the scene of the Marxist-utopian debacle. Yet the ever-shifting, self-ironic, and brilliantly original style of analysis that Foucault eventually developed can also be regarded in part as a solipsistic Nietzschean travesty of Marxism.[7]

According to Foucault, power is all-pervasive, "knowledge" is its malleable servant, and "reality" is sheer discourse, organized differently in each era according to *epistemes* or paradigms that are presumed to dictate the very structure of perception and mentation. (Foucault never explained how he himself had managed to slip out from under such determinism.) The idea of a succession, within capitalist Europe, of discrete and increasingly sinister epistemes allowed Foucault to exercise the Marxists' own appetite for antagonistic explanation without the awkwardness of having to identify a specific class of exploiters, to say how they had learned the means of manipulating or minds for their unstated purposes, or to engage in risky predictions about a better future.

Again, Foucault retained the Marxist privileging of the Left intelligentsia's unique insight, but by declining to call that insight veridical he endeared himself to people who could no longer swallow Althusser's scientific pretensions, much less Lukács's personification of truth in the proletariat-to-be. Declaring that intellectual activity has nothing to do with truth—or, in a more radical moment, that such activity is "sacrificial, directed against truth" (Foucault, 160)—Foucault resolved the theory-practice dilemma altogether on the side of practice. Thus, when asked whether history "really" displayed the features he claimed for it, he could deem the question moot; his purpose, he insisted, had not been to make accurate statements but merely to manifest his unstinting resistance to the entire order of things. Indeed, if he had tried to tell the truth he would have been acceding to what he considered the most insidiously tyrannical feature of that order, its demand for Cartesian objectivity. By combining such nihilism with activism—he privately worked for prison reform and gay rights—Foucault turned himself into the model antihegemonic leftist, one whose long-term program was immune to disappointment because, so far as anyone could tell, it did not exist.

In Foucault and his emulators, then, we witness not only a decisive turn away from Marxist expressive causality—a turn we can welcome in itself—but also an intensification of the Marxist blurring of thought and action. It was Marxism, remember, that first taught modern intellectuals to be cynical toward the notion of seeking knowledge for its own sake. From Marx's insistence on valuing ideas for their capacity to change the world, through Gramsci's belief that "[m]ass adherence or non-adherence . . . is the real test of the rationality and historicity of modes of thinking . . ." (Gramsci, 341), to Althusser's grudging avowal that philosophy is "class struggle in the field of theory" (Althusser 1976, 37) and Jameson's eager endorsement of that same dictum (Jameson 1981, 12), Marxism has urged us to allot considerations of truth a place below our instrumental goals. Foucault merely carried that principle a step further, suggesting that the most purehearted leftist is the one who remains totally unaccountable either to truth or to the Left itself. In Foucault, perhaps, we are looking at the Marxist to end all Marxists.

Notes

1. Though the toll can never be more than approximately tallied, it is certain that the Soviet Union, in the first four decades of its existence, established itself as the bloodiest tyranny in history. In just one episode, Stalin's Great Terror of the later Thirties, some nineteen million Soviet citizens were done away with. One observer estimates that deliberate state policies have resulted in eighty million internal deaths since 1917 (Antonov-Ovseyenko)—and this is to leave the rest of the "socialist" world out of account.

2. I am also indebted to the cited works by Adamson and Callinicos, though my point of view is quite different from theirs.

3. Elsewhere Dowling avers that Jameson "has been anticipated" by Althusser; that "there is a parallel" between Jameson and Lacan, who "has made Jameson's point more available to us"; and that Jameson's notion of the ideologeme "participates in" the Foucauldian episteme (Dowling, 55–56, 56, 34, 132–33). What Dowling means is that Jameson has appropriated some of those thinkers' heterogeneous ideas while analogizing from others.

4. An informed reader could also find symptomatic interest in Jameson's waffling over Althusser's Stalinist leanings (39) and his queasy half-endorsement of Althusser's favorite movement, the "incomplete" (95) Chinese Cultural Revolution, which a few years earlier he had embraced more cordially as "the rich collective innovations of the Chinese experience" (Jameson 1977, 394).

5. For a penetrating critique, see Gallagher.

6. Jameson even carries the Church Fathers' approach to knowledge beyond the domain of texts, maintaining in his *summa marxologica* that Christianity itself and "the pretheological systems of primitive magic" must be understood as "anticipatory foreshadowings of historical materialism" (285). Not even the most mystically inclined of previous Marxists ever dared to advance such a quaintly anti-intellectual contention.

7. For especially keen insight into Foucault's playfulness, see Megill.

Works Cited

Adamson, Walter L. 1984. *Marx and the Disillusionment of Marxism.* Berkeley: University of California Press.

Althusser, Louis. 1976. *Essays in Self-Criticism,* trans. Grahame Lock. London: New Left Books.

Anderson, Perry. 1985. *In the Tracks of Historical Materialism.* Chicago: University of Chicago Press.

Antonov-Ovseyenko, Anton. 1980. *The Time of Stalin: Portrait of a Tyranny.* New York: Harper & Row.

Callinicos, Alex. 1982. *Is There a Future for Marxism?* London: Macmillan.

———. 1983. *Marxism and Philosophy.* Oxford: Clarendon.

Descombes, Vincent. 1980. *Modern French Philosophy,* trans. L. Scott-Fox and J. M. Harding. Cambridge: Cambridge University Press.

Dowling, William C. 1984. *Jameson, Althusser, Marx: An Introduction to* The Political Unconscious. Ithaca: Cornell University Press.

Eagleton, Terry. 1976. *Criticism and Ideology: A Study in Marxist Literary Tradition.* London: Atlantic Highlands/Humanities.

Foucault, Michel. 1977. *Language, Counter-Memory, Practice: Selected Essays and Interviews,* ed. Donald F. Bouchard; trans. Donald F. Bouchard and Sherry Simon. Ithaca: Cornell University Press.

"Fredric Jameson—The Political Unconscious." 1982. *Diacritics,* Special Issue. Vol. 12, no. 3.

Gallagher, Catherine. 1980. "The New Materialism in Marxist Aesthetics." *Theory and Society,* 9: 633–646.

Gramsci, Antonio. 1971. *Selections from the Prison Notebooks,* ed. and trans. Quintin Hoare and Geoffrey Nowell Smith. New York: International Publishers.

Jameson, Fredric. 1971. *Marxism and Form: Twentieth-Century Dialectical Theories of Literature.* Princeton: Princeton University Press.

———. 1972. *The Prison-House of Language: A Critical Account of Structuralism and Russian Formalism.* Princeton: Princeton University Press.

———. 1977. "Imaginary and Symbolic in Lacan: Marxism, Psychoanalytic Criticism, and the Problem of the Subject." *Yale French Studies,* 55–56: 338–395.

———. 1981. *The Political Unconscious: Narrative as a Socially Symbolic Act.* Ithaca: Cornell University Press.

Jay, Martin. 1984. *Marxism and Totality: The Adventures of a Concept from Lukács to Habermas.* Berkeley: University of California Press.

LaCapra, Dominick. 1982. Review of Fredric Jameson, *The Political Un-conscious. History and Theory,* 21, no. 1: 83–106.

Lindenberger, Herbert. 1984. "Toward a New History in Literary Study." *Profession 84.* New York: Modern Language Association. Pp. 16–23.

Megill, Allan. 1985. *Prophets of Extremity: Nietzsche, Heidegger, Foucault, Derrida.* Berkeley: University of California Press.

Polanyi, Michael. 1964. *Personal Knowledge: Towards a Post-Critical Philosophy. New York:* Harper Torchbooks.

Thompson, E. P. 1978. *The Poverty of Theory and Other Essays.* New York: Monthly Review Press.

9

The Grand Academy of Theory

This chapter, the most recently written one, grew out of an opportunity to review a collection of essays intriguingly called The Return of Grand Theory in the Human Sciences. *My essay became a general assessment of "theoreticism," the most notable—and, I believe, the most noxious—change in academic intellectual style over the past quarter-century. "The Grand Academy of Theory" appeared in* The New York Review of Books *in May 1986.*

It has been more than a quarter-century now since C. P. Snow first told us that we educated Anglo-Americans belong to two mutually uncomprehending and antagonistic cultures, one scientific and the other humanistic. In 1959, with the beeping of Sputnik still echoing in the public ear, no one expected Snow to accord the two camps equal sympathy, and he did not. The forbidding technical intricacy of the sciences, he declared in *The Two Cultures and the Scientific Revolution*, was hardly a sufficient reason for humanists to turn their backs on science, retreating into spiteful ignorance and misrepresentation. Nonscientists grumbled under Snow's tongue-lashing, but many of them secretly agreed with the consensus that they had better mend their ways. Certainly it would have been an unpropitious moment for anyone to launch a major counteroffensive against scientific authority.

That episode came to mind as I was reading the Cambridge political scientist Quentin Skinner's introduction to a collection of essays by various hands on influential recent thinkers, portentously titled *The Return of Grand Theory in the Human Sciences* (Skinner 1985; hereafter *RGT*). Snow's name is never invoked, but the idea of the two estranged cultures pervades Skinner's introduction, which spells out for us how radically the academic mood has altered. Moreover, Skinner begins his story just around the time that Snow's polemic appeared.

In those days, we are reminded, the most prestigious general model of explanation was logical positivism, the view that the meaningfulness of a statement is vouchsafed by its testability. Judged by that criterion, much of what had long passed for important discourse had to be dismissed as vacuous. Consequently, a generation of no-nonsense philosophers abandoned metaphysics for more modest pursuits, including, for example, clarification of the exact meaning of scientific terms. Social scientists, caught in the same wave, declared an "end of ideology" and steeled themselves to perceive only narrow empirical issues. And historians followed Sir Lewis Namier in rejecting all theoretical "flapdoodle," as he had called it, and in fixing their attention on "the detailed manoeuvres of individual political actors at the centres of political power" (RGT, 3). Thus, while most academics may have been as scientifically illiterate as Snow alleged, their own work implicitly honored what they took to be the heart of science, namely, deference to the almighty fact.

But by now, Skinner reports, a dramatic change has occurred. Among recent "general transformations" in the "human sciences,"[1] "perhaps the most significant has been the widespread reaction against the assumption that the natural sciences offer an adequate or even a relevant model for the practice of the social disciplines. The clearest reflection of this growing doubt has been the revival of the suggestion that the explanation of human behaviour and the explanation of natural events are logically distinct undertakings . . ." (RGT, 6). Thus,

> During the past generation, Utopian social philosophies have once again been practised as well as preached; Marxism has revived and flourished in an almost bewildering variety of forms; psychoanalysis has gained a new theoretical orientation with the work of Lacan and his followers; Habermas and other members of the Frankfurt School have continued to reflect on the parallels between the theories of Marx and Freud; the Women's Movement has added a whole range of previously neglected insights and arguments; and amidst all this turmoil the empiricist and positivist citadels of English-speaking social philosophy have been threatened and undermined by successive waves of hermeneuticists,

structuralists, post-empiricists, deconstructionists and other invading hordes. (*RGT*, 5–6)

Anyone who has been close to the Anglo-American humanities
and social sciences in recent decades will know what Skinner is
talking about here. The paragraph, however, is arresting as an
index both to the feelings stirred by its subject matter and to a
resultant confusion in *RGT*. A quick reading could give the impression that Skinner is caught up in the irresistible energy of an
ascendant movement, but his choice of language points elsewhere:
to bewilderment, turmoil, threats, underminings, successive waves,
invading hordes. Skinner sounds rather like a hostage on video-
tape, assuring the folks at home that he is being exposed to a lively
new slant on things, meanwhile signaling with grimaces, *These
people mean business!*

This mixed impression deepens when we realize that the "invading hordes," clearly of uppermost concern to Skinner, are only
spottily represented by the nine figures treated in the volume he
has edited: Hans-Georg Gadamer, Jacques Derrida, Michel Foucault, Thomas Kuhn, John Rawls, Jürgen Habermas, Louis Althusser, Claude Lévi-Strauss, and Fernand Braudel.[2] What, for example,
do Marxists, Freudians, feminists, and deconstructionists have to
do with Gadamer, the tradition-minded seeker of interpretive certainty, or with Rawls, the Kantian ethical philosopher who deduces
rules of justice from an imagined social contract, or with Braudel,
the student of geographic necessities that transcend and outlast all
linguistic networks? Why, on the other hand, are such idolized system builders as Jacques Lacan and Gilles Deleuze not afforded
chapters of their own? Lacan is mentioned only in passing, Deleuze
not at all. One wonders if Skinner wants to allay his doubts about
the "invading hordes" by putting them into the most respectable
company he can find.

Not surprisingly, some of the contributors to *RGT* appear less
than comfortable with Skinner's vague notion of Grand Theory.
Thus Barry Barnes deems it "ironical" to include Thomas Kuhn,
whose "mental universe could scarcely be more distant from that
of Althusser, or even Habermas" (*RGT*, 98). And Mark Philp observes that Michel Foucault's presence in the book "might seem
paradoxical," since "his work is above all iconoclastic in intent"
(*RGT*, 67). Skinner himself perceives this latter problem, confessing that it "may well sound dangerously like missing the point" to

characterize as grand theorists those extreme relativists who seek "to demolish the claims of theory and method to organize the materials of experience" (*RGT*, 12).

This anomaly remains in place after Skinner has lamely tried to banish it, first by claiming that iconoclasm is itself Grand Theory, then by calling its *influence* grand, and finally by hazarding that the iconoclasts at any rate "cleared the ground" (*RGT*, 13) for other thinkers who have reopened such classic topics as "the character of the good life and the boundaries of a free and just society" (*RGT*, 14). Here we are apparently being invited to imagine that a figure like Rawls must have been made possible by groundbreakers like Derrida and Foucault. But even a surface acquaintance with the latter pair would show the absurdity of such a suggestion. If Derrida and Foucault lead anywhere, it is not to social contracts and laws of human nature but to a ban on recourse to such flagrantly bourgeois concepts.

As a set of introductions to important figures, *RGT* is a sober and useful work, distinguished for the most part by clarity, fairmindedness, and bibliographical helpfulness. In one contribution, James Boon's on Lévi-Strauss, it passes beyond utility to significant insight and eloquence. But as a case for a specific return of Grand Theory within determinate limits of time and place, the book is drastically fuzzy. It cannot even make up its collective mind about the meaning of its basic terms or the scope of their application.

In France and Germany, the homelands of all but two of the figures treated, modern philosophical and sociopolitical thought never surrendered to positivism and thus never reverted to sweeping speculation. Heidegger and Sartre, for instance, surely had more to say about "grand" issues of human fate than Foucault and Derrida do. If the new movement arrived with, say, Gadamer's *Truth and Method* in 1960, then we must exclude Lévi-Strauss, whose anthropological researches were already under way in the Thirties. And if Braudel is to be counted, Grand Theory began at least as early as 1947, the year that *The Mediterranean* was submitted as a *thèse,* and possibly as far back as 1929, when the *Annales* school of historiography first became known. What kind of "return" would that be?

The editorial muddle behind *RGT* is worsened by a general reluctance to admit that some currents of theoretical enthusiasm are already weakening in their Continental homelands. In one instance, Susan James's chapter on the structuralist Marxist Louis

Althusser, such discretion passes over into apparent disingenuousness. Not only does James fail to report that Althusser's intricately deterministic and top-heavy system of thought has come to be almost universally repudiated in France; she employs the present perfect tense (Althusser "has revised," "has held fast," etc.) to suggest that his position is still being articulated at this hour. But as every "Western Marxist" knows all too well, the curtain rang down on Althusser's career in 1980 when he strangled his wife and was judged mentally incompetent to stand trial. That culminating shock, in Martin Jay's words, "spelled the end [in France] of structuralist Marxism, whose obituary some observers in fact had written as early as 1969" (Jay, 397).

Again, the diffuse idea of Grand Theory obscures a crucial shift of values within the career of Jürgen Habermas, the leading successor to the Frankfurt School, whom Skinner can appreciate only as the harbinger of our brisk Freudian and Marxist renaissance. Anthony Giddens's chapter on Habermas, though competent and informative so far as it goes, is less candid about Habermas's self-oppositions than is a still more recent essay of his (Giddens 1985). In *RGT* Giddens appears to be restrained by the book's kid-gloves decorum and by the group effort to accentuate "grandeur." His newer essay, by contrast, is more attuned to Habermas's dilemma of trying to reconcile traditional intellectual loyalties with a nascent impulse to ideologize knowledge.

For whatever reason, Skinner has confounded two reactions against positivism, one thematic and the other attitudinal, that are only casually and inconsistently related. The first is Grand Theory proper, the addressing of those general ethical and political questions that positivism had declared senseless. The other is a new peremptoriness of intellectual style, emboldening thinkers to make up their own rules of inquiry or simply to turn their whim into law. Such liberation from the empirical ethos can result in Grand Theory, but it can just as easily lead to a relativism that dismisses the whole idea of seeking truth. Skinner has chosen to minimize the fact that one thinker (Rawls, for example) can be "grand" in scope but flexible in intellectual style, whereas another (Derrida, for example) can be "anti-grand" in a way that brooks no dissent.

It seems obvious which of Skinner's themes is the more significant for an understanding of our present intellectual climate. The major shift we have witnessed over the past generation is not a growing taste for big ideas but a growing apriorism—a willingness to settle issues by theoretical decree, without even a pretense of evidential appeal. In 1960 nearly everyone, despite the widening fissure between Snow's two cultures, would have concurred with R. S. Crane's observation that one of the most important marks of the good scholar is "a habitual distrust of the a priori; that is to say, of all ways of arriving at particular conclusions which assume the relevance and authority, prior to the concrete evidence, of theoretical doctrines or other general propositions . . ." (Crane, 29). But today we are surrounded by *theoreticism*—frank recourse to unsubstantiated theory, not just as a tool of investigation but as anti-empirical knowledge in its own right.

To appreciate the theoreticist climate, it is essential to recognize a distinction between two related conceptions of empiricism. Philosophers have used the term in several senses, one of which is a faith in "scientific method" or a "logic of verification"—that is, in the availability of neutral grounds for infallibly showing which of several hypotheses or theories is "closest to the truth." For excellent reasons, belief in that "foundationalist" empiricism has all but vanished in the past twenty years.[3] In a broader sense, however, science remains thoroughly empirical; even its most formalized reasoning is ultimately answerable to the testing of predicted consequences. Thus we both do and don't live in a "post-empiricist" age, depending on which kind of empiricism is intended.

The empiricism that stands in some jeopardy today is simply a regard for evidence—a disposition to consult ascertainable facts when choosing between rival ideas. In practice, of course, the individual investigator never collects enough evidence to guarantee that a given idea is the best one going. Consequently, the heart of empiricism consists of active participation in a community of informed people who themselves care about evidence and who can be counted on for unsparing criticism.

Now, our theoreticists pride themselves on being resolutely "anti-positivist"—that is, opposed to the restriction of meaningfulness to verifiability in the foundationalist or "scientific method" sense. They think of themselves as staving off a persistent threat of positivist incursion upon human studies. But there must be something else going on here, since by now one might have to repair to the graveyard to find an authentic positivist to kick around. What "anti-positivism" really comes down to is a feeling of non-obligation toward empiricism in the broad sense—that is, toward the community that expects theory to stay at least somewhat responsive to demonstrable findings.

In the rhetoric of theoreticism, that community often gets conveniently merged with "science." To be a good contemporary antipositivist, then, is to resist the encroachment of science on human studies—to deny, as Skinner puts it, "that the natural sciences offer [us] an adequate or even a relevant model." This can be done in either of two ways. First, one can *declare the human studies off-limits to scientific rigor* by saying, in Skinner's phrase, that they are "logically distinct" from science. Or, more radically, one can *deny that science itself is really empirical.* Both methods make ample room for willful assertion, but the second, as we will see, leads to more spectacular theoretical claims.

We can observe the first of these strategies at work by looking at the early Habermas's so-called hermeneutic argument for making use of Marxism and psychoanalysis in social thought. According to hermeneutics, science seeks permanent cause-effect relations between physical objects, whereas hermeneutic insight consists of empathy with social-historical actors or with texts. Some hermeneuticists go on to assert that different standards of corroboration therefore apply to the two realms. Habermas's novelty in his first major treatise, *Knowledge and Human Interests* (1968), was to redescribe Marxism and psychoanalysis as *non*scientific so that they could be absolved from empirical scrutiny and employed for utopian speculative ends.

Freud and Marx thought of themselves as scientific lawgivers, of psychic etiology and cure in the one case and of political economy and historical development in the other. Habermas, however, managed to convince himself and quite a few readers that Freud and Marx had made causal claims only through a kind of inadvertence or "scientistic self-misunderstanding." Properly understood, he explained, their visions must be regarded as context-dependent, self-certifying interpretive techniques, or "historical-hermeneutic disciplines." Their justification thus resides not in whatever empirical plausibility they may possess—an issue Habermas unceremoniously swept under the rug—but rather in their capacity to produce experiences of liberating "self-reflection."

In retrospect it seems clear that the acclaim bestowed on this argument owed much to the *Zeitgeist*—the emerging climate of theoreticism—and little to Habermas's reasoning, which was wishful in the extreme. As Adolf Grünbaum has shown, Habermas first misconstrued the bounds of science, wrongly decreeing that any historical phenomenon, such as a patient's therapeutic progress, automatically falls outside the scientific purview. Then he entangled himself in such absurdities as the claim that the *etiological causality* behind a neurotic symptom is rendered void once the symptom has been cured—as if determinism itself, fully efficacious at one early time, could then be retroactively unraveled (Grünbaum, 7–44). In short, Habermas had sacrificed logical cogency to his overriding value in the Sixties, "emancipation."[4]

Nonetheless, we can see that Habermas, whose political evolution soon caused him to begin rethinking the whole liberationist approach to knowledge, had scarcely gotten started down the theoreticist path. He was quite satisfied, for example, with the relatively mild epistemic relativism professed by Marx and Freud. That is, both of those observers faulted the majority for dwelling in occluded consciousness, but they did so—and Habermas approved—in the name of a truer, unrepressed consciousness that could be made accessible through private or mass re-education. Habermas was already placing his faith in human powers of cognitive adjustment to conditions that could be rationally brought to light.

Moreover, even in 1968 Habermas was concerned to employ only the most plausible-looking features of Marxism and psychoanalysis—which is to say, necessarily, the least deterministic ones.[5] His affinity was not for iron laws either of history or of psychobiological compulsion but for holistic humanism, ego psychology, and the mundane actualities of the therapeutic transaction. In all these respects he was showing resistance to theoreticism, whose purest impulse is toward positing ineluctable constraints on the perceptiveness and adaptability of everyone but the theorist himself.[6] Habermas's ethic of widening the individual's range of conscious choice armed him against that temptation.

It was fitting, however, that Habermas was trying to advance the particular doctrines of Marxism and psychoanalysis when he took his first tentative steps toward theoreticism. Of course the immediate explanation lies in his involvement with the Frankfurt School, which had already diluted Marx with Freud to explain the unfulfillment of Marx's prophecies. (If the Western proletariat was not arising on schedule, its unconscious must have been in thrall to the oppressor.) Yet it is surely no coincidence that when more committed theoreticists than Habermas have laid claim to anti-empirical "sciences" of their own, their choice has almost always been for some permutation of Freudianism or Marxism. It is important to understand why.

While classic Marxism and psychoanalysis insist upon their observational basis, they also constitute inside critiques of received knowledge (it is distorted by "false consciousness" or "repression"), and they bestow epistemic privilege on a group of deep knowers (the revolutionary vanguard, the analyzed) who possess an antidote to chronic error. Try as they may to blend into the wider scientific community, Marxists and Freudians know they have a head start toward truth; and they also know why the uninitiated may be compelled (by class interest, by fear of the repressed) to resist that truth. These two movements may have accumulated some well-founded tenets along their troubled roads, but in origin and spirit they are *counter-sciences*—creeds that use a dry mechanistic idiom and an empirical facade to legitimize "deep," morally engaged revelations, which can always be placed on some new footing if their original claims turn out to be baseless.

We have seen that Habermas's way of shielding his counter-sciences from empirical audit was to shift them to the nonscientific or hermeneutic side of the ledger. Such an evasion cannot satisfy an all-out theoreticist, since it leaves unchallenged the sovereignty of established science. The more thoroughgoing "anti-positivist" strategy, then, is to defy empiricism in general by declaring it inoperative even within science. Practitioners of human studies need only catch distant rumors of philosophers' assaults on the foundationalist logic of verification to leap to a happy conclusion: we now live in a time "when science itself is recognizing that its own methods are ultimately no more objective than those of the arts" (Felperin, 88).

When this obituary for empiricism is accompanied by an argument, the later usually rests on a loose reading of Thomas Kuhn's *The Structure of Scientific Revolutions* (1962), the most frequently cited academic book of modern times. Kuhn, we are told, demonstrated that any two would-be paradigms, or regnant major theories, will be incommensurable; that is, they will represent different universes of perception and explanation. Hence no common ground can exist for testing their merits, and one theory will prevail for strictly sociological, never empirical, reasons. The winning theory will be the one that better suits the emergent temper or interests of the hour. It follows that intellectuals who once trembled before the disapproving gaze of positivism can now propose sweeping

"Kuhnian revolutionary paradigms" of their own, defying whatever disciplinary consensus they find antipathetic and trusting that tomorrow's "sociology" will validate their choice.

One can gauge the emotional force of theoreticism by the remoteness of this interpretation from what Kuhn actually said, especially in the second edition of his book and in subsequent clarifying articles (Kuhn 1970, 1974a, 1974b, 1974c). Kuhn happens to be a fervent believer in scientific rationality and progress, which, he argues, can occur only after a given specialty has gotten past the stage of "theory proliferation" and "incessant criticism and continual striving for a fresh start" (Kuhn 1974b, 246, 244). By incommensurability Kuhn never meant that competing theories are incomparable but only that the choice between them cannot be entirely consigned to the verdict of theory-neutral rules and data. (What looks like a "mistake" in one theory's terms may be a legitimate inference in the terms of its rival.) Transitions between paradigms—which in any case are mere problem solutions, not broad theories or methodologies—must indeed be made globally, through "gestalt switches," but the rationality of science is not thereby impaired. As Kuhn asked, and as he has continued to insist with mounting astonishment at his irrationalist fan club, "What better criterion than the decision of the scientific group could there be?" (Kuhn 1970, 169).

Nothing Kuhn can say, however, will make a dent in theoreticism, which is less a specific position than a mood of antinomian rebellion and self-indulgence. That mood comes down to us from the later Sixties—from a sense of criminal inhumanity in science and technology, a revulsion against dry rationality, a cherishing of direct intuitive belief, and a willing surrender to intellectual, political, and spiritual counter-authorities. Such inwardness can include an unarticulated feeling that one at least deserves the haven of an all-explanatory theory, a way of making the crazy world cohere.

Of course the direct intellectual inspiration for most theoreticism has come from such French thinkers as Lévi-Strauss, Barthes, Lacan, Althusser, Foucault, and Derrida, representing various currents of structuralism and poststructuralism. Anglo-American academics, who seem only dimly aware that structuralism became *vieux jeu* in Paris shortly after they discovered it around 1966, continue to draw liberally on both structuralist and poststructuralist authorities. In doing so they have absorbed a dogmatism of intellectual style that is plainly apparent in their sources. For, while the gurus of theoreticism differ sharply among themselves, in another sense they are much alike: all of them neglect or openly dismiss the principle of intersubjective skepticism, the core of any empirical commitment.[7]

Consider, for example, the "structural-Marxist" Althusser and the "structural-psychoanalyst" Lacan. Unlike Habermas, both were absolutists who aimed at cleansing Freud's and Marx's founding texts of their bourgeois-accommodationist elements, establishing by fiat what was truly scientific in them, and cross-breeding the result with a rigid structural determinism. Observational considerations were totally extraneous to those projects. Indeed, Althusser's bookish "return to Marx" was explicitly modeled on the equally scholastic "return to Freud" effected by his sometime psychoanalyst, Lacan.

Althusser, reacting against Sartre's sentimental "Marxist humanism," arbitrarily excised Marx's own Hegelian humanism from the corpus of his work, claiming that Marx was being himself only when he was coldly systematic and structuralist—in other words, when he was Althusser. (Hence the title of the most damaging attack on Althusser by a former disciple: André Glucksmann's "A Ventriloquist Structuralism.") *Capital*, Althusser brazenly decreed, expounds a science as fundamental as physics and mathematics. Then, taking his methodized and depersonalized *Capital* as irrefutably true, Althusser found within it proof that the philosophy of dialectical materialism is itself scientifically validated. With some changes of terminology, the whole circular argument could have been devised in the thirteenth century.

Similarly, Lacan, repelled by the emphasis on middle-class normality in Freudian ego psychology, concocted a suitably "rigorous" counter-pyschoanalysis. The concepts of Freud's that he endorsed (repression, the castration complex, the death instinct) were not ones that he had winnowed through his own clinical trial and error, but rather those he deemed most powerful—that is, most subversive of appearances. They represented the real, courageous Freud; ego psychology had come into being when a lesser, bourgeois Freud *repressed* those same unnerving notions. That act of diagnosis-at-a-distance epitomized Lacan's disdain for corroboration. Moreover, by then mapping the arbitrarily favored concepts, along with newly invented ones, onto a grid of Saussurean linguistic oppositions and paradoxes, Lacan largely abandoned the original reference of Freud's vision to actual neurotic suffering.

In Althusser's and Lacan's hands, then, both Marxism and psychoanalysis exchange an adaptive materialism for allegory. There is no point at which they unambiguously intersect experience and therefore no point where one of their contentions could be modified by behavioral data. They have become, not critiques of inhumane arrangements or guidelines for practical intervention, but master transcoding devices which will sort any text or problem into sets of formally opposed categories. And that is exactly how they have been used by phalanxes of humorless acolytes.

After the student uprising of 1968, neither Althusser nor Lacan could secure a compliant audience in France. To activists who felt betrayed by the conservative Communist party and by Althusser personally, every intellectual scheme, including the most radical-looking structuralist models, suddenly appeared complicit with a totalitarian principle uniting Right, Left, and Center against the anarchic young. "Anything devoted to 'order,'" as James Boon remarks, "even covert marginalised orders of the social and linguistic unconscious, tended to be indicted as part of the establishment's will to oppress and repress" (*RGT*, 167).[8] The cry then arose for an end not just to oppression but to *theories about* oppression. The immediate beneficiaries on the intellectual *bourse* were poststructuralists, or cognitive minimalists, such as Derrida, Foucault, Jean-François Lyotard, and Gilles Deleuze.

At first glance, an advocate of empirical prudence might perceive such doubters as welcome allies. They have seen with pitiless clarity, for example, that Marxism is intellectually hobbled by its pseudo-objectivity, its moralized vision of history, its ineradicable utopianism, and its economic reductionism. Similarly, they have been largely immune to the scientific pretensions of psychoanalysis. To be sure, their complaint is an idiosyncratic one: that even Lacanian psychoanalysis wrongly presumes to posit real psychic energies and agencies beyond the play of signifiers, meanwhile referring all of its activity of finding structures to a falsely serene contemplative consciousness. But some wariness toward arbitrary claims is certainly better than none.

Unfortunately, however, poststructuralist cynicism is by no means the same thing as empirically based skepticism. We can see that divergence quite clearly in the writings of Derrida, whose "deconstructionist" viewpoint dominated vanguard opinion on both sides of the Atlantic throughout the Seventies. Deconstruction, the technique of laying bare the metaphorical nature of all attempts to establish referential terms, holds that any use of language points only to further language and that the whole Western "metaphysics of presence" from Plato onward is erroneous. This is an arguable position, but in Derrida's hands it becomes an inverted metaphysics of its own, an unsupported contention that "*différance*," or the endless deferral of meaning, "constitutes the essence of life" (Derrida 1978, 203).

Derrida's judgment that "there is nothing outside the text" (Derrida 1976, 158) automatically precludes recourse to evidence. Hence he has no way of arriving at more fruitful ideas than the inherited ones he has doomed himself to deconstruct ad infinitum and thus to retain in a limbo of combined attention and nonassertion. His contentment with that annotative role marks him as an intellectual nihilist, though a learned and exuberant one. Both Derrida and his myriad followers think nothing of appropriating and denaturing propositions from systems of thought whose premises they have already rejected.[9] Why not, after all, when Western knowledge in general is an exercise in self-deception?

By now many theory-conscious academics are willing to admit the monotony and hermeticism of Derrida's "carrying off each concept into an interminable chain of differences" (Derrida 1981, 14). All that is behind us now, they say, thanks to Foucault, who showed us a way out of the Derridean maze and back to concrete social reality. But Foucault's concreteness, such as it was, by no means entailed a belief in regulating his ideas according to the evidence he encountered. Indeed, though his historical works attach portentous significance to certain developments and details, his epistemological pronouncements appear to rule out the very concept of a fact.[10]

For Foucault the whole Enlightenment was a continuing nightmare of ever-harsher social control—a movement to draw "reasonable" distinctions (rational–irrational, sane–insane, innocent–criminal, normal–abnormal) so as to stigmatize and punish behavior that threatens bourgeois self-regard. Foucault's own delicate mission was to trace the origins of that mania without at the same time enlarging its dominion. Such a feat called for a determination not just to "escape the grasp of categories" but to "play the game of truth and error badly" (Foucault, 190)—in other words, to remain unbound by any norms of evidence and logic. Foucault could only hope that his books might serve as "Molotov cocktails, or minefields" that would "self-destruct after use" (quoted by

Megill, 243). The guerrilla imagery, evoking the Romantic anti-rationalism of May 1968, points not only to the wellsprings of the continuing Foucault cult but also to the common denominator of all theoreticism: a refusal to credit one's audience with the right to challenge one's ideas on dispassionate grounds.[11]

It is hard in any case to attach positive significance to the replacement of one revered master by another, when the very appetite for unquestioning belief is the heart of the problem. In the human studies today, it is widely assumed that the positions declared by structuralism and poststructuralism are permanently valuable discoveries that require no further interrogation. Thus one frequently comes upon statements of the type: "Deconstruction has shown us that we can never exit from the play of signifiers"; "Lacan demonstrates that the unconscious is structured like a language"; "After Althusser, we all understand that the most ideological stance is the one that tries to fix limits beyond which ideology does not apply"; "There can be no turning back to naïve pre-Foucauldian distinctions between truth and power." Such servility constitutes an ironic counterpart of positivism—a heaping up, not of factual nuggets, but of movement slogans that are treated as fact.

Our intellectual practices, rather than our choice of idols, will show whether we have begun to recover from our twenty-year romance with theory for theory's sake. Reasons for optimism are as yet hard to come by. I see no decline, for example, in the most curious practice of all, the Derridean habit of simultaneously using a theory and disclaiming responsibility for its implications. Many "human scientists" still assume that the only mistake you can make with a borrowed theory is to "privilege" it—that is, to take its ruling terms as a transcendent foundation or ultimate reality. If you aver that you wouldn't dream of privileging theory x but are merely admitting it into the unsupervised playground of your mind, then any weakness in theory x itself is not your problem. Typically, the writer announces that neither his theoretical methodology nor his subject matter will be privileged; each will keep the other from getting out of hand. Whereupon, of course, the methodology is put to work like a jackhammer.

The same license to subscribe to a theory without actually believing what it says also permits the ideologically committed to combine two or more doctrines which look to be seriously incompatible. Sectarian zeal, which now appears stronger than ever in the academy, provides all the guidance required to tell which tenets should be discarded or updated to match the latest political wisdom. Since no one is comparing a given theory to the state of research in its original domain, problems of empirical justification simply don't arise.

Take, for example, the use of imported theory in American academic film studies, which are now dominated by a pugnacious clique that regards itself as at once Lacanian, Marxist, and feminist. Its journals, which are as fawning toward radical system builders as they are implacable toward the patriarchal-capitalist order, allow little room amid the manifestoes for discussion of actual movies. To an outsider such fierce parochialism can be astonishing, and doubly so because it seems bizarre to commit the flamboyantly sexist Lacan into the care of feminists. But to an engaged theoreticist, that very discrepancy of consciousness offers opportunities for useful labor, namely, sex surgery on Lacan's "phallogocentrism" until it has been rendered suitably "gynocentric." No one suggests that a system needing such drastic repair might be unreliable in other respects as well; to do so would be to manifest a retrograde interest in connections between theory and observation.

Nor, unfortunately, is such insouciance restricted to ideologues. Many otherwise canny humanists and social scientists would now think it boorish and intolerant to care whether the ideas they invoke have received any corroboration, since only a soulless positivist would want to pass judgment on a theory before seeing what illuminating effects its application can provoke. A trial of sensibility is the only precaution needed: the theory will have demonstrated its cogency if it brings out meaning and coherence in a given text or problem. Of course such bogus experiments succeed every time. All they prove is that any thematic stencil will make its own pattern stand out.

With this self-centered approach to ideas—"everything comes together for me when I'm using this theory!"—we reach the mildest and most elusive refinement of theoreticist apriorism. But it is apriorism all the same: a refusal, this time on a pretext of open-mindedness, to adapt one's method to the intellectual problem at hand. And a subtle but ultimately impoverishing price is paid for it: a sense of artifice and triviality, of disconnection from the wider enterprise of rational inquiry.

Some readers, I know, will acknowledge this isolation but suspect that it is unavoidable in the value-laden and fashion-sensitive human studies. They should realize, however, that the global antithesis between scientific rigor and nonscientific diffuseness has been crumbling in recent years. We now know that individual subdisciplines, not the sciences en masse, become coherent and progressive when their practitioners have developed solutions to major problems and acquired a feeling for what Thomas Kuhn calls the "good reasons" that tacitly inhabit those solutions: "accuracy, scope, simplicity, fruitfulness, and the like" (Kuhn 1974b, 261). Each of the human studies contains comparable specialties—research traditions that generate well-focused debate, high standards of reasoning, and even a degree of consensus. I suggest, not that we stop theorizing and expressing our sociopolitical views, but that we notice where our most substantial theories always originate: in concrete disciplinary engagement.

The age of positivism lies well behind us, and we are aware today that there is no algorithm for truth in any field. Science and nonscience are in the same epistemic fix: all we can ever rely on is a dedicated subcommunity that will address shared problems in rationally evolving ways. There can be no question, *pace* Quentin Skinner, of our deciding whether to humble ourselves before *the* scientific model of research. No such model exists. Across the intellectual spectrum, each subdiscipline hews to its uniquely appropriate way of addressing characteristic issues—except, of course, where the anti-investigative mood of theoreticism has taken hold.

In the Grand Academy of Lagado, where "projectors" are busy trying to soften marble for pillows and extract sunbeams from cucumbers, Lemuel Gulliver comes across "a most ingenious architect who had contrived a new method for building houses, by beginning at the roof and working downwards to the foundation." Presumably that project is as insensate as the others. But if Gulliver were to visit our own grand academy of theory, he could witness a like feat accomplished daily, with conceptual gables and turrets suspended on hot air and rakishly cantilevered across the void. And if C. P. Snow is perchance observing from a nearby cloud, it may occur to him that his two cultures stack up somewhat differently by now: not scientists versus nonscientists, but the builders of those floating mansions on one side and, on the other, empirical inquirers of every kind.

Notes

1. When John Stuart Mill's *System of Logic* (1843) was translated into German in 1863, his term "moral sciences" was rendered as *Geisteswissenschaften*, which in its turn got retranslated as "human sciences." As a thoroughgoing empiricist and determinist, Mill believed that "the phenomena of human thought, feeling, and action [and of society] cannot but conform to fixed laws" (Mill, 607). Though such positivism on Mill's part was ill-advised, we should note that the "human sciences" in their early development sought the protection *of* scientific authority, not protection *from* it. I will use the more neutral term "human studies" below, meaning the social sciences and the humanities as usually understood.

2. The contributors, in the same order, are William Outhwaite, David Hoy, Mark Philp, Barry Barnes, Alan Ryan, Anthony Giddens, Susan James, James Boon, and Stuart Clark. Most of the essays originated in a series of BBC radio talks organized by Skinner.

3. "Today," as Hilary Putnam has remarked, "virtually no one believes that there is a purely formal scientific method" (Putnam, 125). The reasons are many, ranging from a consensus that theories are invariably "underdetermined" by data; to W. V. O. Quine's demonstration that scientific propositions are interlocked in networks and thus are never tested "sentence by sentence"; to a widespread realization that whole theories are not overturned by single failed predictions and that "counternormal" tenacity is essential for progress; to an awareness that, for the most part, scientists simply *don't* submit very many of their beliefs to rigorous tests.

4. And this is to pass over the recklessness of granting any doctrine an intrinsic superiority to logical and empirical objections. As a fabric of mutually entailed reality claims, a "historical-hermeneutic" system stands at the same risk of incoherence or disconfirmation as any other.

5. I follow Donald Davidson (1976) and Jon Elster (1984) in believing that deterministic schemes of explaining human motives and deeds are in principle unlikely to be well supported. What Davidson calls "psycho-physical laws" overlook the fact that human beings, as "strategically rational actors" (Elster, 18), are forever adjusting their plans to cope with a changing environment, including the changes wrought by the popular diffusion of those very "laws." As Elster maintains, deterministic schemes could at most account for the evolution of human *capacities* to behave strategically, not for specific strategic acts (Elster, 3).

6. Indeed, we could say with hindsight that in the very act of "hermeneutically" misrepresenting Freud and Marx as not having meant their causal claims very seriously, Habermas was presaging his later withdrawal to still safer ground: from Freudian ego psychology to Piaget's developmental theory, from Marx's sociology of oppression to Talcott Parsons's bland interactionism, from the privileged knowledge of the class-conscious and the analyzed to the common-sense universalist communication of speech act theory, and from "hermeneutic" special pleading to a virtual fetishizing of the empiricism advocated by that scourge of all radicals, Sir Karl Popper. It is hardly surprising that Habermas's admirers on the intellectual Left have by now been reduced to a puzzled and edgy little band.

7. That attitude is traceable in part to an anti-experiential school of reflection about science. In the Cartesian tradition, French scientific philosophers have tended to downplay recourse to experience, instead treating observations as mere applications of previously given theoretical postulates. Gaston Bachelard and Georges Canguilhem especially, who decisively influenced both Althusser and Foucault, presented the history of science as a sequence of ruptures between one self-exhausted "discourse" and its successor. They claimed, in fact, that every science begins precisely by breaking with experience—by turning away from evidence of the senses and constructing a rival conceptual scenario that must follow out its internally plotted course. This helps to explain why an American Althusserian, for example, can declare in an axiomatic spirit that empiricism is only "the mirage of an utterly nontheoretical practice" (Jameson, 58). See Gutting and Lecourt.

8. When Gilles Deleuze and Felix Guattari devastated the already shrinking Lacanian camp in Paris with *The Anti-Oedipus* (1972), for example, they did not point out the complete absence of empirical controls in Lacan's work, but concentrated instead on his illicit wish to bring the irrational under intellectual domination. Deleuze and Guattari indicted Lacanian psychoanalysis as a capitalist disorder, and they pilloried analysts as the most sinister priests-manipulators of a psychotic society. The demonstration was widely regarded as unanswerable.

9. Thus, in the same essay in which he calls psychoanalysis "an unbelievable mythology," one that must be cited "in quotation marks" (Derrida 1978, 228, 197), Derrida credits Freud with the "discovery" of "the irreducibility of the 'effect of deferral'" (203)—in other words, with a realization that "the present is not primal but . . . reconstituted" (212). The "discovery" thus welcomed, drawn from such whimsical sources as Freud's abandoned "Project for a Scientific Psychology" and his "Note on the Mystic Writing-Pad," requires no more proof than the reflection that Freud was in this respect an early Derridean. And Derrida goes on to lay his blessing on Freud's creakiest psychophysical concepts, such as "repressed memory traces" and "cathectic innervations," simply because they evoke his own central notion of *différance*. In this manner he encourages the theoreticist habit of treating one's own system as received truth while dividing all other tenets into those that miss one's point (owing, perhaps, to "repression") and those that can be borrowed to adorn it.

As for Derrida's own "discoveries" of (a) an infinite regress of signifiers, rendering any intended meaning unstable, (b) the constitution of every "signified" by "traces" of its opposite, and (c) the "repression" of writing in all philosophy since Plato, see the decisive rebuttal by Searle.

10. Once having been rebuked by Derrida himself for implying, in his *Madness and Civilization*, that insanity was a dimension of actual (pre-linguistic) experience that the modern West had attempted to disown (Derrida 1978, 31–63), Foucault thenceforth outdid his critic in proclaiming that all of existence is produced by discourse. "There is nothing absolutely primary to be interpreted," he wrote, "since fundamentally, everything is already interpretation . . ." (quoted by Descombes, 117). As one commentator ob-

serves, in Foucault's works after 1963 "one is struck by the total disappearance of the concept 'experience'" (Megill, 202).

11. Not coincidentally, it was immediately after 1968 that Foucault switched from his quasi-structuralist "archaeologies" of Western "epistemes" to more drastic Nietzschean "genealogies" reducing all truth claims to exercises of power. The attractive new ingredient in Foucault's thought was Sixties paranoia toward the hidden, all-powerful oppressors whom he never attempted to identify.

Works Cited

Crane, R. S. 1967. "Criticism as Inquiry; or, The Perils of the 'High Priori Road.'" In *The Idea of the Humanities and Other Essays*, 2 vols. Chicago: University of Chicago Press. II: 25–44.

Davidson, Donald. 1976. "Psychology as Philosophy." In *The Philosophy of Mind*, ed. Jonathan Glover. Oxford: Oxford University Press. Pp. 101–110.

Derrida, Jacques. 1976. *Of Grammatology*, trans. Gayatri Chakravorty Spivak. Baltimore: Johns Hopkins University Press.

———. 1978. *Writing and Difference*, trans. Alan Bass. Chicago: University of Chicago Press.

———. 1981. *Positions*, trans. Alan Bass. Chicago: University of Chicago Press.

Descombes, Vincent. 1980. *Modern French Philosophy*, trans. L. Scott-Fox and J. M. Harding. Cambridge: Cambridge University Press.

Elster, Jon. 1984. *Ulysses and the Sirens: Studies in Rationality and Irrationality*. Cambridge: Cambridge University Press.

Felperin, Howard. 1985. *Beyond Deconstruction: The Uses and Abuses of Theory*. Oxford: Clarendon Press.

Foucault, Michel. 1977. *Language, Counter-Memory, Practice: Selected Essays and Interviews*, ed. Donald F. Bouchard. Ithaca: Cornell University Press.

Giddens, Anthony. 1985. "Reason without Revolution? Habermas's *Theorie des kommunikativen Handelns*." In *Habermas and Modernity*, ed. Richard J. Bernstein. Cambridge: MIT Press, 1985. Pp. 95–121.

Grünbaum, Adolf. 1984. *The Foundations of Psychoanalysis: A Philosophical Critique*. Berkeley: University of California Press.

Gutting, Gary G. 1979. "Continental Philosophy of Science." In *Current Research in Philosophy of Science: Proceedings of the P.S.A. Critical Research Problems Conference*, ed. Peter D. Asquith and Henry E. Kyburg, Jr. East Lansing: Philosophy of Science Association. Pp. 94–117.

Habermas, Jürgen. 1971. *Knowledge and Human Interests*, trans. Jeremy J. Shapiro. Boston: Beacon Press.

Jameson, Fredric. 1981. *The Political Unconscious: Narrative as a Socially Symbolic Act*. Ithaca: Cornell University Press.

Jay, Martin. 1984. *Marxism and Totality: The Adventures of a Concept from Lukács to Habermas.* Berkeley: University of California Press.

Kuhn, Thomas S. 1970. *The Structure of Scientific Revolution,* 2nd ed. (1st ed. 1962.) Chicago: University of Chicago Press.

———. 1974a. "Logic of Discovery or Psychology of Research?" In Lakatos and Musgrave, 1–23.

———. 1974b. "Reflections on My Critics." In Lakatos and Musgrave, 231–277.

———. 1974c. "Second Thoughts on Paradigms." In *The Structure of Scientific Theories,* ed. Frederick Suppe. Urbana: University of Illinois Press. Pp. 459–482.

Lakatos, Imre, and Alan Musgrave. 1974. Eds., *Criticism and the Growth of Knowledge.* Cambridge: Cambridge University Press.

Lecourt, Dominique. 1975. *Marxism and Epistemology: Bachelard, Canquilhem and Foucault,* trans. Ben Brewster. London: NLB.

Megill, Allan. 1985. *Prophets of Extremity: Nietzsche, Heidegger, Foucault, Derrida.* Berkeley: University of California Press.

Mill, John Stuart. 1884. *A System of Logic, Ratiocinative and Deductive: Being a Connected View of the Principles of Evidence and the Methods of Scientific Investigation,* 8th ed. New York: Harper and Brothers.

Putnam, Hilary. 1981. *Reason, Truth and History.* Cambridge: Cambridge University Press.

Searle, John R. 1983. "The Word Turned Upside Down." *New York Review of Books,* 27 October, pp. 74–78.

Skinner, Quentin. 1985. Ed., *The Return of Grand Theory in the Human Sciences.* Cambridge: Cambridge University Press.

Snow, C. P. 1959. *The Two Cultures and the Scientific Revolution.* Cambridge: Cambridge University Press.

III

At Closer Range

10

Roth into Kafka:
The Metamorphosis
That Wasn't

In turning now to discussions of individual authors and critics rather than of general problems, I begin with a review of Philip Roth's novella The Breast, *published in* The New York Review *in 1972. This piece bears some thematic relevance to Part I, in that it could be regarded as my final piece of psychoanalytic criticism. In fact, however, I was no longer a Freudian at the time; it was Roth who, quite consciously I am sure, seeded his book with diagnostic clues that would require every reader to play Dr. Spielvogel.*

The case of The Breast *may illustrate a general problem in recent American fiction: a conflating of the roles of author and critic, whereby the novelist labors to implant ingredients that are sure to strike exegetes as "symbolic." Some such preoccupation, in any case, probably accounts for Roth's distraction from the moral and psychological ironies that remain only half developed in his story.*

We seem to be on familiar ground in the opening pages of *The Breast* (Roth, 1972a). The hero, David Alan Kepesh, has Alex Portnoy's verbal gifts, his irony, his apparent public success, and his private hypochondria. If his life appears more stable than Portnoy's, so much the better, for Roth's specialty is pulling out the rug. We can be fairly sure that this Stony Brook professor of comparative literature, with his regular bowels and his tidy, if monotonous, modus vivendi with a nice young schoolteacher, is in for some awful surprise. When Kepesh gets an itch in the groin and becomes a kind of monogamous debauchee, grateful to be able to take the initiative with patient, neglected Claire, we know we won't get any Lawrentian smarm about the dark wisdom of the body. In Roth's work strong feelings, especially in the pelvic region, are always symptoms.

Kepesh deteriorates, all right, but not in a foreseeable way. In a few cataclysmic hours he suffers "a hermaphroditic explosion of chromosomes" and wakes up in Lenox Hill Hospital to find himself transformed into a 155-pound, dirigible-shaped female breast, with a five-inch nipple that is histologically reminiscent of his lamented penis. At the time of the soliloquy that constitutes the narrative, he has been living in a hammock for fifteen months, blind but not deaf, fed and drained by tubes, with his world constricted to doctors and nurses and a few visitors who do their best to treat this freak as the man he still is beneath his areola.

But the novelty of *The Breast* doesn't lie in its situation. Roth's work since *Portnoy* (1969) has been full of comic surrealism, and what happens to Kepesh is no more implausible than the fate of the talent scout Lippman, for example, in the brilliant story "On the Air" (1970). What is noteworthy is that Roth, having chosen a story line that looks ideally suited to his taste for outrageous sexual farce, has side-stepped the opportunity and instead written a work of high seriousness. *The Breast* has its laughs, but they seem like indulgences Roth has permitted himself along the way to an oblique, cryptic statement about human dignity and resourcefulness.

Kepesh's plight quickly ceases to be funny as attention is diverted from his physical state to his agony of spirit. How can a man accommodate himself to the unthinkable? Why does the will refuse to surrender when the mind sees no escape? Kepesh's complaint, unlike Portnoy's, begins to subside as his dormant courage stirs. At the end Kepesh, now acquainted with his strength, dares to quote us Rilke's sonnet, "Archaic Torso of Apollo," with its bald concluding imperative: "You must change your life." Even hedged with sarcasm and ambiguity, the message is striking. It is as if Roth had wearied of the querulous, sardonic Portnoy and had decided to let Dr. Spielvogel have his say.

The shift of emphasis comes with notable suddenness after Roth's venture into political satire in *Our Gang* (1971). The protagonist of that work, a president named Trick E. Dixon, is assassinated in the nude and stuffed into a water-filled baggie, to the approval of everyone but his widow, who "thinks that at the very least the President should have been slain in a shirt and a tie and a jacket, like John F. Charisma." Roth's humor in *Our Gang* is literally atrocious; his sense of being politically in the right licenses him to create a depersonalized, paranoid world in which sadistic fantasies are considered chic so long as they are directed against despised figures. To skim the book is to understand it. In describing *The Breast*, however, Roth speaks of his "distrust of 'positions,' including my own" (1972b), and the book itself moves fitfully toward transcendence, denying us one easy conclusion after another until we are finally prepared to grasp Kepesh's humanity without any overlay of ideas.

Reviewers who never cared for Roth's startling frankness and iconoclasm have already expressed pleasure with what they take to be his reformation. Even Trick E. Dixon, if he were a student of ideological currents in the arts, might be gratified to see our author moving from the aesthetic of Barbara Garson toward that of Henry James. To my mind, however, *Our Gang* and *The Breast* stand roughly equidistant from Roth's best mode, which is neither "political" nor "moral."

From the very beginning—from the moment when Neil Klugman, on the opening page of "Goodbye, Columbus" (1959), gets a glimpse of Brenda Patimkin's rear—Roth's forte has been the portrayal of compulsives whose humane intelligence cannot save them from their irrationality. The sharpness and energy of his work have to do with a fidelity to petty idiocies of self-betrayal. In *Our Gang* he takes a holiday from characterization and simply lets fly at the Republicans; in *The Breast* he goes to the other extreme and, without detectable irony, subjects his hero to earnest lecturing from a psychoanalyst about "strength of character," "will to live," and even "Mr. Reality." What connects these seemingly opposite books is their common flight from the elements of Roth's finest art.

To be sure, those elements are not absent from *The Breast*. Though Kepesh tells us that "reality has more style" than to punish wishes in a fairy-tale way, it is possible to infer that his fate is profoundly congruent with his disposition. Roth offers at least one obvious clue: once on Nantucket, with his mistress Claire's breast in his mouth, Kepesh wanted to leave it there instead of making orthodox love, and he confessed to an envy of her. Lesser indications of slippage in his male identity are scattered through the text. His ego has been bruised in a disastrous marriage; his arrangement with Claire (they have slept together but lived apart) looks like a phobic defense against what he calls the "dependence, or the grinding boredom, or the wild, unfocused yearning" of married couples; he has placed an unusual value on nonvaginal forms of intercourse; and he has almost entirely lost erotic interest in Claire before getting his premonitory itch. It is still quite a leap from these facts to becoming a female gland—but it also seems unlikely that Kepesh was selected at random by the prankster gods.

If we suppose that Kepesh's change is an exact condensation of his wishes and fears, the story does make detailed Freudian sense. Kepesh's fetishizing of Claire's breast has turned her into a fantasy-mother and himself into a nursing infant; now, it seems, he regresses further and merges himself with the breast as if there were no boundary between self and nurturing world. The breast is the womb and they are both Kepesh. To reach this apparent paradise, though, one must accept castration: the hero becomes blind, limbless, and encased in female tissue like a eunuch. Yet paradoxically, the mutilation permits a regrouping of masculine aims on a safer level: the Kepesh who had formerly submitted to Claire's advances "two, maybe three times a month" is now an imposing, permanently inflated organ, a quasi-penis, and he wants it serviced around the clock.

This isn't just intricate dream logic; it is potentially rich irony. *The Breast* reads like a Midas story for an age whose mystagogues have seriously proposed that the Oedipal film be run backwards until we find ourselves polymorphous, guilt-free infants once again. Kepesh as breast is an object of constant mothering, with feeding and elimination looked after by others, with nonorgasmic pleasure in being rubbed and washed, and with a chance to "sleep the sleep of the sated" as he sways in his hammock. But what is it really like to have an infant's clamorous needs, and his powerlessness to get them satisfied on his own initiative, and his rage when he understands that a mother's patience is finite and her love divided?

Roth achieves real pathos in the moments when Kepesh, believing Claire to be too pure for inclusion in his new erotic script, fears he will lose her. Eventually he consents to a form of weaning, restricting himself to a fixed daily period of stimulation, having himself anesthetized before washing, and even accepting a male nurse, who can't arouse him because, in spite of everything, that would be "homosexual." Regression looks tempting, Roth seems to say, but—wait till you try it! Adult scruples aren't so easy to blot out, and stimulation of the skin "from a source unknown to me, seemingly immense and dedicated solely to me and my pleasure," is finally no substitute for freely exchanged love.

But has Kepesh actually regressed at all? Roth's irony is blunted by the tendency of his plot to deny any linkage between the hero's psyche and his outward state. Kepesh's heroism is measured by his increasing ability to forgo explanations and simply acknowledge the technical fact that he is a breast in a hospital. His soliloquy thus has a curious, unintended effect of filibuster. Thanks to Roth's precise evocations, we as readers have never doubted since page 12 that Kepesh is a breast, and our minds move ahead to consider the poetic justice of this fate. But Roth scorns analysis and insists that his hero is a Job, not a Midas, and we eventually have to agree. Discerning a psychological feast, we are handed an "existential" crumb: isn't it grand to endure the absurd?

"You must change your life"—but first, Mr. Reality might add, you must decide what is wrong with it. Nothing at all is wrong with Kepesh; as the victim of a colossal misfortune he need only keep a stiff upper nipple and exit to applause. By having even the psychoanalyst veto Kepesh's tentative efforts at self-awareness, by making his hero into a noble survivor, Roth loses control over the half-developed themes that would have saved his story from banality. It is as if Kafka were to bludgeon us into admitting that Gregor Samsa is the most stoical beetle we have met, and a wonderful sport about the whole thing.

What makes an image telling, Roth accurately observed in his interview about *The Breast*, is not how much meaning we can associate to it, but the freedom it gives the writer to explore his obsessions. But has he explored his obsessions in this book, or has he simply referred to them obliquely before importing a *deus ex machina* to whisk them away? In a sense *The Breast* is a more discouraging work than the straightforwardly vicious *Our Gang*. Aspiring to make a noble moral statement, Roth quarantines his best insights into the way people are imprisoned by their impulses. What would Alex Portnoy have had to say about *that*?

Works Cited

Roth, Philip. 1959. *Goodbye, Columbus: And Five Stories*. Boston: Houghton Mifflin.

————. 1969. *Portnoy's Complaint*. New York: Random House.

————. 1970. "On the Air." *New American Review*, 10 (August), 7–49.

————. 1971. *Our Gang (Starring Tricky and His Friends)*. New York: Random House.

————. 1972a. *The Breast*. New York: Holt.

————. 1972b. "On *The Breast*: An Interview." With Alan Lelchuk. *New York Review of Books*, 19 October, pp. 26–28.

11

Kinetic Art

Near the end of Henry Miller's long career, his admirer Norman Mailer put together a compendium of his representative work, adding an ample commentary of his own. The result, Genius and Lust: A Journey Through the Major Writings of Henry Miller *(1977), implicitly invited readers to contemplate Miller and Mailer as twin figures. My discussion in* The New York Review *suggested that their resemblances, though extensive, were less compelling than Mailer preferred to think. Mailer—for good or ill—has been by far the more self-conscious and calculating author, and his remoteness from Miller's dervishlike nihilism helps us to grasp how very strange a phenomenon Henry Miller was.*

In that overbearing but fertile treatise, *The Anxiety of Influence* (1973), Harold Bloom tells us that "strong poets" get that way by implicitly diminishing the great predecessors who most threaten to intimidate them into silence. To be a powerful writer one must first be a misreader, exaggerating or inventing a weakness in the forebear that calls for the remedy of one's own gestating work. But despite all his swerving, an insecure writer may remain unconvinced of his right to exist. As an instance, Bloom cites Mailer: "any reader of *Advertisements for Myself* may enjoy the frantic dances of Norman Mailer as he strives to evade his own anxiety that it is, after all, Hemingway all the way."

True enough for the Mailer of the 1950s. Now, however, Mailer seems far less preoccupied with Hemingway than with another figure, Henry Miller, who became important to him well after his formative period was over. And Mailer treats Miller with an empathy and a magnanimity that seem quite opposite to the Bloomian author's struggle to get out from under. Given Bloom's suspicion of efforts to deny influence, I imagine he would be reluctant to close the case of Mailer and Hemingway on the basis of this distracting evidence. The canny thing to say would be that Mailer's homage to Miller is an indirect way of exorcizing Hemingway, the undead; one writer, a harmless decoy, is overpraised with all the generosity that must still be withheld from the other.

A more straightforward and plausible interpretation would be that Hemingway, after his suicide in 1961 and the subsequent revelations about his long nervous debility, is no longer the towering authority of masculine style for Mailer or for anyone else. Our fictive prose in general has turned away from the clipped and bittersweet Hemingway manner and has become loose, expansive, fantastic—in short, Milleresque; and Mailer in particular has positively courted Miller's stylistic guidance since the early Sixties. Now in *Genius and Lust* (1977) he goes out of his way to mark the change in allegiance:

> The eye of every dream Hemingway ever had must have looked down the long vista of his future suicide—so he had a legitimate fear of chaos. He never wrote about the river—he contented himself, better, he created a quintessentially American aesthetic by writing about the camp he set up each night by the side of the river—that was the night we made camp at the foot of the cliffs just after the place where the rapids were bad.
>
> Miller is the other half of literature. He is without fear of his end, a literary athlete at ease in earth, air or water. I am the river, he is always ready to say, I am the rapids and the placids, I'm the froth and the scum and twigs—what a roar as I go over the falls. Who gives a fart. Let others camp where they may. I am the river and there is nothing I can't join.

It is clear that Mailer, as the onrushing, graphic, deliberately heedless mode of his recent books would corroborate, wishes to be identified with "the other half of literature" represented by Miller.

In most external respects, of course, Miller and Mailer are anything but kin. Miller is the last of the great bohemians, anarchistic through and through, a romantic visionary who has always followed his inclination without regard for censors, critics, or royalties. Mailer, as everyone knows, is a "Left conservative" journalist-novelist-personage who thrives on controversy, takes a position on every issue, candidate, and fellow celebrity, and is constantly enmeshed in the toils of big-time publishing. Compare a free spirit like Miller to one who has accepted a million dollars in advances on the slender likelihood that his enormous novel about ancient Egypt, contemporary America, and outer space will become the twentieth-century equivalent of *Moby-Dick*. Think of Mailer at his typewriter, feeling on his neck the collective breath of the reviewers, the stockholders, the movie moguls, the yet unravished Nobel committee. It would be hard to imagine Miller, that insouciant satyr and rebel, allowing himself to become so hedged with contingencies.

Yet the choice of Miller as hero is plausible on several counts, one of which is precisely his self-directedness. In Mailer's estimation Miller is the archetype of the uncompromising, uninhibited artist, "daring to live at the deepest level of honesty he could endure in his life," working always at the edge of his fear of failure, yet aiming at nothing less than to "alter the nerves and marrow of a nation." This may be rather too strenuous an account of Miller, at least after 1934, but it captures Mailer's ideal sense of himself. And that sense surely needs reinforcing as Mailer tries to keep his incidental, bill-paying, publicity-generating work—of which *Genius and Lust* is paradoxically an example—from blunting his vocation.

Then, too, Miller and Mailer have some obsessions in common: with taboo-breaking, with the (literally) cancerous effects of technology, above all with woman as a fortress to be assaulted by the phallic battering ram. It was as fellow sexists—which they assuredly are—that they were jointly reprimanded by Kate Millett (1970); and the several briefs for Miller that Mailer has prepared from *The Prisoner of Sex* (1971) until now have inevitably been defenses of his own right to follow his imagination wherever it may lead. When Mailer pushes Miller forward too insistently, as he often does in the editorial pages of *Genius and Lust*, the explanation would seem to be, not that he is trying to obscure Hemingway, but that he wants the strongest possible blocker in front of himself.

It is not surprising, then, that the passages Mailer chooses for excerption, heavily weighted as they are toward *Tropic of Cancer*, *Black Spring*, and *Tropic of Capricorn*, show us a distinctly Mailer-like Miller, as opposed, say, to the mere pornographer of *Quiet Days in Clichy* or the excitable philosopher-critic of *The Time of the Assassins*. And the effect is reinforced by Mailer's introductions, which, emulating Miller's style, underscore his courage, his energy, his wild metaphors, his nose for sewer gas—in a word, all the traits that would make us think at once of Mailer. At times *Ge-*

nius and Lust appears less like a "journey" than like a tandem attempt to scale Mons Veneris, almost as if these perennially boyish explorers were being incited by one another's pneumatic prose.

In view of the tepid tradition of Miller criticism, however, Mailer's frank participation in his mind is welcome and salutary. Though many of Miller's fellow authors, from Pound and Eliot to Orwell, Edmund Wilson, and Durrell, felt his power as soon as they were exposed to it in *Cancer*, most critics have preferred either to tiptoe past him, to call him a buffoon, or to dwell on the undoubted tiresomeness of his later work. Our Anglo-American criticism, schooled in those stoic moderns who made winningly circumscribed affirmations about endurance, perception, and grace under pressure, has found no use for a writer of total cynicism and total exuberance, one who sees this planet as a "mad slaughterhouse" and finds it personally congenial. Nor has criticism known what to make of someone who moves between autobiographical rambling, surreal fantasy, and sardonic philosophizing with no care for logic or structure. (Ravel, said Miller disdainfully in *Cancer*, "sacrificed something for form, for a vegetable that people must digest before going to bed.") It takes someone like Mailer to read Miller undefensively—to savor his extremes of drollery and aggression without worrying prematurely about good taste or moral seriousness.

To do justice to Miller we must accept him on his own terms, which are announced plainly enough in *Cancer*. They are terms of hostility to "literature"—the same hostility that runs from Miller's beloved Rimbaud through Mallarmé, Jarry, Tzara, Breton, Cendrars, Artaud, and Céline. "Everything that was literature has fallen from me," Miller tells us at once:

> This then? This is not a book. This is libel, slander, defamation of character. This is not a book, in the ordinary sense of the word. No, this is a prolonged insult, a gob of spit in the face of Art, a kick in the pants to God, Man, Destiny, Time, Love, Beauty . . . what you will. I am going to sing for you, a little off key perhaps, but I will sing. I will sing while you croak, I will dance over your dirty corpse. . . .

Spit, kick, sing, dance: Miller's intent is perpetual activity, one kinetic display after another. It is the prescription laid down by Tzara in his "Dada Manifesto 1918": "Every page must explode, either by profound heavy seriousness, the whirlwind, poetic frenzy, the new, the eternal, the crushing joke, enthusiasm for principles. . . ." Or as Miller puts it himself, "If you start with the drums you have to end with dynamite, or TNT." The author of *Why Are We in Vietnam?* would hardly demur. Both as anthologizer and as commentator, he lays his stress on spectacular local effects.

Morceaux choisis alone, however, cannot rescue Miller's reputation from its current limbo. The case for a writer's greatness must be made on the basis of whole works. It seems fair to say that Miller's claim on posterity, like that of most literary revolutionaries, comes down to the one work in which the revolution was manifested. Yet even *Cancer* is crammed with what Orwell wonderingly called "monstrous trivialities." Does the book really set Miller apart as a major figure of his generation?

Orwell certainly thought so, and his essay of 1940 tells us more on the subject than we learn from Mailer. For one thing, Orwell showed how Miller's wholehearted anarchism gave him a surer purchase on reality than either the "cosmic despair" of the wastelanders or the "Boy Scout atmosphere" of the newly Marxized. As an expert in being down and out in Paris, Orwell registered the authenticity of Miller's observation and description. He also remarked on *Cancer*'s amazingly fluid prose, in which "English is treated as a spoken language, but spoken *without fear, i.e.* without fear of rhetoric or of the unusual or poetical word." The same features recur in *Black Spring*, of course. There, however, they lack the force of novelty; and more importantly, by the time of that next book Miller's purpose as a writer has been weakened for good.

What *Cancer* uniquely possesses is a coherent, animating vision of life—one that justifies the book's disjunctions of form, binds together its stark literalism and its reverie, and spares Miller's adventures the drabness of mere anecdote. The vision is of manic nihilism, of hunger for experience combined with scorn for the cowardly, illusion-drugged human race, which has to dream of miracles while "all the while a meter is running inside and there is no hand that can reach in there and shut it off." Miller has given up on value—and, along with it, on any obligation to steel his narrative manner against the ironic fates or to tease meaning from the world with modernist devices of myth and symbol. He is simply talking, much as he will talk through thousands of subsequent pages, but with the difference that here the talk is an act of liberation, a registering of the discovery that no care need be taken to seek order, make discriminations, or check one's impulses. "If I am a hyena I am a lean and hungry one: I go forth to fatten myself."

After *Cancer* everything seems to become too easy. The mental circumstances in which Miller apparently composed that book—detaching himself from his wife June by painful degrees, dissolving his wounded ego in identification with squalor, bursting from self-doubt into unchecked expression—produced an intensity that could never be recaptured. Miller's most ambitious books thereafter merely resume his personal history in fatiguing detail, as if the appetite aroused in readers of *Cancer* had been a simple wish to hear more of his exploits and vicissitudes.

Now, too, Miller begins to write like a man with a repertoire of sure-fire stunts: prodigies of sexual gymnastics, bombast against authority, set pieces of surrealistic fancy. And his opinion of himself and others undergoes a fatal softening. "Man, every man everywhere in the world," he writes in *Capricorn* (1961b), "is on his way to ordination," and in *The Colossus of Maroussi* (1941) he declares that his life is now "dedicated to the recovery of the divinity of man." As a hyena tearing at the still-nutritious corpse of a civilization, the Miller of *Cancer* had a certain magnetism; as a savior he has none.

The chief flaw in Miller's "auto novels," however, is not complacency but garrulous circumstantiality, an attempt to make exhaustiveness stand in the place of significance. As we see in the trite pages that Mailer reprints from *Sunday After the War* and *Big Sur and the Oranges of Hieronymous Bosch*, the problem becomes more acute when Miller's story ceases to be that of a total outsider. In the Forties and Fifties, restraints crowd upon him in the form of marital woes, parental responsibilities, and obnoxious disciples, all faithfully but pointlessly set down. No longer a demon enveloped in incandescent language, he becomes just a guy, Henry Miller from California, full of commonplace ideas and superstitions but a charming talker and a loyal friend.

This is not the whole record, but it is a sad one to contemplate, as bleak in its way as Hemingway's long decline. It hardly serves to encourage a fellow writer with a stake in Miller's permanence. Mailer's difficulties on this score are evidenced in certain attempts to wish away the clichés and confusions that he elsewhere fully acknowledges. "There is not one Henry Miller," he ventures, "but twenty, and fifteen of those authors are very good." Miller's late portraits strike "the tone of that rare writer who ends as a skilled moral craftsman"; the best of them "give every promise they willl live on so long as print remains a nutrient of culture." Mailer thinks it possible that, were it not for the baleful influence of June, *The Rosy Crucifixion* "could have been the most important American novel ever written." If he had never met her, says our editor in his wildest surmise, we might have had "an American Shakespeare capable of writing about tyrants and tycoons (instead, repetitively, of his own liberation)."

It is absurd, of course, to speculate about events that might have turned Miller into a chronicler of tyrants and tycoons. His only possible subject has been himself in the full blossom of his egoism, and his method, as he explained in *My Life and Times* (1971), has always been direct, cathartic self-expression:

> I don't care if I miss the target or not. I'm writing, that's the important thing. . . . *What* I say is not so important. Often it's foolish, nonsensical, contradictory—that doesn't bother me at all. Did I enjoy it? Did I reveal what was in me? That's the thing.

Miller's serenity is awesome, but it is hardly the stuff from which a novelistic Shakespeare could be fashioned. It is Mailer himself who aspires to the honors he barely refrains from conferring on his propped-up master.

For all his studied abandon, it would seem, Mailer hasn't altogether left Hemingway's camp for Miller's river. As a writer in the spotlight he is far from being "without fear of his end." To continue questing after the great American novel is not only to be committed, as Miller would never be, to a form and a subject matter beyond oneself; it is necessarily to remain within the vortex of "influence," where the voices of all past contenders (not just Hemingway) seem ready to preempt one's own. A writer as reflective as Mailer will never become a redundant bore; neither, I suspect, by any exertion will he produce a book like *Cancer*, which marks out fundamentally new possibilities for fiction.

In Miller at his earliest and best we meet a liberator, one of those eccentrics of literature who, like Whitman, break every law and become a law unto themselves. Mailer's view of him, wrong in some particulars, is emphatically right in spirit: the gifts he mostly squandered have been those of a giant. If Miller has done much to provoke us into dismissing him, the fact of his originality remains. We will have to learn to read him as he himself reads "the great and imperfect ones." "When I reflect that the task which the artist implicitly sets himself is to overthrow existing values, to make of the chaos about him an order which is his own, to sow strife and ferment so that by the emotional release those who are dead may be restored to life, then it is that I run with joy to the great and imperfect ones, their confusion nourishes me, their stuttering is like divine music to my ears."

Works Cited

Bloom, Harold, 1973. *The Anxiety of Influence: A Theory of Poetry*. New York: Oxford University Press.

Mailer, Norman. 1971. *The Prisoner of Sex*. Boston: Little, Brown.

———. 1977. *Genius and Lust: A Journey Through the Major Writings of Henry Miller*. New York: Grove.

Miller, Henry. 1941. *The Colossus of Maroussi*. New York: New Directions.

———. 1961a. *Tropic of Cancer* (1st ed. 1934.) New York: Grove.

———. 1961b. *Tropic of Capricorn*. (1st ed. 1939.) New York: Grove.

———. 1971. *My Life and Times*. Chicago: Playboy.

Millett, Kate. 1970. *Sexual Politics*. Garden City, N.Y.: Doubleday.

Orwell, George. 1954. "Inside the Whale." In *A Collection of Essays*. New York: Doubleday Anchor.

Tzara, Tristan. 1951. "Dada Manifesto 1918." In *The Dada Painters and Poets: An Anthology*, ed. Robert Motherwell. New York: Wittenborn, Schultz. Pp. 76–82.

12

The Partisan

This essay-review first appeared in The New York Review *in 1978. It tried to assess what Philip Rahv and his circle both provided and failed to provide for three generations of American readers.*

The references to Freudianism in these pages sound quite different from my assessments of psychoanalytic theory and therapy in Part I. There I address psychoanalysis as its protagonists have understood it; here I touch on a diffuse Freudian atmosphere within a literary-intellectual circle. One of the ironies surrounding the persistence of psychoanalysis in our "high culture" is that its most influential champions have had no very clear notion of what it actually asserts.

So, too, the Marxism of the Partisan Review *group, with the single exception of Sidney Hook, was largely a matter of pious gestures; the critics who came of age in the Thirties were too busy being good leftists to read Marx with any care. Even so, in the light of slick Eighties-style academic Marxism (Chapter Eight), one must be impressed by the earnestness of the New York intellectuals as they tried to dissociate themselves from Stalin's crimes without losing all political commitment. Here at least was a generation that never doubted the connection between utopian ideas, bloodshed, and moral responsibility.*

"Little magazines" are, for the most part, the mayflies of the literary world. Launched on implausibly idealistic manifestoes, briefly sustained by charity and overwork, and imperiled by an ever-worsening ratio of creditors to subscribers, they soon complete their scarcely noticed flights and sink away, to be replaced by swarms of others. Ephemerality is the little magazine's generic fate;

by promptly dying it gives proof that it remained loyal to its first program. Conversely, when such a journal survives for decades and effects a change in the whole temper of cultural debate, we may be sure that a metamorphosis has occurred. In outward respects— format, financing, even the number of paying readers—the magazine may still be technically "little," but its editors will have shown a quite untypical gift for retreating from untenable positions, anticipating new currents of opinion, and harmonizing interests that would seem on their face to be incompatible.

This rule applies nowhere more strikingly than to *Partisan Review*, the longest-lived and most influential of all our magazines that began by being "little." At its inception in 1934 it was not much more than a strident house organ of the Communist party and one of its literary brigades, the John Reed Club of New York City. The numerous members of its editorial board were to all appearances obedient Stalinists who would promote the official line of proletarianism—or, a little later, the relative latitudinarianism of the Popular Front. But by 1936 the most active of those editors, William Phillips and Philip Rahv, had learned all they would ever need to know about the nature of the Soviet dictatorship and the folly of allowing ideologues to enforce critical judgments. They ceased publication; the mayfly seemed to have fallen on schedule.

In fact, however, Rahv and Phillips were busy gathering collaborators, most of whom were recent converts to anti-Stalinism like themselves. In 1937, with the help of F. W. Dupee, Dwight Macdonald, Mary McCarthy, and George L. K. Morris, they reconstituted the magazine, now advocating at once a purer radicalism than·the Party's and devotion to the highest critical standards irrespective of ideology. Before long *Partisan* had attracted contributions not only by such survivors of leftist militancy as Sidney Hook, Meyer Schapiro, Lionel and Diana Trilling, Isaac Rosenfeld, Delmore Schwartz, Clement Greenberg, Irving Howe, Lionel Abel, and Harold Rosenberg, but also by figures as eminent and diverse as Malraux, Ortega, Silone, Eliot, Auden, and Dylan Thomas.

No one could deny that the new *Partisan* was a success, even though no one could explain how neo-Marxist political commentary was to be reconciled with "The Dry Salvages" and highbrow discussion of the modern masters. Not even Trotsky, the idol of the hour for intellectuals who wished to regard themselves as having moved to Stalin's left and not his right, could make room for James, Proust, and Gide on the revolutionist's bedtable. But Phillips and Rahv's eclectic policy was psychologically appropriate both for themselves and for their generation of former Communists. After years of monotonous proletarianizing, bright leftists were aching to do critical justice to complex and resistant texts—but they were not ready to admit that there is nothing especially radical about such activity. They gravitated to *Partisan* as the one journal in which they could bid good riddance to the Thirties without seeming to do so.

Partisan also became the vehicle for another and closely related adaptation. In the Forties and Fifties, the period of its greatest sway, the magazine was among other things a forum for debate about making one's peace with America. Nearly all of its older mainstays had believed at one time that fascism was a logical development of capitalism and that any war joined by the United States would shift the country definitively into its totalitarian phase. But no prior dogmas could prevent well-informed Jewish intellectuals from grasping the special character of Hitlerism. In the pages of *Partisan* and in hairsplitting private encounters, they inched their way from pacifism toward lukewarm support of the war— a process that was capped by the pacifist Dwight Macdonald's resignation in protest from the editorial staff in 1943. Less than a decade later, in a famous symposium canvassing the most prominent members of the *Partisan* circle, all but a few of twenty-four respondents concurred with Phillips's and Rahv's proposal that America had indeed become "Our Country and Our Culture."[1]

Such a rapprochement with the patriots amounted to a conspicuous and at times mortifying compromise of the *Partisan* writers' vanguard identity. It should be noted, however, that they had never constituted an avant-garde in the usual sense of the term. Politically, they had been drifting ambiguously toward the liberalism they professed to despise. Culturally, they welcomed association with such established and unradical personages as Eliot, Stevens, Tate, and Ransom. The poetry and fiction they wrote themselves were hardly experimental. And as judges of contemporary literature they shunned extremes, saving their approval for manifestly dignified ironists like the early Lowell and the early Bellow. For a supposed little magazine, *Partisan* was concerned to an unusual degree with previously established literary values such as complexity, moral seriousness, and a sense of the past.

In retrospect it seems evident that after about 1940, the radicalism of the *Partisan* writers was largely a matter of style. Their progress, at least until they became polarized by McCarthyism, was a fairly steady movement toward the American center; but they camouflaged that movement by drawing around themselves every available form of disciplined pessimism, from psychoanalysis and existentialism to the arid, elusive visions of Kafka and Eliot. As Alfred Kazin (1965) has said of them, "They would never feel that they had compromised, for they believed in alienation, and would forever try to outdo conventional opinion even when they agreed with it." In this manner assimilation retained much of the urgency and energy of revolt.

In a society still rife with anti-Semitism and suspicion of radicals, however, the early *Partisan* critics were by no means assured of a friendly audience. As Lionel Trilling could attest from bitter experience, university departments of English not only had a narrow gentlemanly idea of "the tradition" but also a gentleman's agreement about blood qualifications for discussing that tradition. The championing of modernism in *Partisan* can be understood in part as a turning of the tables on the professors. Of course the *Partisan* writers were sincere in their taste for the thorny moderns. Yet we cannot fail to notice that by placing extremity and alienation at the very heart of modern experience, they were in effect supplanting one tradition with another—one that they were already better prepared to gloss than were the salaried connoisseurs of Keats and Browning.

In view of their standing as outsiders on probation, however, it is not surprising that the *Partisan* critics preferred their pessimism well diluted with cultural decorum. Writers like Céline and Henry Miller, irreverent beyond all civility, were not celebrated in *Partisan*; the ideal figures would be those who already had a foothold on respectability and who emanated more, not less, portentous allusiveness than the favorites of the academy. When a *Partisan* critic set out to analyze such a model modern, the journal's usual tone of iconoclasm was apt to give way to a strangely incautious awe.

Thus Delmore Schwartz, a co-editor at the time, ingenuously entitled a 1945 essay "T. S. Eliot as the International Hero." Schwartz does not ask us to regard Eliot as a hero; he reminds us why we already do. The reason is that Eliot happens to be the quintessential modern cosmopolite, belonging to all and therefore none of the world's capitals, haunted by war and decay, attuned to the defining feature of modernity, namely impotence. "We ought to remember," wrote Schwartz, "that the difficulty of making love . . . is not the beginning but the consequence of the whole character of modern life." Modern man is like Gerontion:

> He lives in a rented house, he is unable to make love, and he knows that history has many cunning, deceptive, and empty corridors. The nature of the house, of love and of history are interdependent aspects of modern life.

Such remarks, absurd in their literal content, tell us something about the anxieties and mannerisms to which *Partisan* writers could be susceptible. To treat "Gerontion" as an accurate picture of "our" condition was both to play one's role as a bearer of grim tidings and to take social shelter beneath Eliot's none too capacious umbrella. Readers were not reminded that Schwartz's nondenominational mournfulness over "modern man" differed notably from Eliot's exclusivism. Not a word about Hakagawa bowing among the Titians, or, more significantly, about the "Jew" squatting on Gerontion's window sill. To be fully critical about such details would have been to strike too personal and querulous a note—and before an audience not devoid of prejudices like Eliot's. It was more prudent to write in universal terms, to ascribe prophetic souls to the gloomier modernists, and insofar as possible to overlook their often reactionary views.

The need to appropriate alienation, whether or not one still felt alienated oneself, also exacted a price in the *Partisan* critics' ability to consider ideas on their merits, apart from their usefulness in conferring adversary status. This holds even for the mildest, subtlest, and most peripheral member of the circle, Lionel Trilling. He called Freud and Nietzsche to the witness stand to vouch for our imperiled condition, but he could not afford to cross-examine them about the cogency of their propositions; they were, after all, his spiritual guardians against such paddlers of the mainstream as Van Wyck Brooks and the *New York Times Book Review*'s vox populi, J. Donald Adams. Trilling needed little coaxing in order to rehearse the terrible antinomies of modern existence and the stern tasks allegedly confronting "us." It seemed that liberalism, meaning the bureaucratic progressivism to which he was in fact quite reconciled, had to be fertilized by imagination; imagination had to be sobered by an unspecified political concern; the ego was not master in its own house; and modern literature was at once our finest possession and a seedbed of libidinous and nihilistic anarchy. The recompense for living with such difficult knowledge, such conflicting imperatives, was of course an awareness that the philistines of the mass culture were not up to doing so.

In the Fifties and Sixties, when the social climate had become less invidious and the *Partisan* writers had gained the recognition they deserved as our first and only intelligentsia, they could afford to begin dissociating themselves from what Bellow's *Herzog* (1967) called "the commonplaces of the Wasteland outlook, the cheap mental stimulants of Alienation, the cant and rant of pipsqueaks about Inauthenticity and Forlornness." Yet even then their bias toward modernism remained strong, for only the great moderns stood between them and a more threatening wasteland, the culturally chaotic one inhabited by trolls like Ginsberg and Kerouac. By the Sixties some *Partisan* graduates were looking back to the modernist classics with an almost professorial nostalgia, as the last serious writing our demotic Western world was likely to produce.

That may look like an oddly patrician stance for one-time champions of proletarianism to assume. In truth, however, the seeming paradox of combining more or less left-wing sociopolitical commentary with lofty aesthetic discourse had never been much of a paradox at all. Behind both kinds of enterprise lay the same animus against the bland middle class, and more especially against "nativism"—the distinctly WASPish idea that American civilization is culturally rich in just those respects where it most sharply diverges from European precedent. What united Marx and Proust, Nietzsche and Joyce, Freud and Camus was their equidistance from Iowa. The lapsed Marxists surrounding *Partisan* disputed many points with one another, but they all seemed to agree, as did the writers they most admired, that literary value was not a matter for the people to decide.

Yet if *Partisan* was held together by elitism, as a magazine of debate it was also significantly open to interaction with outsiders. The "we" so frequently invoked in its pages was meant to designate, not the immediate clique in favor with the editors, but all readers willing to acknowledge the modern crisis of values and the necessity of lodging belief elsewhere than in the Soviet Union on the one hand and warmed-over Christianity on the other. That was a numerous group, and *Partisan* helped to make it more so. Phillips and Rahv were always more concerned to publish intelligent speculative discourse than to promote modernism or any other fashionable cause.

Nevertheless, we are far enough removed from the Forties and Fifties to perceive that for a long while there was not only a recognizable *Partisan* style—wide-ranging, cutting, self-assured—but also a *Partisan* world view. It was a complex of attitudes and positions derived in part from the debacle of the American Left, in part from the concurrence of separatist and assimilationist impulses within the so-called New York family, and in part from the personality of Philip Rahv, by all accounts the ruling figure at *Partisan* during its most influential period.[2]

Rahv, indeed, was in most respects the quintessential *Partisan* contributor. He was anti-nativist and pro-modernist; he distrusted the academy and its weakness for "idealistic" spiritual transports; he felt permanently betrayed by Stalin; he endorsed psychoanalysis as a body of truths too upsetting for optimists and literary professors to comprehend; he craved disputation and was ever watchful for new trends that would bear denouncing; and he treated well-known authors and problems as if no one had discussed them before, or never adequately. Most importantly, he tried in his own criticism to do what he and Phillips as editors were doing only by juxtaposition, namely to bring together sociopolitical consciousness and sensitivity to great literature. In making that effort, Rahv epitomized the magazine's project of freeing analytic intelligence from party-mindedness without stripping it completely of radical purpose.

Before the *Partisan* critics broke with Stalinism they had been practitioners of revolutionary subordination: books were weapons in the class war, and the chief function of criticism was to identify which side was served by a given work. Once that phase was over, the question became how far to go in the direction of sheer aestheticism. Should one now praise *The Golden Bowl* as fervently as one had recently been praising *The Lower Depths*? Were an author's ideas and attitudes nothing more than a *donnée* after all, incidental to the produced sensations that really mattered? What, if anything, could an ex-Stalinist say about literature that wasn't already being said by the suave and ingenious New Critics?

Rahv's answer was that ideas and attitudes counted as much as before, but no longer in the same way. An author lacking a sense of history or an awareness of the social issues of his time was still to be faulted—not, however, because of his deviation from Marx and Engels but because his imagination was incomplete. The critic's task was first to submit himself to that imagination without making fixed ideological demands of it, but then, rather than lose himself in some contrived ecstasy, to draw back and ask what dimensions of the world were being ignored or distorted. Thus, for example, Rahv, who did much to revive interest in Henry James and wrote perceptively about him, eventually decided that James was too narrow, for he took his society for granted and "made a metaphysic of private relations, giving the impression that they are immune to the pressures of the public and historical world." Other critics might challenge Rahv's judgment, but all could recognize that he was writing from a thoroughly considered position. It was a kind of shadow Marxism, whereby one could still value mimesis and social compassion without insisting on determinism or dogmatizing about "structure" and "superstructure" or issuing veiled threats in the name of history.

The most important literary value for Rahv, however, was more Shakespearean than Marxian: a tolerance for contradiction, a capacity to grant full imaginative reality to people not of one's own party. He found that value supremely exemplified in Tolstoy and Dostoevsky, two writers whose more particular opinions he largely rejected. And he found it undeveloped in D. H. Lawrence, who tended to pit his "mouthpiece" characters against contemptible adversaries, and utterly lacking in the recent work of Norman Mailer, whose vacuous superhero Rojack rapes and murders his way through a world that exists only as a field of megalomaniac desire. If Rahv was huffy about such cases, it was because he had learned from the major developments of his age that unmediated will and a failure to credit one's opponents with humanity are defects that can entail appalling mass criminality.

It would seem, then, that Rahv had survived the Thirties with a rare combination of concrete historical awareness and individual morality, the best fruits of both Marxism and conservatism. To be sure, that fact did not make him a great critic. His ideas were mostly derivative, his range of literary interests was restricted to the novel from Gogol onward, and he was too much given to humorless scorn, righteously condemning tendencies he had managed to avoid himself. Yet he was also capable of sustained and generous appreciation; witness the five completed chapters of his projected book on Dostoevsky, which his new editors, Arabel Porter and Andrew Dvosin, have now printed in sequence for the first time (Rahv 1978). Those chapters show a fine subtlety and empathy, interrupted only by the occasional squeaking of Rahv's hobbyhorse: settling scores with the Soviet Union. By reading selectively in this last collection—combining, say, the pieces on Tolstoy, Kafka, and Dostoevsky with such influential essays as "The Cult of Experience in American Writing," "The Dark Lady of Salem," "The Heiress of All the Ages," and "Religion and the Intellectuals"—one can come away with the impression of a mind whose irritability and unforgivingness were more than overbalanced by possession of a coherent yet flexible outlook, neither as prescriptive as the ideologues' nor as indeterminate as the aesthetes'.[3]

A rather different picture of Rahv emerges, however, when we attend to his strictly political writings, which until now have formed an inconspicuous part of the record. For reasons we can only surmise, he completely omitted them from his *summa*, *Literature and the Sixth Sense* (1969). But Porter and Dvosin want to call attention to those writings, which Dvosin in his introduction claims to be pregnant not only with documentary value but also with "great political insight." More than seventy pages of the new *Essays* are given over to such items as a 1932 declaration of Communist militancy, a 1938 indictment of the Moscow Trials, a 1939 autopsy on literary proletarianism, a 1952 denunciation of mass philistinism, a 1964 appreciation of Trotsky, a 1967 blast at liberal anti-Communists, and a 1971 assessment of the New Left as insufficiently revolutionary.

Taken individually, these pieces make lively reading. Rahv was implacably and persuasively contemptuous of Stalin's show trials, of the conformist atmosphere in postwar America, and of the zeal of penitents like Whittaker Chambers, who could pass so readily from Stalin to Jesus because they had been unworldly absolutists all along. Yet when considered together, the political writings make us conscious of a persistent and damaging evasion. More than anyone else in his circle, Rahv showed himself incapable of understanding that values as well as tactics were entailed in the general backing-off from revolutionary activism.

Even in the most superficial terms, Rahv's politics were inconsistent. In his own view he had changed direction only once, when he repudiated Stalin as a traitor to Marx. Thereafter he considered himself an independent Marxist or, as he sometimes said, a democratic socialist. Little was heard of this Marxism in the Forties and Fifties, however; in that period Rahv conveniently simplified things by referring to himself and *Partisan* as "anti-Communist." He and

Phillips, for example, wrote in 1953 that their "ideal reader" would be someone "concerned with the structure and fate of modern society, in particular with the precise nature and menace of Communism" (Rahv 1953). But in 1967, emboldened by the newer collegiate radicalism, Rahv defiantly told *Commentary* that he had never broken with "communism, in its doctrinal formulations by Marx *or even by Lenin*" (emphasis added). He professed himself scandalized that official America still rejected "not the Stalinist aspect of communism but communism as such, authoritarian or not."

One might say that the unclarity here could be resolved merely by attending to the difference between capital and lower-case *c*'s. Rahv was a communist, not a Communist. Fair enough—but apart from disapproving of mass murder and slave-labor camps, what difference in principle was involved? Was Lenin a nonauthoritarian, a communist with a small *c*? And hadn't Marx himself accepted the necessity of concerted violence against those who stand to lose by the revolution? To ascribe Soviet terror entirely to Stalin was to indulge in an inverse cult of personality, a flight from essential issues.

Toward the end of his life, sizing up the imprudent radicals of the Vietnam era, Rahv began to sound like a born-again Leninist of the familiar type. In "What and Where Is the New Left?" he declared that "violent assaults on the class-enemy" are inadvisable "if undertaken prematurely, . . . before the challengers of the status quo can count on at least an even chance of victory in an armed struggle with the police." With avuncular sagacity he pointed to the need for "a guiding organization—one need not be afraid of naming it a centralized and disciplined party," practically and ideologically alert "so as not to miss its historical opportunity. . . ." Rahv neglected to say how such a party, once its "armed struggle" was over, would wither away in favor of nonauthoritarian democracy. A lifetime of political argument and observation had failed to teach him that repression flows naturally from defining others as "the class-enemy."

If we ask why Rahv was so obtuse on this point, I think the answer must be sought in an irrational appeal that Marxism makes to people of a certain prickly, combative, and power-hungry disposition. Where others need friends, they need class-enemies. Lacking such hateful antagonists, they would no longer be able to connect their will to domination with an ultimately benign historical drama, guided by transpersonal forces. In a word, they would be just plain bullies. By retaining faith, however inactively, in what he called "the principles of classic Marxism, its knowledge and foresight," Rahv succeeded in mistaking his native Manicheism for revolutionary vigilance. But he paid a price in squandered bile, not just against the capitalists (for in fact he had little to say about them) but more especially against everyone who struck him as following an incorrect line: Stalinists and professional anti-Stalinists, pacifists and patriots, McCarthyites and fellow travelers, ideologues and idealizers. Dissociation on all sides was his one strategy for retaining a sense of mission.

Like other Americans who rejected Stalin only because he was a counter-revolutionary, Rahv never admitted the extent of his debt to liberal capitalism. As an editor, he stood behind the shield of the First Amendment. As a judge of literature, he upheld a magnanimity of vision that could never flourish in a state founded on the victory of one former underclass. And as both editor and critic, he took for granted a readership of people who would believe that values can be absorbed from unorthodox books, and who would be free to change their minds and indeed their lives if they agreed with his own independent reasonings. The contemporary world offered no basis for imagining that such readers would be available under a Marxist dispensation.

The irony of Rahv's political nondevelopment is that, unlike the sophists who warned against "repressive tolerance," he actually did appreciate guaranteed liberties. After World War II he had to admit that America had thus far "sustained that freedom of expression and experiment without which the survival of the intelligence is inconceivable in a modern society." Meanwhile the record of entrenched Marxism in the management of culture was unambiguous. But for Rahv to embrace the liberal institutions that protect "freedom of expression and experiment" would have been to jeopardize his adversary identity; he could no more do that than Trilling could question Freud's gratuitously tragic ideas about civilization, or than Schwartz could reject Eliot on the grounds of his anti-Semitism. It was easier to keep hoping that history would one day give birth to a true realm of freedom as described by Marx, in which one would not have to thank the class-enemy for revocable favors.

Fortunately, the shallowness of Rahv's political thought had little effect on his best literary criticism. We can now understand, however, why nearly all of that criticism was written in the Forties, when he and others were under maximum pressure to show that they could reach a nonsectarian audience. The Rahv we see in earlier and later periods reveals a sensibility dissociated between revolutionary impulses and a belief in cultural hierarchy.

Toward the end of his life that dissociation became painful; the New Left had re-ignited his wrath against the ruling class, but it had also quickly dissolved into a "counterculture" utterly alien to his temperament. Meanwhile, under new leadership, *Partisan* had turned its back on the great moderns and was flirting with pornography, rock music, and the newest of liberties, freedom from interpretation. Fulminating against "swinging reviewers" and "our contemporary porno-aesthetes," Rahv sounded just like the academic traditionalists he had always disprized. Was there no way to restore cultural norms and simultaneously continue to struggle against the system? *Modern Occasions* was founded, and soon foundered, on that dim prospect.

Some cultural conservatives have argued that promoters of literary nihilism such as they claim the early *Partisan* critics were have only themselves to blame for the anarchy they now oppose. Trilling himself, appalled by the mood of the Sixties, is known to have spoken ruefully of "modernism in the streets." Such remorse, however, betrays a teacher's illusion that mostly unread books are more determinative of mass conduct than are wars and baby booms. In any case, the tasteful kind of modernism favored by *Partisan* was always less likely to lead to Molotov cocktails than to dry martinis. It would be especially far-fetched to accuse Philip Rahv of having incited the new anti-authoritarianism, for, unlike some of his contributors, he had never equated modernity with the overthrow of moral restraint. As for his political militancy, it slumbered for three decades before being briefly aroused by the New Left.

Rahv's program of political and literary seriousness was exactly the same in 1970 as it had been in 1940, but everything else had changed. In the early years he and his friends were sufficiently close to their leftist past for their devotion to literature to be seen as a courageous break with the party line, a more high-minded radicalism. Again, modernism was still a tradition to conjure with, not a staple of every curriculum. Above all, *Partisan* was just beginning its spectacularly successful work of propagating its cultural position. As the word from New York radiated outward, the adversary fever which had been so essential to the magazine's self-image necessarily subsided. Then the veterans of the Forties found themselves inhabiting a larger world, full of prosperity, compromise, and chatter about the authors they had once claimed as their own. Rahv and his associates had helped to shape a new literary establishment, more democratic and sophisticated than its predecessor. In doing so, they phased themselves irreversibly out of business as spokesmen for an alien vision.

Notes

1. For a concise account of this history, see Longstaff (1976).

2. I do not mean to slight William Phillips's steadying influence, but former associates make it clear that equal collaboration was not Rahv's normal *modus operandi*. According to Alfred Kazin (1965), "He was naturally a talker rather than a writer, a pamphleteer, a polemicist, an intellectual master of ceremonies and a dominator. . . ." William Barrett (1974) rather grudgingly calls Rahv an extraordinary editor but describes him as cliquish, overbearing, easily offended, and dismissive—a portrait largely anticipated in Mary McCarthy's self-important Will Taub in her *roman à clef*, *The Oasis* (1949). More recently, in an obituary memoir reprinted in the collection just published (Rahv 1978), McCarthy wrote less satirically of "a powerful intellect, a massive, overpowering personality and yet shy, curious, susceptible, confiding." As for Delmore Schwartz, he considered Rahv "a manic impressive" and was fond of repeating, "Philip does have scruples, but he never lets them stand in his way" (Barrett).

3. Readers who find Rahv congenial may want to supplement the named essays with important pieces that Porter and Dvosin do not supply, notably "Freud and the Literary Mind," "The Myth and the Powerhouse," "Fiction and the Criticism of Fiction," and "The Native Bias." All of them can be found in the third and last of Rahv's own collections, *Literature and the Sixth Sense* (1969).

Works Cited

Barrett, William. 1974. "The Truants: *Partisan Review* in the 40's." *Commentary*, June, pp. 48–54.

Bellow, Saul. 1967. *Herzog*. (1st ed. 1964.) New York: Viking.

Kazin, Alfred. 1965. *Starting Out in the Thirties*. Boston: Little, Brown.

Longstaff, S. A. 1976. "The New York Family." *Queen's Quarterly*, 83 (1976), 556–73.

McCarthy, Mary. 1949. *The Oasis*. New York: Random House.

Rahv, Philip. 1953. Foreword. *The New Partisan Reader 1945–1953*, ed.
    William Phillips and Philip Rahv. New York: Harcourt.
———. 1969. *Literature and the Sixth Sense*. Boston: Houghton Mifflin.
———. 1978. *Essays on Literature and Politics 1932–1972*, ed. Arabel J.
    Porter and Andrew J. Dvosin. Boston: Houghton Mifflin.
Schwartz, Delmore. 1945. "T. S. Eliot as the International Hero." *Partisan
    Review*, 12: 199–206.

13

Pop Goes the Critic

This chapter can be regarded in part as a sequel to the previous one. Leslie Fiedler's early career, like that of Philip Rahv, was bound up with the literary culture surrounding The Partisan Review. *But whereas Rahv decisively shaped that culture, the much younger Fiedler grew up within it and, as we now perceive, never wholly subscribed to its values.*

"Pop Goes the Critic" was first published in The New Criterion *early in 1983.*

Leslie Fiedler we have always with us. For roughly two decades now he has been intellectually stagnant and muddled, prolifically redundant, obsessed with shoring up his ever more dubious fame, pitching one-liners to an empty house. It would be a kindness if he were to declare a moratorium on self-promotion, but nothing appears less likely. Indeed, in his twenty-second and most autobiographical book, *What Was Literature?* (1982), he has made his most sustained effort yet to convince us that history is on his side. Though the book leaves a quite opposite impression, there can be little hope that Fiedler will be deterred by the cold welcome it has already received. He is like a bag lady permanently camped on the doorstep of criticism, muttering imprecations at the insiders and keeping warm by waving enthusiastically to oblivious passers-by.

Part I of *What Was Literature?*, characteristically titled "Subverting the Standards," is Fiedler's retrospect on the years since World War II, with particular reference to his own part in the struggle between high and popular culture. We follow him from humble origins—proletarian-Jewish in Newark, then miserable in Missoula, having to pass for a fellow traveler of WASP academic pretensions—through persecution and exile following the famous pot bust in Buffalo, to his present status as a living legend who is free to declare that his cultural affinities have been, all along, those of an impressionable teenager. And in Part II, "Opening Up the Canon," he argues that the popular tradition which he now wishes to champion has its own shelf of worthy classics—best sellers whose lasting appeal rebukes the insufferable professors of literature who, throughout the book, play the bad guys arrayed against the Lone Fiedler.

Because Fiedler is more concerned to settle old scores than to think consecutively, his case for an American counter-canon is rather haphazardly assembled. His analyses of books like *Uncle Tom's Cabin* and *Gone With the Wind*, furthermore, read like parodies of the Fiedler method, with its abundant "archetypes" and stock figures and its loose way of arriving at titillating inferences. And his account of the cultural wars from the Fifties until now, though sometimes lively and frank, is vitiated by his need to score easy points off opponents who are identified only by denigrating epithets that settle their inferiority without the nuisance of debate.

Why bother to write about such a book? I have asked myself that question more than once. But there are two matters here that bear pausing over. In the first place, the latter half of *What Was Literature?* does raise a legitimate issue about the reasons why "perennial best sellers" retain their appeal. If classics are known by their longevity, on what grounds can we deny that *Gone With the Wind*, say, is a classic? Fiedler at least challenges us to come up with an answer. And more generally, Fiedler's memoirs, however self-serving, invite a reassessment of his whole career—a career whose direction he understands quite well but whose decade-by-decade claim on our interest he seems to have exactly backwards.

Such a reassessment would be a sterile exercise if Fiedler had not once been an important figure in our cultural life. But that is indeed what he was, most notably in his first three books: *An End to Innocence* (1955), *Love and Death in the American Novel* (1960), and *No! in Thunder* (1960). Throughout the Fifties he was considered the *enfant terrible* of American social and literary criticism—a reputation that, though he sought it out and cherished it, did less than justice to his actual contribution. Before the Sixties Fiedler was never simply a maverick; he was a cogent analyst of traits that he followed from the classics of our fiction through the political hypocrisies of his own time. His decline is more than an arresting case history; it is a commentary on the passing of a sub-culture that had encouraged a rare combination of literary and social engagement.

To begin seeing what has been lost, let me recall my own introduction to Fiedler, which occurred when I was a graduate student at Princeton and he was in fullest stride. The Gauss Seminar committee selected him as its annual lecturer for 1957—a controversial choice and, I imagine, a great comic opportunity for Fiedler. Princeton in those days was a coldbed of something called, in all ethnic obtuseness, "Christian Humanism," a peculiarly rigid conception of literary study which presumed that literary works were attempts to instruct us in commonplace verities of their authors' time. "Christian" referred broadly to the theological climate that was thought to have survived, *mutatis mutandis*, from the Beowulf poet through "Mr. Eliot," whose tonal influence was everywhere—though of course, being still alive, he was not yet a fit subject for a dissertation.

Into this churchly atmosphere breezed Fiedler, looking not a bit like an awestruck supplicant. Bearded, rotund, robust, ironically genial, eyes twinkling with wary merriment at the effect he was provoking, he lectured about classic American fiction and the *real* themes—misogyny, sadomasochism, sublimated homoeroticism, incest, necrophilia, and miscegenous rape—that had rescued our most cherished books from their sappy manifest content. This was the scandalous material that would be elaborated in *Love and Death in the American Novel*, that bumptious, mischievous tract which, as one of my Princeton professors would have remarked with an air of taking an exact measurement, "went too far"—but in a direction that badly needed to be taken.

The word about Fiedler in Princeton's corridors was that he was a barbarian—dirty-minded, sloppy with facts and theory, disrespectful of tradition. It was hard to disagree, but I remember feeling that this kick in the pants was just what Christian Humanism deserved. Those among us who harbored secret sympathies for "the critics" in their war against "the scholars"—that is, for clever and surprising verbal analysis as opposed to the prevailing blend of pedantry and cultural reverence—saw in Fiedler a potential ally. And though we did not realize it at once, he was supplying an exhilarating intellectual agenda for some of us who felt drawn toward the furtive, inhibited-demonic strain within an American civilization that was outwardly ruled by optimism and materialism. Is there an essential violence in our collective imagination? Are the American classics anti-female? Should we read those books not as plotted sermons but as testaments to ambivalence? To have broached such previously unthinkable questions, with or without fully convincing answers, was in itself a critical landmark.

Fiedler has by no means repented of the jolt he administered to American studies, yet his present rhetorical purpose requires that his best decade of work—when he still cared about literary quality and had not yet turned his mythifying into a methodological tic— be passed over lightly. Instead, he calls our attention to his most conformist period in the Forties, when, we learn, he cut his teeth on Brooks and Warren, wrote his first long paper on Hopkins's verse, produced an orthodox dissertation on "The Medieval Backgrounds of John Donne's 'Songs and Sonnets,' " and accepted without question the professional consensus about "first-rank" literature and "the canon" of great American fiction. That was the hero bound and gagged with old school ties. In the "after" picture we are to discern someone who is free at last from the imposed role of "culture-climbing Jewish boy" or imitation WASP.

While this account is true enough to Fiedler's current sense of himself, it leaves us wondering why his reputation has continued to rest almost entirely on work that was complete by 1960. Such books as *Waiting for the End* (1964) and *The Return of the Vanishing American* (1968), presumably written in a more liberated state, sound by comparison like amiable chitchat, animated by no more urgent purpose than to catalogue some themes and to lay some personal blessings and curses on recent literature. Fiedler in those years was beginning not only to repeat himself and to coast on his notoriety but also to lose the moral incisiveness that had spared his early work from being merely sensationalistic.

Now, "moral incisiveness" may sound like an unnecessarily stuffy compliment to pay the critic who is thought to have tried, in "Come Back to the Raft Ag'in, Huck Honey!," to make us believe that the major American novelists of the mid-nineteenth century were closet homosexuals. But in fact Fiedler's essay made no such claim. Its actual subject was white racial guilt and the outlet it finds in a pathetic dream of remission. Given the persistence of bigotry, Fiedler proposed, the races can be reconciled only symbolically, through a fantasy of chaste, boyish love between a white nonconformist (Natty, Ishmael, Huck) and his black or red companion in adventure. Fiedler blamed our national "nostalgia for the infantile" on the bad faith and escapism of the dominant whites:

> In each generation we *play out* the impossible mythos, and we live to see our children play it: the white boy and the black we can discover wrestling affectionately on any American sidewalk, along which they will walk in adulthood, eyes averted from each other, unwilling to touch even by accident. The dream recedes; the immaculate passion and the astonishing reconciliation become a memory, and less, a regret, at last the unrecognized motifs of a child's book. "It's too good to be true, Honey," Jim says to Huck. "It's too good to be true."

Here is the prose of a man with something more important on his mind than his own self-image or his ability to ferret out prurient themes; his analytic powers remain in the service of his sense of humanity and justice.

That same sense also informs Fiedler's once controversial political essays from the Fifties, notably "Hiss, Chambers, and the Age of Innocence," "Afterthoughts on the Rosenbergs," and "McCarthy and the Intellectuals." Those pieces have so often been denounced for unseemly red-baiting that one hesitates to cite their virtues. Admittedly, no great courage was needed in the McCarthy years to chide liberals for having deceived themselves about the Soviet Union. Yet Fiedler was not in fact leaping onto an ideological bandwagon. He was holding his fellow intellectuals accountable to their consciences and doing so through richly persuasive analysis of events and public personalities. What strikes one on reacquaintance with his political writing is the openness and alertness of the sensibility it displays—at once tough, engaged, empathetic, and fair.

The vigor of that sensibility can be explained in part by reference to Fiedler's most immediate audience in the Fifties. In appealing to an ideal reader who would be skeptical, liberal, humane, and cosmopolitan, the early Fiedler was also addressing a circle of real readers whose approval he strove to earn. I mean the so-called New York intellectuals—those mostly Jewish literary and social critics who, in the Forties and Fifties, were beating a dignified retreat from their former leftism. When Fiedler argued for artistic integrity, judged American literature to be "immature" by European standards, and skewered both the know-nothings of the Right and the sentimentalists of the Left, he was emulating such *Partisan Review* elders as Philip Rahv and Lionel Trilling. Emulating, but by no means parroting, for while Trilling was wont to vaporize and Rahv was given to peremptory, defensive, bullying pronouncements, Fiedler was nearly always shrewd, concrete, and implicitly democratic in his sympathies.

In retrospect, we can see that the "adversary culture" of the *Partisan* circle owed its existence to a unique moment in American social and political history. The discrediting of Stalinism, the emergence of the United States as custodian *pro tempore* of a shattered European civilization, and the weakening of class and ethnic barriers after the Depression all helped to coax would-be revolutionaries into uneasy reconciliation with capitalism and nativism. In that reconciliation, the old anti-bourgeois impetus survived in derivative forms: as an advocacy of international literary modernism and of "difficulty" generally, as an insistence on tragedy and irony as opposed to middle-class shallowness, as a suspicion of dogma in whatever form. Both the pretensions and the accomplishments of the New York intellectuals, then, reflected the conflicting claims of assimilation and exclusivity in a period of political realignment and widening social opportunity.

In order to understand what happened to Fiedler in the Sixties and thereafter, it is essential to grasp that he was a second-generation participant in the adversary culture, one who had barely flirted with Communism and whose arena from the outset was the semibureaucratic world of the literary academy. Thus he experienced none of the anxiety that older New York intellectuals felt about losing their vanguard status when they were belatedly welcomed into the universities. For them, as Fiedler points out in *What Was Literature?*, the essential thing was to continue exposing provincialism and kitsch. Though they had no reason to trust the clubby Anglophiles of the English departments, they also had no fundamental quarrel with the idea that literary education should be elitist in spirit. But for Fiedler, a self-described "Jewish-American academic arriviste," things were significantly different. In his world the anti-Semitic professors, the connoisseurs of beauties in Keats and Pater, were the gatekeepers to success. He had to start out by playing their game—and, for self-respect, by undermining it in every way that would not jeopardize his toehold in the academy.

Fiedler's *Partisan* predecessors had approached literary problems with the solemn urgency of men who had lost a secular faith and who wanted to balance a cutting-edge skepticism against a need for order and certitude. The Freud and Marx whom they somewhat airily invoked were not just presences that could help them withdraw from Trotsky to Kafka without appearing to stumble. They were also thought to be repositories of hard-won knowledge about mass repression and false consciousness—knowledge, in short, of the modern soul and the enduring human condition. But Fiedler had no desire to traffic in such woolly abstractions. Since his primary aim was to upstage his academic colleagues, he would avail himself of Marxian and Freudian concepts, along with those of the seemingly antithetical Jung, in an ad hoc, opportunistic spirit, knowing but not caring, as he said in the preface to *Love and Death in the American Novel*, "how syncretically I have yoked together and how cavalierly I have transformed my borrowings."

Already in the Fifties, it is clear, Fiedler's egoism and theatricality were chafing to break free from the purposes he shared with the New York intellectuals. And from the outset he was never steadied by the university's ideals of patient research, objectivity, and deference to pertinent work by other scholars. For him those ideals would always be tainted by their association with the old guard of the Modern Language Association. Although that old guard disappeared long ago, in Fiedler's mind the academy would always remain a bastion of WASP privilege. He could therefore conceive of himself only as an enemy agent within its walls.

We can see, then, that Fiedler was well primed for the gestural radicalism that was to blossom in the later Sixties. By the time that Trilling-style liberalism had lost its cachet in the Vietnam era, Fiedler no longer had any stake in it. When high culture came under attack as an instrument of social control, he was ready to declare that he had never really believed in it—that only protective mimicry had prompted him, for example, to condemn the Beat writers "in the court of high art for flagrant immorality, an immorality of form." And when a generation of college students sided with "the people" against "the establishment," Fiedler could claim to have been there first. Although his idea of "the people" was the very middle class against whom the Haydens and the Rubins were rebelling, Fiedler already shared the activists' taste for simplistic contrasts between the oppressors and the oppressed.

It is not surprising, then, in turning to *What Was Literature?*, to discover that Fiedler's sociopolitical observations no longer show any regard for fairness or nuance. By now he thinks nothing of slandering the New Critics as "proto-fascist"; of fingering Saul

Bellow as "a spokesman for the New Right, vilifying the young, blacks and insubordinate women"; and of hinting that *Huckleberry Finn* and the unbowdlerized Mother Goose rhymes are no longer available to the young. In a society which happens to be discarding taboos rapidly without any prompting from himself, Fiedler has chosen to depict the Eighties as "our own repressive decade," a time when the retreat from the First Amendment "threatens to turn into a rout." His conception of himself as an embattled liberationist, a Gang of One in the cause of cultural democracy, comes first; actualities must be adjusted to fit the picture.

The same need to represent himself as surrounded by villains now manifests itself in Fiedler's assessment of the English departments, which in his rendering are still bent upon suppressing all things popular and anti-modernist. We must not be lulled, he warns, by the fact that his favorite genres—science fiction, the detective story, the cowboy movie, the soap opera, pornography— have found their way into many a curriculum. He insists that the specialists in popular culture are still being treated as pariahs within their departments. Besides, he says, the mandarins are stubbornly unwilling to relinquish their "last and dearest snobbism, the conviction that print is inherently superior to movies and TV. . . ." If teachers of literature are to satisfy Fiedler that they are true sons of liberty, they will have to get over their atavistic preference for books. At the very least they must avoid "even the semblance of celebrating already established works at the expense of those still despised, much less those preferred by an elite at the expense of those loved by the great majority."

Fiedler labors mightily to convince us, and perhaps himself as well, that he feels right at home with the taste of that "vast majority." Within the literary tradition, he favors Stephen Foster over Emily Dickinson and finds redeeming virtues in "The Bells" and in the poems of Longfellow, whose "Hiawatha," he notes, was "a smash hit" in 1855. He proudly lays claim to having written the first highbrow defense of *Superman* comics and to having extolled hard-core pornography and Grade B movies before their merits had become apparent to other intellectuals. He can testify, further, that he weeps copiously over daytime serials and responds "passionately" to the triumphs of Tarzan. And with what he himself calls a "truly Dickensian sentimentality," he invites the rest of us to join him in embracing "what used to be called 'trash,' . . .

[which] touches us all at a place where we have never been psychically sundered each from each."

Halfway through his book, however, Fiedler lets us see what he really thinks of "the people" and their literary preferences. There the great commoner suddenly lashes out at "the ersatz mystical maunderings of Kahlil Gibran" and "the vapid rhapsodies of Rod McKuen," which apparently exemplify the wrong, or truly trashy, variety of trash. Eventually Fiedler confesses that he is offended by the "majoritarian tyranny" of "the most ill-educated and naïve." "I do not believe," he announces, ". . . that even in an open society like our own everyone is entitled to establish his own rank order of books based on personal preference, whether these lead him to rate *Jonathan Livingston Seagull* higher than *Huckleberry Finn* or vice versa." Fiedler too turns out to believe in a canon—to believe, that is, that "some literary works are better than others, which is to say, more moving, more lasting in their appeal."

What, then, has all the fuss been about in Part I of *What Was Literature*? Fiedler seems gravely confused between his allegiance to "the great novels of our own tradition" and his need to identify with the mass audience. But the contradiction becomes less mysterious when we recall that Fiedler's aesthetic egalitarianism derives, not from untutored responses, but from his continuing vendetta against the genteel professors who once exacted from him a betrayal of his ethnic and class identity. The yearned-for regressive paradise, the "place where we have never been psychically sundered each from each," is not just childhood; it is a *pre-academic* condition antedating the fall into WASP sophistication.

As the not-yet-populist Fiedler himself remarked in 1958, when "the New York intellectual in academia" concentrates on popular literature and affects to "prefer a standard Hollywood Western to an 'art film,'" he is displaying "an inverted snobbism, a resistance to culture-mongering." In this light, the present fan of *Tarzan* is not so distant from the professor who scorns "the most ill-educated and naïve." One Fiedler tries to repudiate the taste-making authority of the academic overlords, the other to preempt their disapproval of him by merging into their company.

But what happens to the self-respect of a thinker whose grudges and compromises have left him with only clashing fragments of an identity? None of his provisional roles, we may imagine, will supply him with the confidence he enjoyed when he felt himself, however marginally, to be a member of a coherent community. His one remaining hope must be to make himself a favorite of those masses he has pretended to admire. If they will give their affection only to a clown who can amuse them by thumbing his nose at the cultural establishment, he will try his hand at being a clown.

There was a time, two decades ago, when Fiedler apparently sensed such an imminent change in his self-conception and cried out against it. "I am a literary man," he warned in *An End to Innocence*, "immune to certain journalistic platitudes"; and in *No! in Thunder* he protested that "I am not, let it be clear, for all my occasional hamminess, an entertainer." But that was 1960. Today, in *What Was Literature?*, Fiedler tells us that "like other entertainers I have been paid to allay boredom—in my case, by making our country and our culture seem more interesting and amusing than most academic accounts would lead us to believe." Now he sees himself as a would-be media star, eager to play the "visiting 'nut'" on television talk shows by twitting the critical stuffed shirts and by parading his affinity for the freakish.

In his own estimation, then, Fiedler is now a performer with an act to keep booked. And like anyone else in show business, he has had to cope with a fickle public. Television, he confesses, "ran out for me after a while"; but since he had never felt entirely comfortable with "the three-, four-, or five-minute shticks television format demands," he was glad enough to return to the college lecture circuit, where, "[t]hough I have not struck it quite as rich as Humboldt, I have been doing all right." "I am not only paid for public performance," Fiedler confides, "but I get free books for which other people pay hard cash, and am invited to attend without paying admission plays and movies for which others must buy tickets at the box office." What does it matter, asks the man who once disclosed a general "failure of the moral imagination" in leftists and rightists alike, if his sponsors have included both the CIA and the Writers Union of Rumania? The show must go on.

When we get to Part II of *What Was Literature?*, however, we find that Fiedler the earnest literary critic is still alive if far from well. There he eases up on the clowning and assembles a reasoned, though revealingly flawed, argument about the merits of certain popular works that the mass audience continues to find compelling. Here at last is Fiedler's bid to reassert his tarnished authority as a student of American literary history.

The pop classics Fiedler scrutinizes are *Uncle Tom's Cabin;* Thomas Dixon, Jr.'s *The Clansman* and D. W. Griffith's adaptation of it, *Birth of a Nation; Gone With the Wind,* the novel and film alike; and, somewhat prematurely it would seem, Alex Haley's *Roots* as both book and television series. Though these works, according to Fiedler, are despised by the fussy professors of literature, they meet the professors' own criterion of durability. They do so, moreover, without being notably complex or verbally distinguished. As Fiedler points out, the perennial best seller may have been collaboratively written or even plagiarized, and it is so little beholden to excellence of language that it can actually gain in power when transposed to other media. What is the secret of its allure?

The puzzle is not necessarily very profound. If he had merely pursued the fact that works like *Uncle Tom's Cabin* and *Gone With the Wind* belong to a mixed genre, at once romantic and realistic, Fiedler could have gone far to explain their resilience. Such books give us the easy thrills of romance while assuring us, through an admixture of candid, sometimes brutal details, that our daydreams pertain to the harsh actual world. And their moral narrowness make them more accessible to the unreflective reader than are doubt-riddled works like *The Scarlet Letter* and *Billy Budd.* It is a luxury to share in the Southern belle's glamour *and* her deserved fall, to stand in judgment of her personal failings while accepting her (and her creator's) politically childish grasp of the larger world. The romantic-realistic best seller allows us to believe that life is both unbearable and wonderful, just and unjust, heroic and base; we are never put to the trouble of trying to hold the extremes within a single tragic, ironic, or satirical apprehension.

For Fiedler to adopt this line of reasoning, however, would be to forfeit his game of overturning the professors' canon. That game calls for a transvaluation of values: the pop classics must come out looking *better* than works of idiosyncratic genius. And since those classics are at least partly sentimental in outlook and technique, this means that Fiedler must discover an innate virtue in what he once called, in *An End to Innocence,* "the ersatz religion of sentimentalism."

But where is such virtue to be found? Clearly, the sentimental dream of the harmonious, monogamous, all-white household is of small interest to a man of Fiedler's thematic preoccupations. Again, while Fiedler still identifies himself with books that "call into question our fundamental assumptions about men and God," the essence of the sentimental is that it generates a maximum of bittersweet emotion while calling as little as possible into question. (Even slavery, as Fiedler acknowledges, escapes condemnation in *Uncle Tom's Cabin*.) And of course sentimental fiction is regularly prudish, euphemistic, and trite—not hearty fare, one would think, for the imperturbable author of *Freaks* (1978).

Fiedler's means of escaping this dilemma is typically bluff and reckless. He simply tells us that he was wrong when, back in 1960, he declared that for the novelist, ineptitude is the one unforgivable sin. Verbal talent, it now transpires, is quite beside the point; it may even impede the mythic power that shines through the great popular novel. And that power emerges not in spite of sentimental clichés of plotting and portraiture but because of them. As Fiedler proclaims with a flourish of self-conscious hokum, "in every stereotype, no matter how weary, there sleeps a true archetype, waiting to be awakened by the majority critic, who, like the majority poet or novelist, screenwriter or composer of popular songs, dares to be simple enough, sentimental enough, passionate enough, absurd enough to try."

Fiedler's response to the timid domestic ideals of sentimental fiction is equally bold. Properly understood, he explains, that fiction is really a species of pornography, since it "impel[s] us toward some kind of orgasmic release." This, of course, is exactly the opposite of what sentimental novels appear to do, but Fiedlerian depth analysis puts us in contact with primordial themes lying beneath the fig leaf of altruism and decorum. Thus we learn that *Uncle Tom's Cabin* is gripping because it pulsates with symbolic rape, while *Gone With the Wind* is "essentially sadomasochistic."

As for Mrs. Stowe's cloying hearthside morality, a little methodological ingenuity can send it out into the storm. If Stowe is female, Fiedler reasons, she must of course be anti-male. Thus the two exemplars of "black phallic power" who flank Simon Legree as he beats Tom to death are really "projections of a misandry otherwise difficult for a dutiful wife, sister and daughter of strong pious males to confess." Similarly, the novel gets more interesting when we realize that "metaphorically, mythically, Tom is female and white"—an identification that leads to many a penetrating inference until we are told, some pages later, that Tom is in fact "the Great Black Mother of us all."

Now, this sort of capriciousness has marred Fiedler's criticism ever since he first grasped that he could import the concepts of repression and sublimation whenever a text looked recalcitrant to his hobbyhorses. Yet over the years an ominous difference has set in. Originally, as we have seen, Fiedler's meditations about the American "archetypes" of racial and sexual bigotry were framed by his avowed liberalism and his neo-Freudian concern for "maturity" in fiction. The idea was that our national literature has *suffered from* an ingrained racism and misogyny that issue in symptomatic polarities: the virgin and the whore, the kindly slave or noble Indian and the foe of white womanhood, the flight into prissy "values" on the one hand and into homoerotic, pre-adolescent male companionship on the other. Before long, however, those themes had become, not marks of a condition that might yet be rectified, but simply Fiedler's stock-in-trade as a traveling salesman of his own reputation. As they did so, Fiedler gradually forgot about "maturity" and social progress and began locating literary merit directly in the "archetypes." The result is a critical mode that could be fairly named redneck-mythic.

Mrs. Stowe, Fiedler now declares approvingly, "was what we call nowadays a 'racist,' which is to say, one who believes that whites and blacks are intrinsically different." The quotation marks are eloquent, as they are again in the following complaint against fellow critics: "they feel free to denounce [Thomas] Dixon [Jr.] for his 'misrepresentation' of slavery and the Negro, or to scold Margaret Mitchell for the 'falsity' of her account of the rise of the Klan."

"The form of a book," Fiedler wrote long ago, "represents either a moral critique of man and society, or a moral surrender." Somewhat later, applying that yardstick, he characterized *The Clansman* as perhaps "the worst book ever written in our country, an inept and hysterical piece of anti-Negro propaganda." If he now holds a different view, it is not because he has evolved into a racist. Rather, having deserted the *Partisan* critics' values and replaced them with nothing but a star-struck worship of success, he hesitates to object to any widely popular author's purposes. It seems that sheer audience excitement—as in the lynch-thirsty chase scenes in *Birth of a Nation*—lays to rest any questions about art in the service of race hatred.

Fiedler becomes uneasy only when confronting a work that is *not* suffused with plantation envy. What can he say about *Roots*? Well, to begin with, he can call it an "anti-anti-Tom book" and sportingly designate its author a " 'good good nigger.' " So much for the main mythic coordinates. But how could millions of white Americans have been entranced by an account of slavery written from the *slaves'* point of view? Could this be a sign of better understanding between the races? On the contrary, Fiedler assures us that *Roots* succeeded through orthodox means, by offering "images of black-white atrocities," by portraying sexual passion as "essentially evil," and by reactivating that guaranteed crowd pleaser, miscegenation horror. Once it is regarded in this light, we can suppose that Haley's book appears worthy after all to join *The Clansman* on the shelf of pop immortals.

There is no need to attach sinister importance to the strange political tenor of Fiedler's latest criticism. He continues to perform his eccentric version of deep thematic analysis, not because he cares where it comes out, but simply because he thinks his public expects him to run through a certain repertoire of interpretive stunts. The thesis he really cares about is that he is still the great Leslie Fiedler—still a rebel, a myth doctor, a man of the people, a kid at heart. It is a message he evidently needs to hear, and so, no doubt, he will go on repeating it. Meanwhile, some of us will prefer our recollections of the early Fiedler—the one who argued so trenchantly against escapism in every guise and who still believed that aesthetic and ethical standards, not gross sales, are the proper measure of an author's excellence.

Works Cited

Fiedler, Leslie A. 1955. *An End to Innocence: Essays on Culture and Politics.* Boston: Beacon.

———. 1960a. *Love and Death in the American Novel.* New York: Criterion.

———. 1960b. *No! in Thunder: Essays on Myth and Literature.* Boston: Beacon.

———. 1964. *Waiting for the End.* New York: Stein and Day.

———. 1968. *The Return of the Vanishing American.* New York: Stein and Day.

———. 1978. *Freaks: Myths and Images of the Secret Self.* New York: Simon and Schuster.

———. 1982. *What Was Literature? Class Culture and Mass Society.* New York: Simon and Schuster.

14

Conrad by Daylight

This review of Zdzisław Najder's Joseph Conrad: A Chronicle *gave me a welcome opportunity not only to assess a heroic work of scholarship but also to retrace some of my own steps. In* Out of My System *(1975) I had reprinted a 1967 essay offering a fairly standard oedipal reading of "Heart of Darkness" and other Conrad texts, and in that essay I had praised Bernard C. Meyer's* Joseph Conrad: A Psychoanalytic Biography *(1967) for correcting the romantic Conrad legend. The legend did need puncturing, but in 1967 I had failed to see that Meyer was substituting a no less arbitrary one: Conrad as helpless Freudian patient, writing fiction so as to flash distress signals from his tortured unconscious. By 1984, when this piece appeared in* The New York Review, *Meyer's book struck me as flagrantly aprioristic. My purpose in reverting to it was not merely to correct the record, but above all to show how, by employing a more humane and substantiated psychiatric model than the Freudian one, a biographer could expose Conrad's mental suffering* and *give ample recognition to his strength of character, his considered judgments on public issues, and his artistic control.*

I

The moment when a definitive biography appears would seem to be especially risky for the fortunes of any writer. Take, for instance, the Nobel prizewinner Sinclair Lewis, whose already waning reputation can scarcely be said to have survived Mark Schorer's comprehensive *Sinclair Lewis: An American Life* (1961). In that case the biographer himself fell to wondering publicly why he had lavished a decade on such an unimposing figure, and most readers who struggled through his bulky tome must have felt as though they were watching a once-brilliant rocket tumble awkwardly and irrevocably to earth. Both Schorer and his audience had learned too much. Why bother oneself further with a man who was so contemptibly understandable as a product of his callow and bumptious age?

Joseph Conrad, who never did receive a Nobel prize, is an incomparably larger figure than Lewis ever was, yet he might be considered even more vulnerable to an onslaught of mundane details and deflating explanations. Conrad, desperately seeking recognition from the xenophobic Pollyannas who dictated British taste, had gradually created for himself a seductive autobiographical legend compounded of small and large misrepresentations. The legend, personally foisted upon his earliest biographers, Richard Curle and Gérard Jean-Aubry, spoke of a hapless orphan and "sea dreamer" from the borderlands of Europe who ran off to illegal and romantic adventures in France and Spain, rose through sheer daring and willpower to the rank of captain in a foreign merchant marine, and then was summoned to a still greater vocation by the sonorities of England's literary language. In the public mind if not among biographical scholars, that dashing figure still *is* Conrad— our modern Sidney, equally at home in the worlds of action and of letters.

The scholars have known for some time, however, that the legend is doomed. It began crumbling in 1960 with Jocelyn Baines's *Joseph Conrad: A Critical Biography*, a book that questioned whether we should rest inferences about Conrad's life on unverified impressions gleaned from his memoirs and his autobiographical fiction. Baines could not free himself altogether from Conrad's spell, but others—notably Zdzisław Najder (1964), Norman Sherry (1966, 1971), William Blackburn (Conrad 1958), Cedric Watts (Conrad 1969), and Ian Watt (1979)—have gradually shown us a Conrad emerging from his times instead of from the mists of self-dramatization.

If we needed reminding that this movement from myth toward history is irreversible, two new books of documents would serve the purpose: Frederick Karl and Laurence Davies's first installment of Conrad's eight-volume *Collected Letters* (1983) and Zdzislaw Najder's *Conrad Under Familial Eyes* (1984b), which gives English-speaking readers a wider basis for exploring Conrad's roots and enduring connections with his homeland. Nor need we wait for the new evidence to be properly weighed. With the appearance of Najder's exhaustive and relentlessly objective biography, *Joseph Conrad: A Chronicle* (1984a), the process of demythification has surely reached its most decisive moment. Before long, all but the most casual of Conrad's admirers will have to take stock of a very different figure from the one they used to revere.

But before considering the problems this new Conrad causes us, let me immediately dispel the impression that Najder is a latecomer to the movement begun by Baines. The truth is that Najder was already making significant contributions to Conrad scholarship before Baines's study was published. For at least two decades now he has been the most knowledgeable Conradian alive, and everyone in the field is indebted to his *Conrad's Polish Background* of 1964. Twelve of the fifteen chapters in his present book, furthermore, were published before 1977, when a slightly different version appeared in Polish. Thus Najder is justified in his claim of precedence over Frederick Karl's *Joseph Conrad: The Three Lives* (1979), which non-Polish readers might otherwise assume to be an earlier work than his.

Najder's biography also takes priority in its wealth of original research, its methodological rigor, and its comprehensiveness of perspective. These traits bear emphasizing because Najder, though testy toward some of his competitors' claims, takes an unnecessarily modest line about the significance of his own work. His "too angular" mind, he says, is unsuited to reproducing the atmosphere of Conrad's times; he merely aspires to give a month-by-month account of what happened to the Polish child Konrad Korzeniowski and his successor, the English author Joseph Conrad. But his book accomplishes a great deal more than that. Far from being a recitation of trivia, it is the richest and most persuasive portrait of Conrad we have had or will probably ever have, created by a man who is uniquely situated to understand Conrad's divided cultural loyalties and who has devoted the greater part of his scholarly career to the task.[1]

Though Najder is by no means reluctant to generalize and speculate, his pursuit of facts for their own sake does compel admiration. No detail has been too small for him to check. Norman Sherry, for example, had proposed that the slowness of Conrad's trek from Matadi to Kinshasa in July 1890 was the cause of his conflict with his superiors in the Société Anonyme Belge pour le Commerce du Haut-Congo, but Najder neutralizes the claim by showing that Conrad's party bettered the standard time proposed in an official itinerary for caravans. More significantly, a report of scars on Conrad's chest leads Najder to review their exact location and shape and to rule them out as evidence for the duel Conrad claimed to have fought in Marseilles in 1878. Thus he reinforces his own previous conclusion, drawn from surviving letters to Conrad from his uncle, that no such duel occurred; Conrad apparently invented it to cover a humiliating suicide attempt and then perpetuated the story in later years to enhance the image of a youthful bravado that would be tempered in due time by manly responsibility.

Nothing in Conrad's memoirs or in those of his well-intentioned but obtuse wife, Jessie, can be taken on faith. To gain a fair account, an inquirer must give less weight to reconstructions than to contemporary documents such as the ones Najder himself has collected in *Conrad's Polish Background* and *Conrad Under Familial Eyes*. And even documents require circumspect interpretation. Najder not only distrusts such obviously legend-building works as *The Shadow Line, A Personal Record, The Mirror of the Sea*, and *The Arrow of Gold;* he also cautions against uncritical reliance on Conrad's letters, which teem with discrepancies and tend to overrepresent his quite genuine states of exasperation, anxiety, and injured pride. And where independent records are skimpy, one must rely on probabilities. This is where Najder truly shines: in wielding common sense against tempting but gratuitous assumptions that make Conrad appear more romantic, possessed, or mysterious—or sometimes simply more English—than he actually was.

Thus Najder reviews the several popular explanations for Conrad's having left Poland for France and a nautical career at age seventeen: that he was fleeing from an unhappy love affair, or from Poland's tragic past, or from gloomy Cracow, or from his late father's revolutionism, or (Conrad's own favorite version) that he was already determined to join the British merchant marine. What these hypotheses have in common is their proleptic slant; they interpret the Conrad of 1874 by reference to a self-representation he cultivated in later years.

Najder, by contrast, is able to address Conrad's motives without anachronism. Not denying the romantic fascination of the sea or Conrad's lifelong restlessness, he reminds us that in going abroad Conrad was being a typical Pole of the privileged class; that no renunciation of national values was implied by seeking one's fortune elsewhere, especially given the scarcity of good prospects in the occupied homeland; that Conrad's prudent uncle and guardian, Tadeusz Bobrowski, blessed his plans and expected them to yield both moral and commercial profit; and that Marseilles was hardly the logical destination for someone intending to join the *British* merchant service.

Consider another key feature of the Conrad legend: his seemingly phenomenal rise from common sailor to captain in a foreign fleet. How can we not admire his grit, his linguistic aptitude, and his nautical skills, tested by such chilling adventures as those of the fledgling skipper in "The Secret Sharer"? But thanks to low wages in the depressed sea trade, many foreigners were able to work on English ships in the 1870s and 1880s, and standards for officers' examinations were lax. Even so, Conrad initially failed his qualifying tests for both first officer and captain, stumbling in navigation and mathematics. At several key moments in his career, furthermore, he advanced himself by lying about his past service. His actual record was far from disgraceful, yet it included his having been fired as second mate of one ship and having had to resign as first mate of another after he had loaded cargo inexpertly, causing hazardous rolling in heavy seas. And throughout his years as mariner Conrad exhibited the delicacy of constitution that, after he was devastated by dysentery, malaria, and a nervous collapse in 1890–91, left him a valetudinarian for the last thirty-four years of his life.

Then there is Conrad's famous decision, apparently made as if by the muses descending in a cart, to abandon sailing for writing. "It was as though all unknowing I had heard a whisper or seen something" (*The Shadow Line*). Yet beyond the artistic stirrings that impelled him to begin writing *Almayer's Folly* in 1889, Conrad also knew that his sea career was heading nowhere. He *had* to find a new livelihood. Even so, he was still fruitlessly seeking officer's work as late as 1894, when a 15,000-ruble inheritance from his uncle Tadeusz finally enabled him to begin affecting the life of a modest country squire. Apparently there was no prior moment when Conrad clearly forsook one profession for the other.

Most commentators have followed Conrad's lead in treating that shift as a wondrous metamorphosis, scarcely within the realm of the explainable. But the wonder evaporates as soon as we inquire dispassionately whether the young Polish aristocrat's heart had truly belonged to the sea and its traditions. Though Conrad gave

nearly twenty years to his first career, Najder reminds us that he
hated the tedium, inconvenience, and base social tone of nautical
life. His lyricism about spars and yards did not oblige him to prefer sail power to steam when his own comfort was involved. He
did not spend a day more at sea than his financial condition required. And, encouraged by his uncle, he was at least as hopeful of
making profitable investments and trade arrangements abroad as
he was of securing the major captaincies that never materialized.

According to the many witnesses cited by Najder, furthermore, Conrad was a most untypical officer—nervous, irritable,
fastidious, and aloof, though abnormally considerate of his crews.
Dressed like a lord, he would spend his many landlocked months
reading Shakespeare, Maupassant, and Flaubert and seeking out
the most cosmopolitan company available. He was, after all, the
son of a noted author and political martyr. That he himself, having
been praised for his elegant epistolary style in both Polish and
French, should have eventually turned to authorship seems entirely
natural.

Consider, finally, Conrad's allegedly supreme mastery of English, a language he scarcely knew at age twenty. In this one area,
at least, must we not bow to the mystery of sheer genius? "I have
a strange and overpowering feeling," he wrote in *A Personal Record*, "that [English] had always been an inherent part of myself."
But once again Najder brings the hero back to earth. Though Conrad often denied it, he had thought of launching his literary persona in French, a language that caused him fewer difficulties. Acci-
dents of circumstance, not some prior Anglicism of soul, pressed
Conrad into the ranks of British authors. For the previous eleven
years he had had to conduct his affairs in English, and he knew
that the experiences he had garnered would be of paramount interest to English readers.

Yet Conrad's spoken English, we now know, was barely deci-
pherable and riddled with pronoun errors. And his stories and novels, even after correction by editors and friends, continued to show
unidiomatic touches that were pounced on by chauvinistic London
reviewers. Conrad in print was a formidable English stylist, but
Najder reminds us that his originality derived partly from a resid-
ual overlay of Polish, which urged his sentences toward greater
length, richer modification, and a more "rhetorical" air than the
English norm. Not even in his syntax was Conrad the captain of
his fate.

II

The adjustments of biographical perspective necessitated by Najder and other recent scholars can hardly be considered a threat to Conrad's reputation as an author. Nor does his revised character look remotely scandalous in its own right. But once this has been said, let us admit that the moment is a delicate one. Do we find ourselves somewhat disappointed with the new Conrad? Once stripped of his legend, is he not a rather small-looking figure—shifty, hypochondriacal, forlorn, afraid of his shadow?

That is precisely the wretch already familiar to us from Jessie Conrad's querulous memoirs, *Joseph Conrad As I Knew Him* (1926) and *Joseph Conrad and His Circle* (1935). And it is, *mutatis mutandis*, the neurotic dissected in Bernard C. Meyer's *Joseph Conrad: A Psychoanalytic Biography* (1967)—a man who was not merely excitable, evasive, peremptory, and petulant, but also allegedly impotent, fetishistic, oral-aggressive, masochistic, exhibitionistic, oedipally fixated on his dead parents, and pathologically afraid of women.

I was once impressed by Meyer's study, which, in my own Freudian phase, struck me as a welcome corrective to the flourishing Conradolatry of the Sixties. But there is really no need to choose between Meyer's Conrad and the sea-dreamer, for both versions are untrustworthy. If the one feeds on cultivated illusions, the other springs from an investigative method at once too dogmatic and too undisciplined to be considered reliable. Not only did Meyer fail to discriminate adequately between facts and gossip; he presumed, like other armchair analysts, that he could plunder Conrad's fiction for direct revelations of that repressed unconscious whose features prove so predictably alike from one posthumous patient to another.

Even if the whole Freudian conception of mind were better established than it is, that strategy would be illegitimate. For, as we can substantiate from Ian Watt's painstaking *Conrad in the Nineteenth Century* (1979), Conrad was a tradition-steeped artist whose writings were affected by a number of literary and intellectual currents, from Naturalism, Symbolism, and popular romance to Social Darwinism and *fin-de-siècle* pessimism. Common prudence forbids us to read the fiction symptomatically without first asking, as Meyer never did, whether its motifs may be more readily accounted for.

But this is not to say that a psychiatric understanding of a dead author must be wrong in principle. Najder himself, as it happens, has an important diagnostic thesis to propound: that throughout his publishing years Conrad was a severe and chronic depressive. No previous biographer, including the clinician Meyer, has embraced that idea, yet the evidence for it appears overwhelming. We know that Conrad was disabled by two full-scale breakdowns— not to mention his apparent suicide attempt—and that he was frequently laid up with possibly psychogenic attacks of gout. But more tellingly, he often manifested combinations of the classic depressive symptoms, which Najder sums up as follows:

> Sadness; a feeling of incapacity; fatigue; heaviness of limbs; anxiety coupled with listlessness; aversion to any mental or physical activity; continuous self-reproach; thoughts of guilt and punishment; inability to concentrate, sometimes to the extent of stupor; a slowing down of the capacity for work, especially when it is beyond the ordinary routine; frequent and exaggerated symptoms of physical ailments, particularly of the digestive tract; sense of loneliness; fear of madness and the disintegration of personality; . . . suicidal tendencies; seeing the bad side of everything; delusions of calamities and disaster; shrinkage of psychological space; loss of vivid imagination; seeing [one's] world in gray and dark colors, and feeling it is unreal and chaotic.

Now, the difference between calling Conrad a depressive, as that term is medically understood today, and calling him a neurotic in the Freudian sense may seem negligible at first. Actually, it is critical to Najder's whole task of reconstructing the historical Conrad in coherent terms. The Freudian neurotic, whether the identified complaint is depression or some other syndrome, is inevitably assumed to have a damaged ego which is relatively helpless against upwellings of "the repressed." He is at best a perpetual juggler, coping more or less ingeniously with irruptions which, because they emanate from momentous childhood trauma, are implicitly awarded a deeper ontological status than the "compromise formations" of his quotidian nervous behavior. The unthinkable is the real, and it rules the mind. Meyer's whole biography exemplifies this downgrading of the neurotic subject's mental integrity. By contrast, an enlightened contemporary view of depression requires no such condescending imputation. Since the most likely source of the malady is currently thought to be biochemical, no stigma is entailed. One can be—Conrad surely was—both a depressive and a person of strong identity and principle.

Those of us who are not chronically depressed can have at most a glimmering, I think, of the depressive's daily struggle to avoid surrender to torpor and self-contempt. Apart from money woes, that struggle is the chief and perennial topic of Conrad's intimate correspondence. As he confided to Edward Sanderson, a friend who helped to run a boys' school,

> try to imagine yourself trying your hardest to save the School . . . from downfall, annihilation, and disaster: and the thing going on and on endlessly. That's exactly how I am situated: and the worst is that the menace . . . does not seem to come from outside but from within . . . in myself alone. . . . I fear! I fear!

In the light of such suffering, Conrad's sheer output—24 volumes within 29 years—suggests an objective correlative for his ideal of fidelity. Perhaps we are looking at a hero after all, though of a different sort than we have hitherto suspected.

III

In a wicked sally, E. M. Forster (1936) taught many of us to believe that Conrad "is misty in the middle as well as at the edges, that the secret casket of his genius contains a vapour rather than a jewel. . . ." The observation stuck because it exposed a real tendency on Conrad's part to philosophize melodramatically, invoking a sense of profundity without having earned it through represented action or cogent reasoning. Insofar as the philosophizing had a definite content, moreover—near nihilism combined with a paradoxical insistence on virtues of character—it has proved troublesome to would-be admirers. Virtue has been out of style among literary people for longer than anyone can remember; and though nihilism has not, Conrad's brand of it looks too easy, as if it were a kind of euphemism or escape from unexpressed concerns. D. H. Lawrence spoke for many readers when he complained in a letter, "Conrad . . . makes me furious—and the stories are *so* good. But why this giving in before you start. . . . I can't forgive Conrad for being so sad and for giving in."

It cannot be denied that pessimism and resignation were part of Conrad's approach to reality. Yet Najder's biography goes far toward showing us why this had to be the case. Though Najder's Conrad remains elusive in certain respects, he is neither the butterfly mounted in E. M. Forster's scrapbook nor the mere merchant of gloom scorned by Lawrence. His politics and ethics were much clearer-headed, less sentimental, and more richly informed by history and personal trial than Forster's or Lawrence's own, and his comprehension of Europe's drift toward dictatorship and cataclysm—as notably analyzed in his great essay of 1905, "Autocracy and War"—deserves to be called prophetic. Indeed, the power cultist Lawrence might have spared himself a good deal of silly bluster if he had been able to grasp the basis of Conrad's "sadness."

Though Conrad was the most deracinated and internally tormented of authors, and though he had to practice a delicate diplomacy every day of his life on English soil, we can now understand that he remained profoundly Polish in his sense of self. This is not to say that he felt welcome when he revisited Poland in 1914. As Najder shows more fully in *Conrad Under Familial Eyes*, by then he was an object of suspicion to activists who had remained at home; and he in turn was annoyed by their advice that he devote himself explicitly to Polish themes and causes, as if that were a way of feasibly supporting his family in England. All the same, Conrad never ceased addressing the world privately, if not always publicly, as a member of the Polish intelligentsia and the *szlachta*—the noble class that had controlled cultural and political life before the country was partitioned and subjugated to three neighboring powers in 1795. Najder shows us that if we appreciate what that self-image entailed, and if we then picture Conrad's plight as a financially vulnerable, suspiciously regarded foreigner in Victorian and Edwardian England, much that looks furtive, insensitive, or contradictory in his pronouncements commands our sympathy.

For Conrad, to be a *szlachcic* meant first of all to know oneself a gentleman in all surroundings, hardships, and embarrassments and to insist on being recognized as one. Hence, for example, his evident attempt to pass off the failed suicide as a duel, which would have been more in keeping with his station; his stand-offishness as a seaman; his refusal either to live in an attic, as he put it, or to prostitute his art to common taste; his touchiness with creditors and rudely impatient publishers; and his recklessness with money, a substance whose scarcity he seemed almost to regard as a flaw in nature implanted to disrupt his concentration on more important things. Hence too, perhaps, his refusal to accept the honorary degrees and the knighthood that were eventually proffered. In his own eyes Conrad had been a nobleman all along.

When Conrad has not been patronized as an old salt—"They want to banish me to the middle of the ocean," he once complained of his reviewers—he has sometimes been patronized as a Slav—that is, as someone thought to be hereditarily disposed toward impulsiveness, mysticism, and a taste for conspiracies. No label evoked more contempt from this firsthand victim of Russian imperialism. The so-called Slavonic spirit, he wrote, is utterly foreign "to the Polish temperament with its tradition of self-government, its chivalrous view of moral restraints and exaggerated respect for individual rights: not to mention the important fact that the whole Polish mentality, Western in complexion, had received its training from Italy and France and, historically, had always remained, even in religious matters, in sympathy with the most liberal currents of European thought."

Too often Conrad has been considered a reactionary on both cultural and political issues. On the contrary, he was a freethinker who rejoiced in Voltaire and Anatole France and who counted among his cherished later friends André Gide and Bertrand Russell. His bête noire was his fellow "Slav" Dostoevsky, who in Conrad's judgment had made a craven, unforgivable peace with autocracy and Christianity. And his dearest friend of all was a militant socialist, R. B. Cunninghame Graham, who shared his loathing for oppressors, his anti-materialism, and his scorn for British jingoism.

To be sure, Conrad himself was a moral traditionalist, a nationalist, and a skeptic toward all egalitarian movements. But those were the stands not of a feudalist but of a patriot who had seen his own country's traditions kicked aside by the czars, who had spent much of his boyhood in a harsh Russian exile, and who lived under the threat of Russian military conscription throughout his long struggle to become a British subject. Like many modern Poles—indeed, like Najder himself, who now works in Munich for Radio Free Europe and who has been sentenced to death by the latest Russian surrogates in Warsaw—Conrad had little patience with the rhetoric of international class brotherhood, mouthed for the most part by people who could not trouble themselves over the fates of captive nations.

As for Conrad's evasiveness, the circumstances of his upbringing and adult life go far toward making it understandable as a survival strategy. We can now see, for example, how he was torn between the extremism of his martyred father, whose banishment to Russia all but deprived Conrad of a childhood, and the accommodationism of that Polish Polonius, Uncle Tadeusz; the result was a fury of inaction, a fatalism laced with self-reproach. And we can appreciate how little freedom Conrad felt to be as candid about British imperialism as he was about the Belgian and Russian varieties. If he sometimes sounds overwrought and barely coherent in his panegyrics on solidarity, fidelity, and the singular merits of the English sailor, the reason can be found not in any naïveté but in the constraints under which he wrote—constraints including the discretion of the grateful guest, the prudence of the closely watched alien, and the pride of the aristocrat who would never disclose the slights he had suffered in England and on English ships because of his "queer" foreign voice and manners.

The legend that Najder and others have laid to rest required us to imagine a supremely romantic figure, the master of two remarkable destinies. Today we see that, on the contrary, Conrad's life from an early age was a series of adaptations to odd circumstances, both of temperament and of history, that kept him perpetually off balance. Even after he had acquired the outward features of a normal existence, his self-awareness—as a Pole and European, as a displaced person, as a melancholic, and as a Flaubertian artist in the land of Kipling—spared him from the smug and stuffy conformism of imperial England and threw him upon his inner resources. Conrad's discomposure, we can gather, was his passport to distinction.

Note

1. How regrettable, then, that this handsome book reached print still showing a good number of typos and Mrs. Najder's lingering uncertainties with English tenses, punctuation, and diction: *as* for *like*, *past* for *previous*, *ago* for *before*, *apart for* for *apart from*, *reticent* for *hesitant*, etc.

Works Cited

Baines, Jocelyn. 1960. *Joseph Conrad: A Critical Biography*. New York: McGraw Hill.

Conrad, Jessie. 1926. *Joseph Conrad As I Knew Him*. London: Heinemann.

———. 1935. *Joseph Conrad and His Circle*. London: Jarrolds.

Conrad, Joseph. 1958. *Letters to William Blackwood and David S. Meldrum*, ed. William Blackburn. Durham, N.C.: Duke University Press.

———. 1969. *Joseph Conrad's Letters to R. B. Cunninghame Graham*, ed. C. T. Watts. Cambridge: Cambridge University Press.

———. 1983. *The Collected Letters of Joseph Conrad: Volume I, 1861–1897*, ed. Frederick R. Karl and Laurence Davies. Cambridge: Cambridge University Press.

Forster, E. M. 1936. "Joseph Conrad: A Note." In *Abinger Harvest*. London: Edward Arnold. Pp. 159–163.

Karl, Frederick R. 1979. *Joseph Conrad: The Three Lives*. New York: Farrar, Straus & Giroux.

Lawrence, D. H. 1962. *The Collected Letters of D. H. Lawrence*, ed. Harry T. Moore. New York: Viking. Quoted letter: p. 152.

Meyer, Bernard C. 1967. *Joseph Conrad: A Psychoanalytic Biography*. Princeton: Princeton University Press.

Najder, Zdzisław. 1964. *Conrad's Polish Background: Letters to and from Polish Friends*. London: Oxford University Press.

———. 1984a. *Joseph Conrad: A Chronicle*, trans. Halina Carroll-Najder. New Brunswick: Rutgers University Press.

———. 1984b. *Conrad Under Familial Eyes*, trans. Halina Carroll-Najder. Cambridge: Cambridge University Press.

Sherry, Norman. 1966. *Conrad's Eastern World*. Cambridge: Cambridge University Press.

———. 1971. *Conrad's Western World*. Cambridge: Cambridge University Press.

Watt, Ian P. 1979. *Conrad in the Nineteenth Century*. Berkeley: University of California Press.

Index